ASPECTS OF CHURCH HISTORY

ABOUT THE COLLECTED WORKS

Fr. Florovsky devoted much attention to his *Collected Works*. Until shortly before his death, he had continued to supply a variety of materials. These included suggestions for the structuring of the volumes; changes in certain texts; new materials; updated materials; notes; revisions; suggestions for revisions; updated bibliography; and several outlines for a new structure to his work on the Byzantine Fathers. Substantial time has been expended to implement his suggestions and instructions. Some materials will be included in the final volume, a volume which also contains an Index to the entire *Collected Works*, Appendices, Notes, Bibliography, and Miscellanea. To publish *The Collected Works* in English has entailed the translation of his works from several languages, including Russian, Bulgarian, Czech, Serbian, German and French.

ASPECTS OF CHURCH HISTORY

VOLUME FOUR
in *THE COLLECTED WORKS* of

GEORGES FLOROVSKY
Emeritus Professor of Eastern Church History
Harvard University

General Editor
RICHARD S. HAUGH
Visiting Scholar
Andover Newton Theological School

BÜCHERVERTRIEBSANSTALT
Postfach 461, FL - 9490 Vaduz, Europa
[Exclusive Sales Agent: Notable & Academic Books
P. O. Box 470, Belmont, MA {USA} 02178]

ASPECTS OF CHURCH HISTORY
ISBN 3-905238-04-7

THE COLLECTED WORKS OF GEORGES FLOROVSKY

Volume I – *Bible, Church, Tradition: An Eastern Orthodox View*
Volume II – *Christianity and Culture*
Volume III – *Creation and Redemption*
Volume IV – *Aspects of Church History*
Volume V – *Ways of Russian Theology: Part One*
Volume VI – *Ways of Russian Theology: Part Two*
Volume VII – *The Eastern Fathers of the Fourth Century*
Volume VIII – *The Byzantine Fathers of the Fifth Century*
Volume IX – *The Byzantine Fathers of the Sixth to Eighth Century*
Volume X – *The Byzantine Ascetic and Spiritual Fathers*
Volume XI – *Theology and Literature*
Volume XII – *The Ecumenical Movement and the Orthodox Church*
Volume XIII – *Philosophy: Philosophical Problems and Movements*
Volume XIV – *Sermons and Writings on Spirituality*

[Additional forthcoming volumes. The final volume contains an Index to the entire *Collected Works,* Bibliography, Appendices, and Miscellanea]

PRINTED IN THE UNITED STATES OF AMERICA

CONTENTS

IN MEMORIAM

FR. GEORGES FLOROVSKY
1893-1979

"Preeminent Orthodox Christian Theologian, Ecumenical Spokesman, And Authority on Russian Letters."

[All quotations are from pages 5 and 11 of the *Harvard Gazette* of October 1, 1982, written by George H. Williams, Hollis Professor of Divinity *Emeritus*, Harvard Divinity School and Edward Louis Keenan, Dean of the Graduate School of Arts and Sciences, Harvard University and "placed upon the records" at the Harvard Faculty of Divinity Meeting on September 16, 1982.]

"Archpriest Professor Georges Vasilyevich Florovsky (1893-1979), preeminent theologian of Orthodoxy and historian of Christian thought, ecumenical leader and interpreter of Russian literature . . . died in Princeton, New Jersey in his 86th year" on August 11, 1979.

Born in Odessa in 1893, Fr. Florovsky was the beneficiary of that vibrant Russian educational experience which flourished toward the end of the 19th century and produced many gifted scholars. His father was rector of the Theological Academy and dean of the Cathedral of the Transfiguration. His mother, Klaudia Popruzhenko, was the daughter of a professor of Hebrew and Greek. Fr. Florovsky's first scholarly work, "On Reflex Salivary Secretion," written under one of Pavlov's students, was published in English in 1917 in the last issue of *The Bulletin of the Imperial Academy of Sciences.*

In 1920, with his parents and his brother Antonii, Fr. Florovsky left Russia and settled first in Sophia, Bulgaria. He left behind his brother, Vasilii, a surgeon, who died in the 1924 famine, and his sister Klaudia V. Florovsky, who became a professor of history at the University of Odessa. In 1921 the President of Czechoslovakia, Thomas Masaryk, invited Fr. Florovsky and his brother Antonii to Prague. Fr. Florovsky taught the philosophy of law. Antonii later became a professor of history at the University of Prague.

In 1922 Georges Florovsky married Xenia Ivanovna Simonova and they resettled in Paris where he became cofounder of St. Sergius Theological Institute and taught there as professor of patristics (1926-1948). In 1932 he was ordained a priest and placed himself canonically under the patriarch of Constantinople.

In 1948 he came to the United States and was professor of theology at St. Vladimir's Theological Seminary from 1948 to 1955, and dean from 1950. From 1954 to 1965 he was professor of Eastern Church History at Harvard Divinity School and, concurrently (1962-1965) an associate of the Slavic Department and (1955-1959) an associate professor of theology at Holy Cross Theological School.

"Although Fr. Florovsky's teaching in the Slavic Department [at Harvard University] was only sporadic, he became a major intellectual influence in the formation of a generation of American specialists in Russian cultural history. His lasting importance in this area derives not from his formal teaching but from the time and thought he gave to informal "circles" that periodically arose around him in Cambridge among those who had read *The Ways of Russian Theology* [then only in Russian], for decades a kind of "underground book" among serious graduate students of Russian intellectual history, and had sought him out upon discovering that he was at the Divinity School . . . During a portion of his incumbency at Harvard . . . patristics and Orthodox thought and institutions from antiquity into 20th century Slavdom flour - ished. In the Church History Department meetings he spoke up with clarity. In the Faculty meetings he is remembered as having ener - getically marked book catalogues on his lap for the greater glory of the Andover Harvard Library! In 1964 Fr. Florovsky was elected a director of the Ecumenical Institute founded by Paul VI near Jerusalem." Active in both the National Council of Churches and the World Council of Churches, Fr. Florovsky was Vice President-at-Large of the National Council of Churches from 1954 to 1957.

"After leaving Harvard, Professor *Emeritus* Florovsky taught from 1965 to 1972 in Slavic Studies at Princeton University, having begun lecturing there already in 1964; and he was visiting lecturer in patristics at Princeton Theological Seminary as early as 1962 and then again intermittently after retirement from the University. His last teaching was in the fall semester of 1978/79 at Princeton Theological Seminary."

"Fr. Florovsky in the course of his career was awarded honorary doctorates by St. Andrew's University . . . Boston University, Notre Dame, Princeton University, the University of Thessalonica, St. Vladimir's Theological Seminary, and Yale. He was a member or honorary member of the Academy of Athens, the American Academy of Arts and Sciences, the British Academy, and the Fellowship of St. Alban and St. Sergius."

Fr. Florovsky personified the cultivated, well-educated Russian of the turn of the century. His penetrating mind grasped both the detail and depth in the unfolding drama of the history of Christianity in both eastern and western forms. He was theologian, church historian, patristic scholar, philosopher, Slavist, and a writer in comparative literature. "Fr. Florovsky sustained his pleasure on reading English novels, the source in part of his extraordinary grasp of the English language, which, polyglot that he was, he came to prefer above any other for theological discourse and general exposition. Thus when he came to serve in Harvard's Slavic Department, there was some disappointment that he did not lecture in Russian, especially in his seminars on Dostoievsky, Soloviev, Tolstoi, and others. It was as if they belonged to a kind of classical age of the Russian tongue and civilization that, having been swept away as in a deluge, he treated as a Latin professor would Terrence or Cicero, not presuming to give lectures in the tonalities of an age that had vanished forever."

Fr. Florovsky's influence on contemporary church historians and Slavists was vast. The best contemporary multi-volume history of Christian thought pays a special tribute to Fr. Florovsky. Jaroslav Pelikan of Yale University, in the bibliographic section to his first volume in *The Christian Tradition: A History of the Development of Doctrine*, writes under the reference to Fr. Florovsky's two works in Russian on the Eastern Fathers: "These two works are basic to our interpretation of trinitarian and christological dogmas" (p. 359 from *The Emergence of the Catholic Tradition: 100-600*). George Huntston Williams, Hollis Professor *Emeritus* of Harvard Divinity School, wrote: "Faithful priestly son of the Russian Orthodox Church . . . , Fr. Georges Florovsky – with a career-long involvement in the ecumenical dialogue – is today the most articulate, trenchant and winsome exponent of Orthodox theology and piety in the scholarly world. He is innovative and creative in the sense wholly of being ever prepared to restate the saving truth of Scripture and Tradition in the idiom of our contemporary yearning for the transcendent."

I
ASPECTS OF PATRISTIC
THOUGHT AND HISTORY

Patristic Theology and The Ethos
of the Orthodox Church

I

IN 1872 WILHELM GASS published his *Symbolik der Griechischen Kirche*. Gass was an expert scholar, especially competent in the field of Byzantine studies. His monographs, *Gennadius und Pletho* (Breslau 1844) and *Die Mystik des Nikolaus Kabasilas* (Greifswald 1849), were notable contributions to the study of late Byzantine theology, little known at that time. His *Symbolik* also was an able book, well written and well documented. Yet, a problem of method was involved in his exposition. It was at this methodological point that Gass was strongly challenged by another distinguished German scholar, Ferdinand Kattenbusch.[1]

In fact, Gass based his exposition of Greek doctrine, mainly and deliberately, on the alleged "symbolic books" of the Eastern Church, in particular on Peter Mogila's *Orthodox Confession* (in its revised Greek version) and the Decrees of the Jerusalem Council of 1672. Now, Kattenbusch contested the adequacy of such an approach. In his opinion, the

This article originally appeared as "The Ethos of the Orthodox Church" in *The Ecumenical Review,* Vol. XII, No. 2 (Geneva, 1960), pp. 183-198. It was a paper presented to the Faith and Order Orthodox Consultation in Kifissia, Greece, August 16-18, 1959. Reprinted by permission of the author.

11

so-called "symbolic books" of the Eastern Church could not be regarded as an authentic source. They were not spontaneous expressions of the Orthodox faith. They were occasional polemical writings addressed primarily to the problems of Western controversy, between Rome and the Reformation, in which the Christian East was not intrinsically involved. The XVIIth century was not, Kattenbusch contended, a creative epoch in the history of the Eastern Church. In order to grasp the genuine spirit of the Orthodox Church one had, according to Kattenbusch, to go back to that crucial epoch—*die Gründungsepoche,* when the distinctive Greek tradition in theology and worship had been formed; that is, to the period of great *Christological* controversies in the Ancient Church. In order to understand the Orthodox Church, at her very heart, one had to turn to the fathers, to St. Athanasius, the Cappadocians, and indeed to Pseudo-Dionysius, rather than to Mogila or Dositheos. Moreover, one could properly understand the Orthodox tradition only out of its own central vision. Kattenbusch rightly stressed the centrality of the Christological vision in the total structure of the Greek theological system: *der Inbegriff aller Themata.* It was this synthetic or comprehensive method that Kattenbusch used in his own exposition of Eastern Orthodoxy, some years later.[2]

Kattenbusch was right. The alleged "symbolic books" of the Orthodox Church have no binding authority, as much as they might have been used by particular theologians and at particular times. Their authority is subordinate and derived. In any case, they have no authority by themselves, but only in so far as they are in agreement with the continuous tradition of the Church. And at certain points they betray an obvious Western influence. This influence was characteristic of certain stages in the history of modern Orthodox *theology,* but in no sense is it characteristic of the Orthodox *Church herself.* We may quote at this point an apt statement by the late Professor Nicholas Glubokovsky. "As a matter of fact, Orthodoxy has no 'symbolic books' in the technical sense of the word. All the talk about them is extremely conditional and conformable only to the Western Confessional schemes, in opposition to the nature and history of Orthodoxy. It considers itself the right or authentic teaching of Christ in all its primitiveness and incorruptibility; but then—what particular distinguishing doctrine can it have except that of the Gospel of Christ? The Orthodox Church herself down to the present time does not make use of any special 'symbolical books', being satisfied with the general traditional documents which have the character of defining the faith."[3]

Gass was not impressed by the arguments of Kattenbusch. His reply was firm and sharp. There was no "Greek Church" in Ancient times: *damals noch gar keine Griechische Kirche gab, d.h., keine Griechische Separatkirche.* The Fathers of the Church, in Gass's opinion, were quite *irrelevant* for the understanding of contemporary Orthodoxy. For Gass, the modern Greek Church was not identical with the Ancient Church: she has widely departed or deviated from the early foundations. Gass made this point quite emphatically in his *Symbolik.* Indeed, Kattenbusch also spoke of the *Griechische Partikularkirche.* But with him it was rather a statement of fact. In his opinion, all the distinctive marks of this *Partikularkirche* were established already in the age of Chalcedon and Justinian. Certain distinctive, but not necessarily divisive, features had developed in the East and in the West already in the early centuries of Christian history, and one speaks legitimately of "particular" traditions: Eastern and Western, Carthaginian and Roman, Alexandrinian and Antiochene. In any case, since the final break with Rome, the "Greek Church" actually existed as a *Partikularkirche,* just as did the "Roman Church." But Gass went much further. In his view, the modern Eastern Church, and probably already the Byzantine, was actually a "new church," a new "denominational" formation, separated from the ancient Church by a long and complex process of decay and deviation. In other words, she was just a particular "denomination," among others, and had to be characterized as such. For this task only the modern "symbolic books" were relevant.[4]

The *Auseinandersetzung* between Gass and Kattenbusch was much more than just an episode in the history of modern scholarship.[5] Nor was their disagreement simply methodological. Again, Gass was not alone in his approach. It is still typical of Western scholarship, both Roman and Protestant, to characterize Orthodoxy on the basis of modern and contemporary documents, without clear discrimination between authoritative statements and writings of individual authors, and without any proper historical perspective. It is enough to mention the various studies of such authors as M. Jugie and Th. Spacil. It is logical from the Roman point of view: the Orthodox Church, as a "schism," must have her distinctive, schismatic features, and cannot be "identical" with the Catholic Church of old, even in her Eastern version. The ultimate question is, therefore, theological. Is the contemporary Orthodox Church *the same church,* as in the age of the Fathers, as has been always claimed and contended by the Orthodox themselves? Is she a legitimate continuation of that ancient Church? Or is she no more than a new *Separatkirche?* This dilemma is of decisive relevance for the contemporary ecumenical conversation, especially between the Protestants and the Orthodox. Indeed, the Orthodox are bound to claim that the only "specific" or "distinctive" feature about their own position in "divided Christendom" is the fact that the Orthodox Church is essentially identical with the Church of all ages, and indeed with the "Early Church," *die Urkirche.* In other words, she is not *a* Church, but *the* Church. It is a formidable, but fair and just claim. There is here more than just an unbroken *historic continuity,* which is indeed quite obvious. There is above all an ultimate *spiritual and ontological identity,* the same faith, the same spirit, the same ethos. And this constitutes the distinctive mark of Orthodoxy. "This is the Apostolic faith, this is the faith of the Fathers, this is the Orthodox faith, this faith has established the universe."

II

Following the Holy Fathers... It was usual in the Ancient Church to introduce doctrinal statements by phrases like this. The great *Decree* of Chalcedon begins precisely with these very words. The Seventh Ecumenical Council introduces its decision concerning the Holy Icons even in a more explicit and elaborate way: *following the Divinely inspired teaching of our Holy Fathers and the tradition of the Catholic Church* (Denzinger 302). Obviously, it was more than just an appeal to "antiquity." Indeed, the Church always stresses the identity of her faith throughout the ages. This identity and permanence, from Apostolic times, is indeed the most conspicuous token and sign of right faith. In the famous phrase of Vincent of Lérins, *in ipsa item catholica ecclesia magnopere curandum est ut id teneamus quod ubique, quod semper, quod ab omnibus creditum est (Commonitorium* c. 2.3). However, "antiquity" by itself is not yet an adequate proof of the true faith. Archaic formulas can be utterly misleading. Vincent himself was well aware of that. Old customs as such do not guarantee the truth. As St. Cyprian put it, *antiquitas sine veritate vetustas erroris est (Epist.* 74). And again: *Dominus, Ego sum, inquit, veritas. Non dixit, Ego sum consuetudo (Sententiae episcoporum numero* 87, c. 30). The true tradition is only the tradition of truth, *traditio veritatis.* And this "true tradition," according to St. Irenaeus, is grounded in, and guaranteed by, that *charisma veritatis certum,* which has been *deposited* from the very beginning in the Church and preserved in the uninterrupted succession of Apostolic ministry: *qui cum episcopatus successione charisma veritatis certum acceperunt (Adv. haereses* IV. 40. 2). Thus, "tradition" in the Church is not merely the continuity of human memory, or the permanence of rites and habits. Ultimately, "tradition" is the continuity of divine assistance, the abiding presence of the Holy Spirit. The Church is not bound by "the letter." She is constantly moved forth by "the spirit." The same Spirit, the Spirit of Truth, which "spake through the Prophets," which guided the Apostles, which illumined the Evangelists, is still abiding in the Church, and guides her into the fuller understanding of the divine truth, from glory to glory.

Following the Holy Fathers... It is not a reference to abstract tradition, to formulas and propositions. It is primarily an appeal to persons, *to holy witnesses.* The witness of the Fathers belongs, integrally and intrinsically, to the very structure of the Orthodox faith. The Church is equally committed to the *kerygma* of the Apostles and to the *dogmata* of the Fathers. Both belong together inseparably. The Church is indeed *"Apostolic."* But the Church is also *"Patristic."* And only by being *"Patristic"* is the Church continuously *"Apostolic."* The Fathers testify to the Apostolicity of the tradition. There are two basic stages in the proclamation of the Christian faith. *Our simple faith had to acquire composition.* There was an inner urge, an inner logic, an internal necessity, in this transition—from *kerygma* to *dogma.* Indeed, the *dogmata* of the Fathers are essentially the same "simple" *kerygma,* which had been once delivered and *deposited* by the Apostles, once, for ever. But now it is— this very *kerygma*—properly articulated and developed into a consistent body of correlated testimonies. The apostolic preaching is not only kept in the Church: it *lives* in the Church, as a *depositum juvenescens,* in the phrase of St. Irenaeus. In this sense, the teaching of the Fathers is a permanent category of Christian faith, a constant and ultimate measure or criterion of right belief. In this sense, again, Fathers are not merely witnesses of the old faith, *testes antiquitatis,* but, above all and primarily, witnesses of the true faith, *testes veritatis.* Accordingly, our contemporary appeal to the Fathers is much more than a historical reference—to the past. "The *mind* of the Fathers" is an intrinsic term of reference in Orthodox theology, no less than the word of the Holy Writ, and indeed never separated from it. The Fathers themselves were always servants of the Word, and their theology was intrinsically exegetical. Thus, as has been well said recently, "the Catholic Church of all ages is not merely a child of the Church of the Fathers, *but she is and remains* the Church of the Fathers."⁶

The main distinctive mark of Patristic theology was its "existential" character. The Fathers theologized, as St. Gregory of Nazianzus put it, "in the manner of the Apostles, and not in that of Aristotle," ἁλιευτικῶς οὐκ ἀριστοτελικῶς (*Hom.* XXIII. 12). Their teaching was still a "message," a *kerygma*. Their theology was still a "kerygmatic theology," even when it was logically arranged and corroborated by intellectual arguments. The ultimate reference was still to faith, to spiritual comprehension. It is enough to mention in this connection the names of St. Athanasius, St. Gregory of Nazianzus, St. Maximus the Confessor. Their theology was a witness. Apart from the life in Christ theology carries no conviction, and, if separated from the life of faith, theology may easily degenerate into empty dialectics, a vain *polylogia*, without any spiritual consequence. Patristic theology was rooted in the decisive commitment of faith. It was not just a self-explanatory "discipline," which could be presented argumentatively, i.e., ἀριστοτελικῶς, without a prior spiritual engagement. This theology could only be "preached," or "proclaimed," and not be simply "taught" in a school-manner; "preached" from the pulpit, proclaimed also in the word of prayer and in sacred rites, and indeed manifested in the total structure of Christian life. Theology of this kind can never be separated from the life of prayer and from the practice of virtue. "The climax of purity is the beginning of theology," in the phrase of St. John Klimakos (*Scala Paradisi,* grade 30). On the other hand,

theology is always, as it were, no more than *"propaideutic,"*
since its ultimate aim and purpose are to bear witness to the
Mystery of the Living God, in word and in deed. "Theology"
is not an aim in itself. It is always but a way. Theology
presents no more than an "intellectual contour" of the
revealed truth, a "noetic" testimony to it. Only in an act of
faith is this contour filled with living content. Yet, the
"contour" is also indispensable. Christological formulas are
actually meaningful only for the faithful, for those who have
encountered the Living Christ, and have acknowledged Him
as God and Saviour, for those who are dwelling by faith in
Him, in His Body, the Church. In this sense, theology is
never a self-explanatory discipline. It appeals constantly to the
vision of faith. "What we have seen and have heard, we
announce to you." Apart from this "announcement" theological formularies are of no consequence. For the same
reason these formulas should never be taken out of their
spiritual context. It is utterly misleading to single out certain
propositions, dogmatic or doctrinal, and to abstract them from
the total perspective in which only they are meaningful and
valid. It is a dangerous habit just to handle "quotations,"
from the Fathers and even from the Scripture, outside of the
total structure of faith, in which only they are truly alive.
"To follow the Fathers" does not mean simply to quote their
sentences. It means *to acquire their mind,* their φρόνημα.
The Orthodox Church claims to have preserved this *mind*
[φρόνημα] and to have theologized *ad mentem Patrum.*

At this very point a major doubt may be raised. The
name of "Church Fathers" is normally restricted to the
teachers *of the Ancient Church.* And it is currently assumed
that their authority, if recognized at all, depended upon their
"antiquity," i.e., upon their comparative chronological nearness to the "Primitive Church," to the initial or Apostolic
"Age" of Christian history. Now, already St. Jerome felt
himself constrained to contest this contention: the Spirit
breathes indeed in all ages. Indeed, there was no decrease

in "authority," and no decrease in the immediacy of spiritual knowledge, in the course of Church History—of course, always under the control of the primary witness and revelation. Unfortunately, the scheme of "decrease," if not of a flagrant "decay," has become one of the habitual schemes of historical thinking. It is widely assumed, consciously or subconsciously, that the early Church was, as it were, closer to the spring of truth. In the order of time, of course, it is obvious and true. But does it mean that the Early Church actually *knew and understood* the mystery of the Revelation, as it were, "better" and "fuller" than all subsequent ages, so that nothing but "repetition" has been left to the "ages to come"? Indeed, as an admission of our own inadequacy and failure, as an act of humble self-criticism, an exaltation of the past may be sound and healthy. But it is dangerous to make of it the starting point of our theology of Church History, or even of our theology of the Church. It is widely assumed that the "age of the Fathers" had ended, and accordingly should be regarded simply as an "ancient formation," archaic and obsolete. The limit of the "patristic age" is variously defined. It is usual to regard St. John of Damascus as "the last Father" in the East, and St. Gregory the Great or Isidor of Seville as the last in the West. This habit has been challenged more than once. For instance, should not St. Theodore of Studium be counted among the Fathers? In the West, already Mabillon suggested that Bernard of Clairvaux, the *Doctor Mellifluus,* was actually "the last of the Fathers, and surely not unequal to the earlier ones."[7] On the other hand, it can be contended that "the Age of the Fathers" has actually come to its end much earlier than even St. John of Damascus. It is enough simply to recall the famous formula of the *Consensus quinquesaecularis* which restricted the "authoritative" period of Church History actually to the period up to Chalcedon. Indeed, it was a Protestant formula. But the usual Eastern formula of "Seven Ecumenical Councils" is actually not very much better, when it tends, as it currently does, to *restrict* the Church's spiritual authority to the eight centuries, as if the "Golden Age" of the Church had already passed and we are now dwelling probably in an Iron Age, much lower on the scale of spiritual vigor and authority. Psychologically, this attitude is quite comprehensible, but it cannot be theologically justified. Indeed, the Fathers of the Fourth and Fifth centuries are much more impressive than the later ones, and their unique greatness cannot be questioned. Yet, the Church remained fully alive also after Chalcedon. And, in fact, an overemphasis on the "first five centuries" dangerously distorts theological vision and prevents the right understanding of the Chalcedonian dogma itself. The decree of the Sixth Ecumenical Council then is regarded just as a kind of "appendix" to Chalcedon, and the decisive theological contribution of St. Maximus the Confessor is usually completely overlooked. An overemphasis on the "eight centuries" inevitably obscures the legacy of Byzantium. There is still a strong tendency to treat "Byzantinism" as an inferior sequel, or even as a decadent epilogue, to the patristic age. Probably, we are prepared, now more than before, to admit the authority of the Fathers. But "Byzantine theologians" are not yet counted among the Fathers. In fact, however, Byzantine theology was much more than a servile "repetition" of Patristics. It was an organic continuation of the patristic endeavor. It suffices to mention St. Symeon the New Theologian, in the Eleventh century, and St. Gregory Palamas, in the Fourteenth. A *restrictive* commitment of the *Seven* Ecumenical Councils actually contradicts the basic principle of the *Living Tradition* in the Church. Indeed, *all Seven*. But *not only* the Seven.

The Seventeenth century was a critical age in the history of Eastern theology. The teaching of theology had deviated at that time from the traditional patristic pattern and had undergone influence from the West. Theological habits and schemes were borrowed from the West, rather eclectically, both from the late Roman Scholasticism of Post-Tridentine times and from the various theologies of the Reformation.

These borrowings affected heavily the theology of the alleged "Symbolic books" of the Eastern Church, which cannot be regarded as an authentic voice of the Christian East. The *style of theology* has been changed. Yet, this did not imply any change in doctrine. It was, indeed, a sore and ambiguous *Pseudomorphosis* of Eastern theology, which is not yet overcome even in our own time. This *Pseudomorphosis* actually meant a certain *split in the soul* of the East, to borrow one of the favorite phrases of Arnold Toynbee. Indeed, in the life of the Church the tradition of the Fathers has never been interrupted. The whole structure of Eastern Liturgy, in an inclusive sense of the word, is still thoroughly patristic. The life of prayer and meditation still follows the old pattern. The *Philokalia,* that famous encyclopaedia of Eastern piety and asceticism, which includes writings of many centuries, from St. Anthony of Egypt up to the Hesychasts of the Fourteenth century, is increasingly becoming the manual of guidance for all those who are eager *to practice Orthodoxy* in our own time. The authority of its compiler St. Nicodemus of the Holy Mount, has been recently re-emphasized and reinforced by his formal canonization in the Greek Church. In this sense, it can be contended, "the age of the Fathers" still continues alive in the "Worshiping Church." Should it not continue also *in the schools,* in the field of theological research and instruction? Should we not recover "the mind of the Fathers" also in our theological thinking and confession? "Recover," indeed, not as an archaic pose and habit, and not just as a venerable relic, but as an existential attitude, as a spiritual orientation. Actually, we are already living in an age of revival and restoration. Yet it is not enough to keep a "Byzantine Liturgy," to restore a "Byzantine style" in Iconography and Church architecture, to practice Byzantine modes of prayer and self-discipline. One has to go back to the very roots of this traditional "piety" which has been always cherished as a holy inheritance. One has to recover the patristic mind. Otherwise one will be still in danger of being internally split—between the "traditional" pattern of "piety" and the un-traditional pattern of mind. As "worshipers," the Orthodox have always stayed in the "tradition of the Fathers." They must stand in the same tradition also as "theologians." In no other way can the integrity of Orthodox existence be retained and secured.

It is enough, in this connection, to refer to the discussions at the Congress of Orthodox theologians, held in Athens at the end of the year 1936. It was a representative gathering: eight theological faculties, in six different countries, were represented. Two major problems were conspicuous on the agenda: first, the "External influences on Orthodox Theology since the Fall of Constantinople"; secondly, the Authority of the Fathers. The fact of Western accretions has been frankly acknowledged and thoroughly analyzed. On the other hand, the authority of the Fathers has been re-emphasized and a "return to the Fathers" advocated and approved. Indeed, it must be a *creative return.* An element of self-criticism must be therein implied. This brings us to the concept of a *Neopatristic synthesis,* as the task and aim of Orthodox theology today. The *Legacy of the Fathers* is a challenge for our generation, in the Orthodox Church and outside of it. Its recreative power has been increasingly recognized and acknowledged in these recent decades, in various corners of divided Christendom. The growing appeal of patristic tradition is one of the most distinctive marks of our time. For the Orthodox this appeal is of special urgency and importance, because the total tradition of Orthodoxy has always been patristic. One has to reassess both the problems and the answers of the Fathers. In this study the vitality of patristic thought, and its perennial timeliness, will come to the fore. *Inexhaustum est penu Patrum,* has well said Louis Thomassin, a French Oratorian of the Seventeenth century and one of the distinguished patristic scholars of his time.[8]

III

The synthesis must begin with the central vision of the Christian faith: Christ Jesus, as God and Redeemer, Humiliated and Glorified, the Victim and the Victor on the Cross.

"Christians apprehend first the Person of Christ the Lord, the Son of God Incarnate, and behind the veil of His flesh they behold the Triune God." This phrase of Bishop Theophanes, the great master of spiritual life in Russia in the last century, may serve appropriately as an epigraph to the new section of our present survey.

Indeed, Orthodox Spirituality is, essentially and basically, Christocentric and Christological. The Christocentric emphasis is conspicuous in the whole structure of Orthodox devotional life: sacramental, corporate, and private. The Christological pattern of Baptism, Eucharist, Penance, and also Marriage, is obvious. All sacraments are, indeed, sacraments of the believer's life *in Christo.* Although the Eucharistic Prayer, the *Anaphora,* is addressed and offered to the Father and has, especially in the rite of St. Basil, an obvious Trinitarian structure, the climax of the Sacrament is in the Presence of Christ, including also His ministerial Presence ("for Thou Thyself both offerest and art offered"), and in the personal encounter of the faithful with their Living Lord, as participants at His "Mystical Supper." The utter reality of this encounter is vigorously stressed in the office of preparation for Communion, as also in the prayers of thanksgiving after Communion. The preparation is precisely for one's meeting with Christ in the Sacrament, personal and intimate. Indeed, one meets Christ only in the fellowship of the Church. Yet, personal emphasis in all these prayers is dominant and prevailing. This personal encounter of believers with Christ is the very core of Orthodox devotional life. It suffices to mention here the practice of the *Jesus Prayer*—it is an intimate intercourse of penitent sinners with the Redeemer. The Akathistos Hymn to the "Sweetest Jesus" should also be mentioned in this connection. On the other hand, the whole of the Eucharistic rite is a comprehensive image of Christ's redemptive *oikonomia,* as it was persistently emphasized in the Byzantine liturgical commentaries, up to the magnificent *Exposition of the Holy Liturgy* by Nicholas Kabasilas. In his other treatise, *The Life in Christ,* Kabasilas interpreted the whole devotional life from the Christological point of view. It was an epitome of Byzantine spirituality.[9]

Christ's Mystery is the center of Orthodox faith, as it is also its starting point and its aim and climax. The mystery of God's Being, the Holy Trinity, has been revealed and disclosed by Him, who is "One of the Holy Trinity." This Mystery can be comprehended only through Christ, in meditation on His Person. Only those who "know" Him can "know" the Father, and the Holy Spirit, the "Spirit of adoption"—to the Father, through the Incarnate Son. This was the traditional way, both of Patristic theology, and of Patristic devotion. The *lex credendi* and the *lex orandi* are reciprocally interrelated. The basic pattern is surely the same in both. The aim of man's existence is in the *"Vision of God,"* in the adoration of the Triune God. But this aim can be achieved only through Christ, and in Him, who is at once "perfect God" and "perfect Man," to use the phraseology of Chalcedon. The main theme of Patristic theology was always the Mystery of Christ's Person. Athanasian theology, as well as Cappadocian theology, was basically Christological. And this Christological concern permeated the whole theological thinking of the Ancient Church. It is still the guiding principle of Orthodox theology today. Indeed, there is actually nothing specifically "Eastern" in this. It is simply the *common ethos* of the Ancient Church. But, probably, it has been more faithfully preserved in the Eastern Tradition. One can evolve the whole body of Orthodox belief out of the Dogma of Chalcedon.

In Patristic theology the Mystery of Christ has been always presented and interpreted *in the perspective of Salva-*

tion. It was not just a speculative problem. It was rather an existential problem. Christ came to solve the problem of man's destiny. This soteriological perspective is conspicuous in the thought of St. Irenaeus, St. Athanasius, the Cappadocians, St. Cyril of Alexandria, St. Maximus, St. Symeon the New Theologian, up to St. Gregory Palamas. Yet, "Soteriology" itself culminates in the concept of "New Creation." It was both the Pauline and the Johannine theme. And the whole dimension of Christology is disclosed only in the doctrine of *the Whole Christ—totus Christus, caput et corpus,* as St. Augustine loved to say. The doctrine of the Church is not an "appendix" to Christology, and not just an extrapolation of the "Christological principle," as it has been often assumed. There is much more than an "analogy." Ecclesiology, in the Orthodox view is an integral part of Christology. There is no elaborate "ecclesiology" in the Greek Fathers. There are but scattered hints and occasional remarks. The ultimate reason for that was in the total integration of the Church into the Mystery of Christ. "The Body of Christ" is not an "appendix." Indeed, the final purpose of the Incarnation was that the Incarnate should have "a body," which is the Church, the New Humanity, redeemed and reborn in the Head. This emphasis was especially strong in St. John Chrysostom, in his popular preaching, addressed to all and to everybody. In this interpretation Christology is given its full existential significance, is related to man's ultimate destiny. Christ is never alone. He is always the Head of His Body. In Orthodox theology and devotion alike, Christ is never separated from His Mother, the *Theotokos,* and His "friends," the saints. The Redeemer and the redeemed belong together inseparably. In the daring phrase of St. John Chrysostom, inspired by Ephes. 1. 23, Christ will be *complete* only when His Body *has been completed.*

It is commonly assumed that, in counterdistinction from the West, Eastern theology is mainly concerned with Incarnation and Resurrection and that the "theology of the Cross," *theologia crucis,* has been under-developed in the East. Indeed, Orthodox theology is emphatically a "theology of glory," *theologia gloriae,* but only because it is primarily a "theology of the Cross." The Cross itself is the sign of glory. The Cross itself is regarded not so much as a climax of Christ's humiliation, but rather as a disclosure of Divine might and glory. "Now is the Son of man glorified, and God is glorified in him." Or, in the words of a Sunday hymn, "it is by the Cross that great joy has come into the world." On the one hand, the whole *oikonomia* of Redemption is summed up in one comprehensive vision: *the victory of Life.* On the other, this *oikonomia* is related to the basic predicament of fallen man, to his existential situation, culminating in his actualized "mortality," and the "last enemy" is identified, accordingly, as "death." It was this "last enemy" that had been defeated and abrogated on the tree of the Cross, *in ara crucis.* The Lord of Life did enter the dark abyss of death, and "death" was destroyed by the flashes of His glory. This is the main motive of the divine office on Easter Day in the Orthodox Church: "trampling down death by death." The phrase itself is significant: Christ's death is itself a victory, Christ's death dismisses man's mortality. According to the Fathers, Christ's Resurrection was not just a glorious sequel to the sad catastrophe of crucifixion, by which "humiliation" had been, by divine intervention, transmuted and transvaluated into "victory." Christ was victorious precisely on the Cross. *The Death on the Cross itself was a manifestation of Life.* Good Friday in the Eastern Church is not a day of mourning. Indeed, it is a day of reverent silence, and the Church abstains from celebrating the Holy Eucharist on that day. Christ is resting in His tomb. But it is the Blessed Sabbath, *requies Sabbati Magni,* in the phrase of St. Ambrose. Or, in the words of an Eastern hymn, "this is the blessed Sabbath, this is the day of rest, whereon the Only Begotten Son of God has rested from all His deeds." The Cross itself is regarded as an act of God. The act of Creation has been completed on the Cross.

According to the Fathers, the death on the Cross was effective
not as a death of an Innocent One, not just as a sign of
surrender and endurance, not just as a display of human
obedience, but primarily as the *death of the Incarnate God,*
as a disclosure of Christ's Lordship. St. John Chrysostom put it
admirably: "I call Him King, *because I see Him crucified,*
for it is appropriate for a King to die for His subjects" (*in
crucem et latronem,* hom. I). Or, in the daring phrase of St.
Gregory of Nazianzus, "we needed a God Incarnate, we
needed God put to death, that we might live" (*Hom.* 45.
28). Two dangers must be cautiously avoided in the interpretation of the mystery of the Cross: *docetic* and *kenotic.* In
both cases the paradoxical balance of the Chalcedonian definition is broken and distorted. Indeed, Christ's death was a
true death. The Incarnate did truly languish and suffer at
Gethsemane and on Calvary: "by His stripes we are healed."
The utter reality of suffering must be duly acknowledged and
emphasized, lest the Cross is dissolved into fiction: *ut non
evacuetur crux Christi.* Yet, it was the Lord of Creation that
died, the Son of God Incarnate, "One of the Holy Trinity."
The Hypostatic Union has not been broken, or even reduced,
by Christ's death. It may be properly said that God died
on the Cross, but in His own humanity. "He who dwelleth
in the highest is reckoned among the dead, and in the little
grave findeth lodging" (Office of Good Saturday, Canon,
Ode IX). Christ's death is a human death indeed, yet it is
death within the hypostasis of the Word, the Incarnate Word.
And therefore it is a resurrecting death, a disclosure of Life.
Only in this connection can we understand adequately the
whole sacramental fabric of the Church, beginning with
Baptism: one rises with Christ from the baptismal font precisely because this font represents the grave of Christ, His
"life-bearing grave," as it is usually described by the Orthodox. The mystery of the Cross can be understood only in the
context of the total Christological vision. The mystery of
Salvation can be adequately apprehended only in the contest

of an accurate conception of Christ's Person: *One Person in two natures. One* Person, and therefore one has to follow strictly the pattern of the Creed: it is the Son of God who came down, became man, suffered and died, and rose again. There was but One Divine Person acting in the story of salvation—yet Incarnate. Only out of this Chalcedonian vision can we understand the faith and devotion of the Eastern Orthodox Church.

IV

Let us turn, in conclusion, to the immediate purpose of our present gathering together. We are meeting now in an ecumenical setting. What is actually our meeting ground? Christian charity? Or deep conviction that all Christians somehow belong together, and the hope that ultimately the "divided Christians" may be re-united? Or do we assume that certain "unity" is already given, or rather has never been lost? And then—what kind of "unity"? In any case, we are meeting now as we are, i.e., precisely *as divided,* conscious of the division and mutual separation. And yet, the "meeting" itself constitutes already some kind of "unity."

It has been recently suggested that basic division in the Christian Word was not so much between "Catholics" and "Protestants," as precisely between East and West. "This opposition is not of a dogmatic nature: neither the West nor the East can be summed up in one set of dogmas applying to it as a whole... The difference between East and West lies in the very nature and method of their theological thinking, in the very soil out of which their dogmatic, liturgical and canonical developments arise, in the very style of their religious life."[10] There is some element of truth in this descriptive statement. We should not, however, overlook the fact that these different "blocs" of insights and convictions did actually grow out of a *common* ground and were, in fact, products of a *disintegration of mind*. Accordingly, the very problem of Christian reconciliation is not that of a *correlation* of parallel traditions, but precisely that of the *reintegration* of a distorted tradition. The two traditions may seem quite irreconcilable, when they are compared and confronted as they are at the present. Yet their differences themselves are, to a great extent, simply the results of disintegration: they are, as it were, *distinctions* stiffened into *contradictions*. The East and the West can meet and find each other only if they remember their original kinship in the *common past*. The first step to make is to realize that, inspite of all peculiarities, East and West belong organically together in the Unity of Christendom.

Now, Arnold Toynbee, in his *Study of History,* contended that "Western Europe," or, as he put it himself, "the Western Christian Society," was an "intelligible," i.e., "self-explanatory" field of study. It was just "self-contained." Obviously, there were also several other fields of study, i.e., certain other "societies," but all of them were also "self-contained" and "self-explanatory." One of them was the Christian East—the Eastern Christian Society, as Toynbee labelled it. Indeed, all these "societies" actually "co-exist," in the same historic space. Yet they are "self-explanatory." This contention of Toynbee is highly relevant for our task. Do we really belong to the two different and "self-explanatory" worlds, as he suggests? Are these worlds really "self-explanatory"? Indeed, Christendom is sorely divided. But are the divided parts really "self-explanatory"? And here lies the crux of the problem.

The basic flaw of Toynbee's conception is that he simply ignores *the tragedy* of Christian disruption. In fact, East and West are not independent units, and therefore are not "intelligible in themselves." They are *fragments* of one world, of one Christendom, which, in God's design, ought not to have been disrupted. The tragedy of division is the major and crucial problem of Christian history. An attempt to view Christian history as one comprehensive whole is already, in a certain sense, a step in advance toward the restoration of the broken unity. It was an important ecumenical achievement when the "divided Christians" realized that they did belong together and therefore had to "stay together." The next step is to realize that all Christians have "common history," that they have had a common history, a common ancestry. This is what I have ventured to describe as "ecumenism in time." In the accomplishment of this task the Orthodox Church has a special function. She is a living embodiment of an uninterrupted tradition, in thought and devotion. She stands not for a certain "particular" tradition, but for the Tradition of ages, for the Tradition of the Undivided Church.

Every scribe which is instructed unto the Kingdom of Heaven is like unto a man that is an householder, which bringeth forth out of his treasure things new and old (Matt. 13. 52).

The Fathers of the Church and
The Old Testament

THE FAMOUS PHRASE of St. Augustine can be taken as
typical of the whole Patristic attitude towards the Old
Dispensation. *Novum Testamentum in Vetere latet. Vetus
Testamentum in Novo patet.* The New Testament is an
accomplishment or a consummation of the Old. Christ Jesus is
the Messiah spoken of by the prophets. In Him all promises
and expectations are fulfilled. The Law and the Gospel
belong together. And nobody can claim to be a true follower
of Moses unless he believes that Jesus is the Lord. Any
one who does not recognize in Jesus the Messiah, the
Anointed of the Lord, does thereby betray the Old Dispensation itself. Only the Church of Christ keeps now the right
key to the Scriptures, the true key to the prophecies of old.
Because all these prophecies are fulfilled in Christ.

St. Justin rejects the suggestion that the Old Testament
is a link holding together the Church and the Synagogue.
For him quite the opposite is true. All Jewish claims must

"The Old Testament and the Fathers of the Church" originally appeared
in *The Student World,* XXXII No. 4 (1939), 281-288. Reprinted by
permission of the author.

31

be formally rejected. The Old Testament no longer belongs to the Jews. It belongs to the Church alone. And the Church of Christ is therefore the only true Israel of God. The Israel of old was but an undeveloped Church. The word "Scriptures" itself in early Christian use meant first of all just the Old Testament and in this sense obviously this word is used in the Creed: "according to the Scriptures," i.e. according to the prophecies and promises of the Old Dispensation.

The Unity of the Bible

The Old Testament is copiously quoted by all early writers. And even to the Gentiles the message of salvation was always presented in the context of the Old Testament. This was an argument from antiquity. The Old Covenant was not destroyed by Christ, but renewed and accomplished. In this sense Christianity was not a new religion, but rather the oldest. The new Christian "Scriptures" were simply incorporated into the inherited Hebrew Bible, as its organic completion. And only the whole Bible, both Testaments together, was regarded as an adequate record of Christian Revelation. There was no break between the two Testaments, but a unity of Divine economy. And the first task of Christian theology was to show and to explain in what way the Old Dispensation was the preparation and the anticipation of this final Revelation of God in Jesus Christ. The Christian message was not merely a proclamation of some doctrines, but first of all a record of mighty acts and deeds of God through the ages. It was a history of Divine guidance, culminating in the person of Christ Jesus whom God has sent to redeem His people. God has chosen Israel for His inheritance, to be His people, to be the keeper of His truth, and to this Chosen People alone the Divine Word was entrusted. And now the Church receives this sacred heritage.

The Old Testament as a whole was regarded as a Christian prophecy, as an "evangelical preparation." Very early some special selections of the Old Testament texts were compiled for the use of Christian missionaries. The *Testimonia* of St. Cyprian is one of the best specimens of the kind. And St. Justin in his *Dialogue with Trypho* made an attempt to prove the truth of Christianity from the Old Testament alone. The Marcionite attempt to break the New Testament away from its Old Testament roots was vigorously resisted and condemned by the Great Church. The unity of both Testaments was strongly emphasized, the inner agreement of both was stressed. There was always some danger of reading too much of Christian doctrine into the writings of the Old Testament. And historical perspective was sometimes dangerously obscured. But still there was a great truth in all these exegetical endeavors. It was a strong feeling of the Divine guidance through the ages.

The Old Testament as Allegory

The history of Old Testament interpretation in the Early Church is one of the most thrilling but embarrassing chapters in the history of Christian doctrine. With the Greek Old Testament the Church inherited also some exegetical traditions. Philo, this Hellenized Jew from Alexandria, was the best exponent of this pre-Christian endeavor to commend the Old Testament to the Gentile world. He adopted for this task a very peculiar method, a method of allegory. Philo himself had no understanding of history whatever. Messianic motives were completely overlooked or ignored in his philosophy of the Bible. For him the Bible was just a system of the Divine Philosophy, not so much a sacred history. Historical events as such were of no interest and of no importance for him. The Bible was for him just a single book, in which he failed to discern any historical perspective or progress. It was treated by him rather as a collection of glorious parables and didactic stories intended to convey and to illustrate certain philosophical and ethical ideas.

In such an extreme form this allegorical method was never accepted by the Church. One has however to recognize a strong influence of Philo on all exegetical essays of the first centuries. St. Justin made a large use of Philo. Pseudo-Barnabas (early 2nd century) once went so far as to deny the historical character of the Old Testament altogether. Philonic traditions were taken up by the Christian school of Alexandria. And even later St. Ambrose was closely following Philo in his commentaries and could be justly described as *Philo latinus.* This allegorical exegesis was ambiguous and misleading.

It took a long time before the balance was established or restored. And still one must not overlook the positive contribution of this method. The best exponent of allegorical exegesis in the Church was Origen and his influence was enormous. One may be shocked sometimes by his exegetical daring and licence. He used indeed to read too much of his own into the sacred text. But it would be a grave mistake to describe him as a philosopher. He was first of all and throughout a Biblical scholar, certainly in the style of his own age. He spent days and nights over the Bible. His main purpose was just to base all doctrine and all theology on a Biblical ground. He was responsible to a great extent for the strength of the Biblical spirit in the entire patristic theology. He did much more for an average believer; he made the Bible accessible to him. He steadily introduced the Old Testament into his preaching. He helped the average Christian to read and to use the Old Testament for their edification. He always stressed the unity of the Bible, bringing both Testaments into a closer relation. And he made a new attempt to build the whole doctrine of God on a Biblical basis.

Origen's limitations are obvious. But his positive contribution was much greater. And it was he who by his example taught Christian theologians to go back always for their inspiration to the sacred text of Scriptures. His line was followed by most of the Fathers. But he met strong opposition at once. There is no room to dwell at length on the controversy between the two exegetical schools in the Early Church. The main features are commonly known. The Antiochene school stood for "history," Alexandrinians rather for "contemplation." And surely both elements had to be brought together in a balanced synthesis.

History or Preaching

The main Alexandrinian presumption was that, as being Divinely inspired, the Scriptures must carry in them some *universal* message, for all nations and ages. Their purpose was just to exhibit this message, to discover and to preach all these riches of Divine wisdom which have been providentially stored in the Bible. Beneath the letter of the Holy Writ there are some other lessons to be learned only by the advanced. Behind all human records of manifold revelations of God one can discern the Revelation, to apprehend the very Word of God in all its eternal splendor.

It was assumed that even when God was speaking under some special circumstances there was always something in His word that passes all historical limitations. One has to distinguish very carefully between a direct prophecy and what one might describe as an application. Many of the Old Testament narratives can be most instructive for a believer even when no deliberate "prefiguration" of Christian truth has been intended by the sacred writers themselves. The main presupposition was that God meant the Holy Writ to be the eternal guide for the whole of mankind. And therefore an application or a standing re-interpretation of the Old Testament was authorized.

The Antiochene exegesis had a special concern for the direct meaning of the old prophecies and stories. The chief exponent of this "historical" exegisis was Theodore of Mopsuestia, known in the East simply as "the Interpreter." And although his authority was gravely compromised by his condemnation for his erroneous doctrines, his influence on the Christian exegesis of the Old Testament was still very considerable. This "historical" exegesis was often in danger of missing the universal meaning of Divine Revelation by overemphasis of the local and national aspects of the Old Testament. And even more, to lose the sacred perspective, to deal with the Old Testament history as if it were merely the history of one single people among the nations of the earth and not a history of the only true Covenant of God.

St. John Chrysostom has combined the best elements of both schools in his exegetical endeavor. He was an Antiochene scholar himself, but he was in many respects a follower of Origen as well. Allegories may be misleading. But one has not to overlook the "typical" meaning of events themselves. Old Testament institutions and personalities were also the "types" or "figures" of the things to come. History was prophetic itself. Events themselves do prophesy, they did and do point out to something else, beyond themselves. The Early Fathers can hardly be described as "fundamentalists." They were always after the Divine truth, after the Divine message itself, which is often rather concealed under the cover of the letter. The belief in Inspiration could rather discourage the fundamentalist tendency. The Divine truth cannot be reduced to the letter even of Holy Writ. One of the best specimens of Patristic exegesis was the *Hexaemeron* of St. Basil, who has succeeded in bringing forward the religious truth of the Biblical narrative of the creation with real balance and sound moderation.

The Old Testament and Christian Worship

The Patristic attitude towards the Old Testament was

reflected in the history of Christian worship. The Jewish roots of Christian Liturgy are obvious. But the whole system of Christian public worship was linked closely to the practice of the Synagogue as well. The Psalms were inherited from the Jews, and they became a pattern of the whole Christian hymnography in the early Church. The Psalms form the skeleton of Christian offices until now. They were the basis of all devotional literature in old days.

The student of public worship in the Eastern Orthodox Church would be impressed by the amount of Old Testament references, hints and images, in all offices and hymns. The unity of the two Testaments is stressed throughout. Biblical motives are superabundant. Many hymns are but variations on the pattern of the Old Testament songs, from the song of Moses at the crossing of the Red Sea up to the song of Zechariah, the father of John the Baptist. On great festivals numerous lessons from the Old Testament are appointed and actually read to stress that Christian perfection was but a consummation of what was pre-figured and foreshadowed, or even directly predicted of old. And specially in the offices of Holy Week this Old Testament preparation is particularly emphasized. The whole worship is based upon this conviction that the true Covenant was always one, that there was a complete agreement between the Prophets and the Apostles. And all this system was established just in the later Patristic age.

One of the most striking examples of this devotional Biblicism is the glorious *Great Canon* of St. Andreas of Crete, read at the Great Compline in Lent. It is a strong exhortation, an appeal for repentance, composed with a real poetical inspiration and based upon the Bible. The whole series of Old Testament sinners, both penitent and impenitent, is remembered. One can be almost lost in this continuous stream of names and examples. One is emphatically reminded that all this Old Testament story belongs to one as a Christian. One is invited to think over again and again this

wonderful story of Divine guidance and human obstinacy
and failures. The Old Testament is kept as a great treasure.
One has to mention as well the influence which the *Song of
Songs* had on the development of Christian mysticism.
Origen's commentary on this book was in St. Jerome's opinion
his best composition, in which he surpassed himself. And
St. Gregory of Nyssa's mystical commentary on the *Song of
Songs* is a rich mine of a genuine Christian inspiration.

The Old Testament as the Word of God

It has been more than once suggested that in the Greek
Fathers the primitive Christian message was hellenized too
much. One has to be very cautious with all such utterances.
In any case it is the Fathers who have kept all the treasures
of the Old Testament and made them the indispensable
heritage of the Church, both in worship and in theology. The
only thing they never did is this: they never kept fast to
the Jewish limitations. The Holy Writ for them was an
eternal and universal Revelation. It is addressed to all mankind now simply because it was addressed to all nations by
God Himself even when the Divine Word was delivered
by the prophets to the Chosen People alone. It means that
one cannot measure the depth of Divine Revelation
with the measure of some past time only, however sacred
those times may be. It is not enough to be sure that the
ancient Hebrews understood and interpreted the Scriptures
in a certain way. This interpretation can never be final. New
light has been thrown on the old revelations by Him Who
came just to accomplish and to fulfil the Law and the
Prophets. The Scriptures are not merely historical documents.
They are really the Word of God, the Divine message to
all generations. And Christ Jesus is the Alpha and Omega
of the Scriptures, both the climax and the knot of the Bible.
This is the standing message of the Fathers to the Church
Universal about the Old Dispensation.

St. Athanasius' Concept of
Creation

I

THE IDEA of Creation was a striking Christian innovation in philosophy. The problem itself was alien and even unintelligible to the Greek mind: *de rerum originatione radicali.* The Greek mind was firmly addicted to the conception of an Eternal Cosmos, permanent and immutable in its essential structure and composition. This Cosmos simply existed. Its existence was "necessary," it was an ultimate or first *datum,* beyond which neither thought nor imagination could penetrate. There was, indeed, much movement within the world—"the wheel of origin and decay." But the Cosmos as a whole was unchangeable, and its permanent structure was repeatedly and unfailingly exhibited in its rotation and self-iteration. It was not a static world, there was in it an intense dynamism: but it was a dynamism of inescapable circulation. The Cosmos was a periodical, and yet a "neces-

This article originally appeared in *Studia Patristica,* Vol. VI, ed. F. L. Cross (Berlin: Akademie Verlag; Texte und Untersuchungen zur Geschichte der altchristlichen Literatur, Band 81, 1962), 36-57. Reprinted by permission of the author.

sary" and "immortal" being. The "shape" of the world might be exposed to changes, it was actually in a constant flux, but its very existence was perennial. One simply could not ask intelligently about the "origin" or "beginning" of the Cosmic fabric in the order of existence.[1]

It was precisely at this point that the Greek mind was radically challenged by Biblical Revelation. This was a hard message for the Greeks. Indeed, it is still a hard message for philosophers.

The Bible opens with the story of Creation. "In the beginning God created the heaven and the earth." This has become a credal statement in the Christian Church. The Cosmos was no more regarded as a "self-explanatory" being. Its ultimate and intrinsic dependence upon God's will and action has been vigorously asserted. But much more than just this relation of "dependence" was implied in the Biblical concept: the world was created *ex nihilo,* i.e., it did not exist "eternally." In retrospect one was bound to discover its "beginning"—*post nihilum,* as it were. The tension between the two visions, Hellenic and Biblical, was sharp and conspicuous. Greeks and Christians, as it were, were dwelling in different worlds. Accordingly, the categories of Greek philosophy were inadequate for the description of the world of Christian faith. The main emphasis of Christian faith was precisely on the radical contingency of the Cosmos, on its contingency precisely in the order of existence. Indeed, the very existence of the world pointed, for Christians, to the Other, as its Lord and Maker. On the other hand, the Creation of the world was conceived as a sovereign and "free" act of God, and not as something which was "necessarily" implied or inherent in God's own Being. Thus, there was actually a double contingency: on the side of the Cosmos— which could "not have existed at all," and on the side of the Creator—who could "not have created" anything at all. In the fine phrase of Etienne Gilson, "it is quite true that a Creator is an eminently Christian God, but a God whose very existence is to be a creator is not a Christian God at all."[2] The very existence of the world was regarded by the Christians as a mystery and miracle of Divine Freedom.

Christian thought, however, was maturing but gradually and slowly, by a way of trial and retraction. The early Christian writers would often describe their new vision of faith in the terms of old and current philosophy. They were not always aware of, and certainly did not always guard against, the ambiguity which was involved in such an enterprise. By using Greek categories Christian writers were forcing upon themselves, without knowing it, a world which was radically different from that in which they dwelt by faith. Thus they were often caught between the vision of their faith and the inadequacy of the language they were using. This predicament must be taken quite seriously. Etienne Gilson once suggested that Christianity has brought the new wine, but the old skins were still good enough, i.e., the skins of Greek Philosophy. "La pensée chrétienne apportait du vin nouveau, mais les vieilles outres étaient encore bonnes."[3] It is an elegant phrase. But is it not rather an optimistic overstatement? Indeed, the skins did not burst at once, but was it really to the benefit of nascent Christian thought? The skins were badly tainted with an old smell, and the wine acquired in them had an alien flavor. In fact, the new vision required new terms and categories for its adequate and fair expression. It was an urgent task for Christians "to coin new names," τὸ καινοτομεῖν τὰ ὀνόματα, in the phrase of St. Gregory of Nazianzus.

Indeed, the radical contingency of the created world was faithfully acknowledged by Christian writers from the very beginning. The Lordship of God over all His Creation was duly emphasized. God alone was mighty and eternal. All created things were brought into existence, and sustained in existence, solely by the grace and pleasure of God, by His sovereign will. Existence was always a gift of God. From this point of view, even the human soul was "mortal," by its own "nature," i.e. contingent, because it was a creature, and was maintained only by the grace of God. St. Justin was quite explicit at this point—in opposition to Platonic arguments for "immortality." Indeed, "immortal" would mean for him "uncreated."[4] But it was not yet clear how this creative "will" of God was related to His own "being." And this was the crucial problem. In early Christian thinking the very idea of God was only gradually released out of that "cosmological setting," in which it used to be apprehended by Greek philosophical thought. The mystery of the Holy Trinity itself was often interpreted in an ambiguous cosmological context—not primarily as a mystery of God's own Being, but rather in the perspective of God's creative and redemptive action and self-disclosure in the world. This was the main predicament of the Logos-theology in the Apologists, in Hippolytus, and in Tertullian. All these writers could not distinguish consistently between the categories of the Divine "Being" and those of Divine "Revelation" *ad extra*, in the world. Indeed, it was rather a lack of precision, an inadequacy of language, than an obstinate doctrinal error. The Apologists were not just pre-Arians or pro-Arians. Bishop George Bull was right in his *Defensio Fidei Nicenae* against the charges of Petavius. And yet, as G. L. Prestige has pointed out, "the innocent speculations of Apologists came to provide support for the Arian school of thought."[5]

The case of Origen is especially significant. He also failed to distinguish between the ontological and cosmological dimensions. As Bolotov has aptly stated, "the logical link between the generation of the Son and the existence of the world was not yet broken in the speculation of Origen."[6] It can be even contended that this very link has been rather reinforced in Origen's thinking. The ultimate question for Origen was precisely this: Is it possible or permissible to think of God without conceiving Him at once as Creator? The negative answer to this question was for Origen the only devout option. An opposite assumption would be sheer blasphemy. God could never have become anything that He has not been always. There is nothing simply "potential" in God's Being, everything being eternally actualized. This was Origen's basic assumption, his deepest conviction. God is always the Father of the Only Begotten, and the Son is co-eternal with the Father: any other assumption would have compromised the essential immutability of the Divine Being. But God also is always the Creator and the Lord. Indeed, if God is Creator at all—and it is an article of faith that He is Lord and Creator—we must necessarily assume that He had always been Creator and Lord. For, obviously, God never "advances" toward what He had not been before. For Origen this implied inevitably also an eternal actualization of the world's existence, of all those things over which God's might and Lordship were exercised. Origen himself used the term παντοκράτωρ, which he borrowed surely from the Septuagint. Its use by Origen is characteristic. The Greek term is much more pointed than its Latin or English renderings: *Omnipotens,* "Almighty." These latter terms emphasize just might or power. The Greek word stresses specifically the actual exercise of power. The edge of Origen's argument is taken off in Latin translation. "Παντοκράτωρ is in the first place an active word, conveying the idea not just of capacity but of the actualization of capacity."[7] Παντοκράτωρ means just κύριος, the ruling Lord. And God could not be παντοκράτωρ eternally unless τὰ πάντα also existed from all eternity. God's might must have been eternally actualized in the created Cosmos, which therefore appears to be an eternal concomitant or companion of the Divine Being. In this context any clear distinction between "generation" and "creation" was actually impossible—both were eternal relations, indeed "necessary" relations, as it were, intrinsic for the Divine Being. Origen was unable, and indeed reluctant and unwilling, to admit anything "contingent" about the world itself, since, in his conception, this would have involved also a certain "change" on the Divine level. In Origen's system the eternal being of the Holy Trinity and the eternal existence of the world are indivisibly and insolubly linked together: both stand and fall together. The Son is indeed eternal, and eternally "personal" and "hypostatic." But He is eternally begotten in relation to the eternally created world.[8]

Origen's argument is straight and consistent, under his basic assumptions. It would be flagrantly impious to admit that God could ever have existed without His Wisdom, even for a single moment—*ad punctum momenti alicujus.* God is always the Father of His Son, who is born of Him, but "without any beginning"—*sine ullo tamen initio.* And Origen specifies: "not only of that kind which can be distinguished by intervals of time—*aliquibus temporum spatiis,* but even of that other kind which the mind alone is wont to contemplate in itself and to perceive, if I may say so, with the bare intellect and reason"—*nudo intellectu.* In other words, Wisdom is begotten beyond the limit of any imaginable "beginning"—*extra omne ergo quod vel dici vel intelligi potest initium.* Moreover, as Origen explained elsewhere, the "generation" of Wisdom could not be interpreted as an accomplished "event," but rather as a permanent and continuous relationship—a relation of "being begotten," just as radiance is perpetually concomitant with the light itself, and Wisdom is, in the phrase of *Sap. Sal.* 7, 26, an ἀπαύγασμα φωτὸς ἀϊδίου (*In Jerem. hom.* IX 4: οὐχὶ ἐγέννησεν ὁ πατὴρ τὸν υἱὸν . . . ἀλλ᾿ ἀεὶ γεννᾷ αὐτόν, 70 Klostermann; cf. Latin translation in the "Apology" of Pamphilus, *PG* 17, 564). Now, according to Origen, in the very subsistence of Wisdom the whole design of creation is already implied. The whole creation, *universa creatura,* is pre-arranged in Wisdom (*De princ.* I 2, 2; 29—30 Koetschau). The text of this important passage might have been somewhat edited by the Latin translator, but surely the main argument was faithfully reproduced (cf. the fragment in Greek, in Methodius, *De creatis,* quoted by Photius,

Cod. 235). Origen spoke of "prevision": *virtute praescientiae.* But, according to his own basic principle, there could be no temporal order or sequence. The world as "pre-viewed" in Wisdom had to be also eternally actualized.[9] It is in this direction that Origen continued his argument. And here the terms "Father" and *"Pantokrator"* are conspicuously bracketed together. "Now as one cannot be father apart from having a son, nor a lord apart from holding a possession or a slave, so we cannot even call God almighty if there are none over whom He can exercise His power. Accordingly, to prove that God is Almighty we must assume the existence of the world." But, obviously, God is Lord from all eternity. Consequently, the world, in its entirety, also existed from all eternity: *necessario existere oportet (De princ.* I 2, 10; 41—42 Koetschau; cf. the Greek quotation in Justinian, *Epist. ad Mennam,* Mansi IX 528). In brief, the world must be always co-existent with God and therefore co-eternal. Of course, Origen meant the primordial world of spirits. Actually, in Origen's conception there was but one eternal hierarchical system of beings, a "chain of being." He could never escape the cosmological pattern of Middle Platonism.[10]

Moreover, Origen seems to have interpreted the Generation of the Son as an act of the Father's will: ἐκ τοῦ θελήματος τοῦ πατρὸς ἐγεννήθη (quoted by Justinian, Mansi IX 525). On the other hand he was utterly suspicious of the phrase: ἐκ τῆς οὐσίας πατρός, and probably even formally repudiated it. For him it was a dangerous and misleading phrase, heavily overloaded with gross "materialistic" associations, and suggesting division and separation in the Divine substance (*In Ioh.* XX 18; 351 Preuschen; *De princ.* IV 4, 1; 348 Koetschau; cf. the quotation by Marcellus, given in Eusebius, *c. Marcellum* I 4; 21 Klostermann). The textual evidence is confused and inconclusive.[11] It may be true that at this point Origen was opposing the Gnostics, especially the Valentinian conception of προβολή, and only wanted to vindicate the strictly spiritual character of every-thing Divine.[12] Yet, there was a flagrant ambiguity. Both the generation of the Son and the creation of the world are equally attributed to the will or counsel of the Father. "And my own opinion is that an act of the Father's will—*voluntas Patris*—ought to be sufficient to ensure the subsistence of what He wills. For in willing He uses no other means than that which is produced by the deliberation of His will—*nisi quae consilio voluntatis profertur*. Thus, it is in this way that the existence of the Son also is begotten of Him—*ita ergo et filii ab eo subsistentia generatur*" (*De princ.* I 2, 6; 35 Koetschau). The meaning of this passage is rather obscure, and we have no Greek text.[13] But, in any case, once again the Son is explicitly bracketed together with creatures.[14]

There was an unresolved tension, or an inner contradic-tion, in the system of Origen. And it led to an inner conflict, and finally to an open split, among those theologians who were profoundly influenced by his powerful thought. It may be contended, indeed, that his trinitarian theology was intrinsically orthodox, that is, pro-Nicene, so that the inter-pretation of his views by St. Athanasius and the Cappa-docians was fair and congenial to his ultimate vision. Indeed, Origen strongly defended the eternity of the Divine Genera-tion and, at this point, was definitely anti-Arian. If we can trust St. Athanasius, Origen explicitly denounced those who dared to suggest that "there was when the Son was not," ἦν ποτε ὅτε οὐκ ἦν ὁ υἱός, whosoever these people might have been (see the quotation from Origen in St. Athan-asius, *De decretis* 27). Yet, on the other hand, the general scheme of his theology was utterly inadequate at many crucial points. In any case, the controversies of the fourth century can be properly understood only in the perspective of Origen's theology and its problematic. The crucial philosophical prob-lem at the bottom of that theological controversy was precisely that of time and eternity. Within the system itself there were but two opposite options: to reject the eternity of the world or to contest the eternity of the Logos. The latter option was taken by Arius and all those who, for various reasons, sympathized with him. His opponents were bound to insist on the temporality of the world. The problem of creation was the crucial philosophical problem in the dispute. No clarity could be reached in the doctrine of God until the problem of creation had been settled. Indeed, the essence of the controversy was religious, the ultimate issue was theological. But faith and piety themselves could be vindicated at this historic juncture only by philosophical weapons and arguments. This was well understood already by St. Alexander of Alexandria: φιλοσοφῶν ἐθεολόγει, says Socrates of him (I 5). St. Alexander made the first attempt to disentangle the doctrine of God out of the traditional cosmological context, while keeping himself still close to the tenets of Origen.[15]

Arius himself contended that the Logos was a "creature," a privileged creature indeed, not like others, but still no more than a κτίσμα originated by the will of God. Accordingly, God for him was primarily the Creator, and apart from that, little, if anything, could be said of the unfathomable and incomprehensible Being of God, unknown even to the Son. Actually, there was no room for "theology" in his system. The only real problem was that of "cosmology"—a typically Hellenic approach. Arius had to define the notion of creation. Two major points were made: (a) the total dissimilarity between God and all other realities which "had beginning," beginning of any kind; (b) the "beginning" itself. The Son had a "beginning," simply because He was a son, that is—originated from the Father, as His ἀρχή: only God (the Father) was ἄναρχος in the strict sense of the word. It seems that with Arius the main emphasis lay on the relation of dependence as such, and the element of time was comparatively irrelevant for his argument. Indeed, in his famous letter to Eusebius of Nicomedia, Arius stated plainly that the Son came into existence "before all times and ages"—

πρὸ χρόνων καὶ πρὸ αἰώνων (apud Epiph., *Haeres.*
LXIX 6; 156 Holl, and Theodoret, *Hist. eccl.* I 4, 63; 25
Parmentier). St. Athanasius himself complained that the
Arians evaded the term χρόνος (*Contra Arianos* I 13). Yet,
they obviously contended that all things "created" did somehow "come into existence," so that the state of "being" has
been preceded, at least logically, by a state of "non-being"
out of which they have emerged, ἐξ οὐκ ὄντων. In this
sense "they did not exist before they came into existence"—
οὐκ ἦν πρὶν γεννηθῇ. Obviously, "creatureliness" meant
for the Arians more than just "dependence": it implied also
an "essential" dissimilarity with God, and a finitude, that
is—some limitation in retrospect. On the other hand, it was
strongly stressed that all Creation was grounded in the will
and deliberation of God: θελήματι καὶ βουλῇ, as Arius
himself wrote to Eusebius. The latter motive was Origenistic.
Indeed, Arius went much further than Origen: Origen
rejected only the Gnostic προβολή, but Arius repudiated any
"natural" affinity of Logos with God. Arius simply had
nothing to say about the life of God, apart from His
engagement in Creation. At this point his thought was
utterly archaic.

It is highly significant that the Council of Antioch in
324/5—that is, before Nicaea—took up all these major points.
The Son is begotten "not from that which is not but from
the Father," in an ineffable and indescribable manner, "not
as made but as properly offspring," and not "by volition."
He existed everlastingly and "did not at one time not exist."
Again, "He is the express image, not of the will or anything
else, but of His Father's very hypostasis."[16] For all these
reasons the Son could not be regarded as "creature." Nothing
has been said about Creation. But one can easily guess what
"Creation" and "creatureliness" meant for the Fathers of
the Council. All elements, of which the later clear distinction
between "begetting" and "creating" (or "making") has
been construed, are already implied in the conciliar statement.

St. Athanasius made a decisive contribution at the next stage of the dispute.

II

Already in his early writings, before the outbreak of the Arian strife, St. Athanasius was wrestling with the problem of Creation. For him it was intimately related to the crucial message of the Christian faith: the redemptive Incarnation of the Divine Word. Indeed, his interpretation of Redemption, as it was expounded in *De Incarnatione Verbi*, is grounded in a distinctive conception of the Cosmos. There was, in the vision of St. Athanasius, an ultimate and radical cleavage or *hiatus* between the absolute Being of God and the contingent existence of the World. There were actually two modes of existence, radically different and totally dissimilar. On the one hand—the Being of God, eternal and immutable, "immortal" and "incorruptible." On the other—the flux of the Cosmos, intrinsically mutable and "mortal," exposed to change and "corruption." The ultimate ontological tension was precisely between the Divine ἀφθαρσία and the φθορά of the Cosmic flux. Since the whole Creation had once begun, by the will and pleasure of God, "out of nothing," an ultimate "meonic" tendency was inherent in the very "nature" of all creaturely things. By their own "nature," all created things were intrinsically unstable, fluid, impotent, mortal, liable to dissolution: Τῶν μὲν γὰρ γενητῶν ἡ φύσις, ἄτε δὴ ἐξ οὐκ ὄντων ὑποστᾶσα, ρευστή τις καὶ ἀσθενὴς καὶ θνητὴ καθ' ἑαυτὴν συγκρινωμένη τυγχάνει. Their existence was precarious. If there was any order and stability in the Cosmos, they were, as it were, super-imposed upon its own "nature," and imparted to created things by the Divine Logos. It was the Logos that ordered and bound together the whole Creation—συνέχει καὶ συσφίγγει—counter-acting thereby, as it were, its inherent leaning toward disintegration. Indeed, the creaturely "nature" itself is also God's creation. But it was inwardly limited by its creaturely condition: it was inescapably "mortal" and mutable. St. Athanasius formally disavowed the notion of seminal λόγοι, immanent and inherent in the things themselves. Creation stood only by the immediate impact of the Divine Logos. Not only was the Cosmos brought into existence "out of nothing," by an initial and sovereign creative *fiat* of God, but it was maintained in existence solely by the continuous action of the Creator. Man also shared in this "natural" instability of the Cosmos, as a "composite" being and originated "out of the non-existing": ἐκ τοῦ μὴ ὄντος γενόμενοι. By his very "nature," man also was "mortal" and "corruptible"—κατὰ φύσιν φθαρτός—and could escape this condition of mortality only by God's grace and by participation in the energies of the Logos: χάριτι δὲ τῆς τοῦ Λόγου μετουσίας τοῦ κατὰ φύσιν ἐκφυγόντες. By himself man was unable "to continue forever"—οὐχ ἱκανὸν εἴη κατὰ τὸν τῆς ἰδίας γενέσεως λόγον διαμένειν ἀεί (*Contra gentes* 40 to 43; *De incarn.* 2, 3, 5). The pattern of this exposition is conspicuously "Platonic." But St. Athanasius used it judiciously. The cosmic or "demiurgic" function of the Logos was strongly stressed in his conception. But His Divine transcendence was also vigorously stressed. Indeed, the Divine character of the Logos was the main presupposition of the whole argument. The Logos was, in the phrase of St. Athanasius, "the Only-begotten God," originating eternally from the Father as from a spring, a πηγή. There was an absolute dissimilarity between the Logos and the creatures. The Logos is present in the world, but only "dynamically," that is, by His "powers." In His own "substance" He is outside of the world: ἐκτὸς μέν ἐστι τοῦ παντὸς κατ' οὐσίαν, ἐν πᾶσι δέ ἐστι ταῖς ἑαυτοῦ δυνάμεσι (*De incarn.* 17). Now, this distinction between "essence" and "powers" can be traced back to Philo and Plotinus, and, indeed, to the Apologists and

Clement of Alexandria. But in St. Athanasius it has a totally new connotation. It is never applied to the relationship between God and Logos, as had been done even by Origen. It serves now a new purpose: to discriminate strictly between the inner Being of God and His creative and "providential" manifestation *ad extra,* in the creaturely world. The world owes its very existence to God's sovereign will and goodness and stands, over the abyss of its own nothingness and impotence, solely by His quickening "Grace"—as it were, *sola gratia.* But the Grace abides in the world.[17]

In his struggle with the Arians St. Athanasius proceeded from the same presuppositions. The main demarcartion line passes between the Creator and the Creation, and not between the Father and the Son, as Arians contended. Indeed, the Logos is Creator. But He is Creator precisely because He is fully Divine, an "undistinguishable Image" of the Father, ἀπαράλλακτος εἰκών. In creation He is not just an "instrument," ὄργανον. He is its ultimate and immediate efficient cause. His own Being is totally independent of creation, and even of the creative design of the world. At this point St. Athanasius was quite formal. The crucial text is in *Contra Arianos* II 31: Ὁ τοῦ Θεοῦ γὰρ Λόγος οὐ δι᾽ ἡμᾶς γέγονεν, ἀλλὰ μᾶλλον ἡμεῖς δι᾽ αὐτὸν γεγόναμεν, καὶ 'ἐν αὐτῷ ἐκτίσθη τὰ πάντα'· οὐδὲ διὰ τὴν ἡμῶν ἀσθένειαν οὗτος, ὢν δυνατός, ὑπὸ μόνου τοῦ Πατρὸς γέγονεν, ἵν᾽ ἡμᾶς δι᾽ αὐτοῦ ὡς δι᾽ ὀργάνου δημιουργήσῃ· μὴ γένοιτο! οὐκ ἔστιν οὕ-τως. Καὶ γὰρ καὶ εἰ δόξαν ἦν τῷ Θεῷ μὴ ποιῆσαι τὰ γενητά, ἀλλ᾽ ἦν οὐδὲν ἧττον ὁ Λόγος 'πρὸς τὸν Θεόν', καὶ ἐν αὐτῷ ἦν ὁ Πατήρ. Τὰ μέντοι γενητὰ ἀδύνατον ἦν χωρὶς τοῦ Λόγου γενέσθαι· οὕτω γὰρ καὶ γέγονε δι᾽ αὐτοῦ, καὶ εἰκότως. Ἐπειδὴ γὰρ Λό-γος ἐστὶν ἴδιος φύσει τῆς οὐσίας τοῦ Θεοῦ ὁ Υἱός, ἐξ αὐτοῦ τέ ἐστι, καὶ 'ἐν αὐτῷ' ἐστιν, ὡς εἶπεν αὐτός· οὐκ ἠδύνατο μὴ δι᾽ αὐτοῦ γενέσθαι τὰ δημιουργή-ματα.—*Even supposing that the Father had never been disposed to create the world, or a part of it, nevertheless the Logos would have been with God and the Father in Him . . .* This was the core of the argument. In fact, St. Athanasius carefully eliminates all references to the οἰκονομία of creation or salvation from his description of the inner relationship between the Father and the Son. This was his major and decisive contribution to Trinitarian theology in the critical situation of the Arian dispute. And this left him free to define the concept of Creation properly. Θεολογία, in the ancient sense of the word, and οἰκονομία must be clearly and strictly distinguished and delimited, although they could not be separated from each other. But God's "Being" has an absolute ontological priority over God's action and will.

God is much more than just "Creator." When we call God "a Father," we mean something higher than His relation to creatures (*Contra Arianos* I 33). "Before" God creates at all, πολλῷ πρότερον, He is Father, and He creates through His Son. For the Arians, actually, God was no more than a Creator and Shaper of creatures, argued St. Athanasius. They did not admit in God anything that was "superior to His will," τὸ ὑπερκείμενον τῆς βουλήσεως. But, obviously, "being" precedes "will," and "generation," accordingly, surpasses the "will" also: ὑπεραναβέβηκε δὲ τῆς βουλήσεως τὸ πεφυκέναι (II 2). Of course, it is but a logical order: there is no temporal sequence in Divine Being and Life. Yet, this logical order has an ontological significance. Trinitarian names denote the very character of God, His very Being. They are, as it were, ontological names. There are, in fact, two different sets of names which may be used of God. One set of names refers to God's deeds or acts—that is, to His will and counsel—the other to God's own essence and being. St. Athanasius insisted that these two sets of names had to be formally and consistently distinguished. And, again, it was more than just a logical or mental distinction. There was a distinction in the Divine

reality itself. God is what He is: Father, Son, and the Holy
Spirit. It is an ultimate reality, declared and manifested in
the Scriptures. But Creation is a deed of the Divine will, and
this will is common to and identical in all Three Persons of
the One God. Thus, God's Fatherhood must necessarily
precede His Creatorship. The Son's existence flows eternally
from the very essence of the Father, or, rather, belongs to this
"essence," οὐσία. The world's existence, on the contrary, is,
as it were, "external" to this Divine essence and is grounded
only in the Divine will. There is an element of contingency
in the exercise and disclosure of the creative will, as much as
His will reflects God's own essence and character. On the
other hand, there is, as it were, an absolute necessity in the
Trinitarian being of God. The word may seem strange and
startling. In fact, St. Athanasius did not use it directly. It
would have embarassed Origen and many others, as offensive
to God's perfection: does it not imply that God is subject to
certain "constraint" or fatalistic determinism? But, in fact,
"necessity" in this case is but another name for "being" or
"essence." Indeed, God does not "choose" His own Being.
He simply is. No further question can be intelligently asked.
Indeed, it is proper for God "to create," that is, to manifest
Himself *ad extra*. But this manifestation is an act of His
will, and in no way an extension of His own Being. On
the other hand, "will" and "deliberation" should not be
invoked in the description of the eternal relationship between
Father and Son. At this point St. Athanasius was definite
and explicit. Indeed, his whole refutation of Arianism
depended ultimately upon this basic distinction between
"essence" and "will," which alone could establish clearly
the real difference in kind between "Generation" and
"Creation." The Trinitarian vision and the concept of
Creation, in the thought of St. Athanasius, belonged closely
and organically together.[18]

Let us examine now in detail some few characteristic
passages in the famous Athanasian *Discourses against the*

Arians. The accurate dating of these "Discourses" is irrelevant for our present purpose.

I 19: God is described in the Scripture as the Fountain of Wisdom and Life. The Son is His Wisdom. Now, if one admits with the Arians that "there was when He was not," this would imply that once the Fountain was dry, or, rather, that it was not a fountain at all. The spring from which nothing flows is not a spring at all.—The simile is characteristic of St. Athanasius. It reappears often in the *"Discourses."* See, for instance, II 2: if the Word was not the genuine Son of God, God Himself would no longer be a Father, but only a Shaper of creatures. The fecundity of the Divine nature would have been quenched. The nature of God would be sterile, and not fertile: ἔρημος . . . μὴ καρπογόνος. It would be a barren thing, a light without shining, a dry font: ὡς φῶς μὴ φωτίζον καὶ πηγὴ ξηρά. See also I 14: ἄγονος ἦν ἡ πηγὴ καὶ ξηρά, φῶς χωρὶς αὐγῆς; or II 33: ἥλιος χωρὶς τοῦ ἀπαυγάσματος.— Both the argument and the imagery can be traced back to Origen. *Otiosam enim et immobilem dicere naturam Dei impium est simul et absurdum* (*De princ.* III 5 2; 272 Koetschau). But, as we have already seen, in Origen the argument was ambiguous and misleading. It was ambiguous because there was no room for any clear discrimination between "being" and "acting." It was misleading because it coupled "generation" and "creation" so closely and intimately together as not to allow any demarcation line. This ambiguity is avoided carefully by St. Athanasius. He never uses this argument—from the Divine "fertility"—in reference to the will of God. On the contrary, he formally refuses to follow Origen at this point,—of course, without quoting him.

I 20: God was never without anything that is His own: Πότε γοῦν τοῦ ἰδίου χωρὶς ἦν ὁ Θεός; On the other hand, created things have no affinity or similarity with the Creator: οὐδὲν ὅμοιον κατ' οὐσίαν ἔχει πρὸς τὸν πεποιηκότα. They are outside God: ἔξωθεν αὐτοῦ. They have received their existence by the grace and appointment of the Word: χάριτι καὶ βουλήσει αὐτοῦ τῷ λόγῳ γενόμενα. And, St. Athanasius characteristically adds, "they could again cease to exist, if it pleased their Creator"—ὥστε πάλιν δύνασθαι καὶ παύεσθαί ποτε, εἰ θελήσειεν ὁ ποιήσας. For, he concludes, "such is the nature of created things"—ταύτης γάρ ἐστι φύσεως τὰ γενητά. See also II 24 and 29: πάντων ἐκ τοῦ μὴ ὄντος ἐχόντων τὴν σύστασιν. Now, at this very point St. Athanasius had to face an objection of his opponents. They said: Is it not so that God must be Creator always, since the "power of creating" could not have come to God, as it were, subsequently? οὐκ ἐπιγέγονεν αὐτῷ τοῦ δημιουργεῖν ἡ δύναμις. Therefore, all creatures must be eternal. It is significant that this counter-argument of the Arians was actually Origen's famous argument, based on the analysis of the term παντοκράτωρ. Only the conclusion was different. Origen's conclusion was that, indeed, creatures were eternal. For the Arians that was blasphemy. By the same argument they wanted to reduce *ad absurdum* the proof of the eternal generation. It was an attack both on Origen and on St. Athanasius. St. Athanasius meets the charge on his own ground. Is there really such a "similarity" between generation and creation—τί ὅμοιον—that what must be said of God as Father must also be said of Him as Creator: ἵνα τὰ ἐπὶ τοῦ πατρὸς ταῦτα καὶ ἐπὶ τῶν δημιουργῶν εἴπωσι? This is the sting of the Athanasian rejoinder. In fact, there is total disparity. The Son is an offspring of the substance: ἴδιον τῆς οὐσίας γέννημα. Creatures are, on the contrary, "external" to the Creator. Accordingly, there is no "necessity" for them to exist eternally: οὐκ ἀνάγκη ἀεὶ εἶναι. But generation is not subject to will (or deliberation): τὸ δὲ γέννημα οὐ βουλήσει ὑπόκειται. It is, on the contrary, a property of the substance: ἀλλὰ τῆς οὐσίας ἐστὶν ἰδιότης. Moreover, a man can be called "a maker," ποιητής, even before he has made anything. But nobody can be

called "a father" before he has a son. This is to say that
God could be described as Creator even "before" Creation
came into existence. It is a subtle but valid point in the
argument. St. Athanasius argues that, although God could,
indeed, have created things from all eternity, yet created
things themselves could not have existed eternally, since
they are "out of nothing," ἐξ οὐκ ὄντων, and consequently
did not exist before they were brought into existence: οὐκ
ἦν πρὶν γένηται. "How can things which did not exist
before they originated be co-eternal with God?"—Πῶς ἠδύνατο συνυπάρχειν τῷ ἀεὶ ὄντι Θεῷ; This turn of the
argument is highly significant. Indeed, if one starts, as
Origen did, with the eternity and immutability of God, it is
difficult to see, how anything truly "temporal" could have
existed at all. All acts of God must be eternal. God simply
could not "have started." But in this case the proper "nature"
of temporal things is ignored and disregarded. This is precisely what St. Athanasius wanted to say. "Beginning"
belongs to the very "nature" of temporal things. Now, it is
the beginning of temporal existence, of an existence in time
and flux. For that reason creatures cannot "co-exist" with
the Eternal God. There are two incomparable modes of
existence. Creatures have their own mode of subsistence:
they are outside God. Thus creatures, by their very nature,
cannot "co-exist" with God. But this inherent limitation of
their nature does not, in any sense, disparage the power
of the Creator. The main point of St. Athanasius was precisely
this. There is an identity of nature in generation, and a
disparity of natures in creation (cf. I 26).

I 36: Since created beings arise "out of nothing," their
existence is bound to be a state of flux: ἀλλοιουμένην
ἔχει τὴν φύσιν. Cf. I 58: Their existence is precarious,
they are perishable by nature: τὰ δυνάμενα ἀπολέσθαι.
This does not imply that they will actually and necessarily
perish. Yet, if they do not actually perish, it is only by the
grace of the Creator. The Son alone, as an offspring of the

substance, has an intrinsic power "to co-exist" eternally with the Father: ἴδιον δὲ τὸ ἀεὶ εἶναι καὶ συνδιαμένειν σὺν τῷ Πατρί. See also II 57: The being of that which has existence "according to a beginning" can be traced back to a certain initial instant.

In the later part of his third "Discourse" St. Athanasius discusses at great length the Arian contention that the Son has been begotten by "the will and deliberation" of the Father: βουλήσει καὶ θελήσει γεγενῆσθαι τὸν Υἱὸν ὑπὸ τοῦ Πατρὸς (III 59). These terms, protests St. Athanasius, are quite out of place in this connection. Arians simply attempt to hide their heresy under the cover of these ambiguous words. St. Athanasius suggests that they borrowed their ideas at this point from the Gnostics and mentions the name of Ptolemy. Ptolemy taught that God first thought, and then willed and acted. In a similar way, St. Athanasius contends, Arians claim that the will and deliberation of the Father preceded the generation of the Word. He quotes Asterius at this point.[19] In fact, however, these terms—"will" and "deliberation"—are only applicable to the production of creaturely things. Now, Arians claim that unless the Son's existence depended upon the "deliberation" of the Father, it would appear that God has a Son "by necessity" and, as it were, "unwillingly"—ἀνάγκῃ καὶ μὴ θέλων. This kind of reasoning, St. Athanasius retorts, only shows their inability to grasp the basic difference between "being" and "acting." God does not deliberate with Himself about His own being and existence. Indeed, it would be absurd to contend that God's goodness and mercy are just His voluntary habit, and not a part of His nature. But does it mean that God is good and merciful unwillingly? Now, what is "by Nature" is higher than that which is only "by deliberation"—ὑπέρκειται καὶ προηγεῖται τοῦ βου-λεύεσθαι τὸ κατὰ φύσιν. The Son being an offspring of the Father's own substance, the Father does not "deliberate" about Him, since it would mean "deliberation" about His

own being: τὸν δὲ ἴδιον Λόγον ἐξ αὐτοῦ φύσει γεννώ-
μενον οὐ προβουλεύεται. God is the Father of His Son
"by nature and not by will—οὐ βουλήσει ἀλλὰ φύσει τὸν
ἴδιον ἔχει Λόγον. Whatever was "created," was indeed
created by the good will and deliberation of God. But the
Son is not a deed of will, like creatures, but by nature is an
offspring of God's own substance: οὐ θελήματός ἐστι
δημιούργημα ἐπιγεγονώς, καθάπερ ἡ κτίσις, ἀλλὰ
φύσει τῆς οὐσίας ἴδιον γέννημα. It is an insane and
extravagant idea to put "will" and "counsel" between the
Father and the Son (III 60, 61, 62).

Let us summarize. The theological writings of St. Athanasius were mainly occasional tracts, tracts for the time. He
was always discussing certain particular points, the burning
issues of the current debate. He was interpreting controversial texts of the Scripture, pondering and checking phraseology, answering charges, meeting objections. He never had
time or opportunity for a dispassionate and systematic exposition. Moreover, the time for systems had probably not
yet come. But there was a perfect consistency and coherence
in his theological views. His theological vision was sharp
and well focused. His grasp of problems was unusually
sure and firm. In the turmoil of a heated debate he was
able to discern clearly the real crux of the conflict. From
tradition St. Athanasius inherited the catholic faith in the
Divinity of the Logos. This faith was the true pivot of his
theological thought. It was not enough to correct exegesis,
to improve terminology, to remove misunderstandings. What
needed correction, in the age of St. Athanasius, was the
total theological perspective. It was imperative to establish
"Theology," that is—the doctrine of God, on its proper
ground. The mystery of God, "Three in One," had to be
apprehended in itself. This was the main preoccupation of
St. Athanasius in his great *"Discourses."* Père Louis Bouyer,
in his admirable book on St. Athanasius, has rightly stated
that, in the *"Discourses,"* St. Athanasius forces the reader

"to contemplate the Divine life in God Himself, before it is communicated to us." This was, according to Père Bouyer, the main emphasis in the book. In this perspective one can see the radical difference between the Divine and the creaturely. One sees the absoluteness of the Divine transcendence: God does not need His creatures. His own Being is perfect and complete in itself. And it is this inner Being of God that is disclosed in the mystery of the Trinity.[20] But the actual mystery is double. There is, indeed, the mystery of the Divine Being. But there is another concomitant mystery, the mystery of Creation, the mystery of the Divine οἰκονο- μία. No real advance can be achieved in the realm of "Theology" until the realm of "Oikonomia" had been properly ordered. This, surely, was the reason why St. Athanasius addressed himself to the problem of Creation even in his early treatises, which constituted, in a sense, his theological confession. On the one hand, the meaning of the redemptive Incarnation could be properly clarified only in the perspective of the original creative design of God. On the other, in order to demonstrate the absolute sovereignty of God it was necessary to show the ultimate contingency of the created Cosmos, fully dependent upon the Will of God. In the perspective of the Arian controversy two tasks were closely related to each other: to demonstrate the mystery of the Divine Generation as an integral feature of the Divine Being itself, and to emphasize the contingency of the creaturely Cosmos, which contingency can also be seen in the order of existence. It was precisely in the light of this basic distinction—between "Being" and "Will"— that the ultimate incommensurability of the two modes of existence could be clearly exhibited. The inner life of God is in no way conditioned by His revelatory self-disclosure in the world, including the design of Creation itself. The world is, as it were, a paradoxical "surplus" in the order of existence. The world is "outside" God; or rather it is precisely this "outside" itself. But it does exist, in its own mode and dimension. It arises and stands only by the will of God. It has a beginning precisely because it is contingent, and moves toward an end for which it has been designed by God. The Will of God is manifested in the temporal process of the Divine Οἰκονομία. But God's own Being is immutable and eternal. The two modes of existence, the Divine and the creaturely, can be respectively described as "necessary" and "contingent," or "absolute" and "conditional," or else, in the apt phraseology of a distinguished German theologian of the last century, F. A. Staudenmeier, as *das Nicht-nicht-seyn-könnende* and *das Nicht-seyn-könnende*. This corresponds exactly to the distinction between the Divine Being and the Divine Will.[21] This distinction was made and consistently elaborated, probably for the first time in the history of Christian thought, in the heat of the Arian debate by St. Athanasius of Alexandria. It was a step beyond Origen. St. Athanasius was not only an expert controversialist, but a great theologian in his own right.

III

The Athanasian distinction between "Generation" and "Creation," with all its implications, was already commonly accepted in the Church in his own time. A bit later, St. Cyril of Alexandria simply repeated his great predecessor. Indeed, his *Thesaurus de sancta et consubstantiali Trinitate* depended heavily upon the Athanasian "Discourses."[22] Only instead of "will" and "deliberation," St. Cyril spoke of Divine "energy": τὸ μὲν ποιεῖν ἐνεργείας ἐστί, φύσεως δὲ τὸ γεννᾶν· φύσις δὲ καὶ ἐνέργεια οὐ ταὐτὸν (*Thesaurus*, ass. 18, PG 75, 313; cf. ass. 15, PG 75, 276: τὸ γέννημα... ἐκ τῆς οὐσίας τοῦ γεννῶντος πρόεισι φυσικῶς—(τὸ κτίσμα)...ἔξωθέν ἐστιν ὡς ἀλλότριον; also ass. 32, PG 75, 564-565). And finally, St. John of Damascus, in his great *Exposition of the Orthodox*

Faith, repeated St. Cyril. "For we hold that it is from Him, that is, from the Father's nature, that the Son is generated. And unless we grant that the Son co-existed from the beginning with the Father, by Whom He was begotten, we introduce change into the Father's subsistence, because, not being the Father, He subsequently became the Father. For the creation, even though it originated later, is nevertheless not derived from the essence of God, but is brought into existence out of nothing by His will and power, and change does not touch God's nature. For generation means that the begetter produces out of his essence offspring similar in essence. But creation and making mean that the creator and maker produces from that which is external, and not of his own essence, a creation which is of an absolutely dissimilar nature." The Divine Generation is an effect of nature, τῆς φυσικῆς γονιμότητος. Creation is, on the contrary, an act of decision and will—θελήσεως ἔργον (*De fide orth.* I 8, PG 94, 812-813). This antithesis: γονιμότης and θέλησις or βούλησις is one of the main distinctive marks of Eastern theology.[23] It was systematically elaborated once more in late Byzantine theology, especially in the theology of St. Gregory Palamas (1296-1359). St. Gregory contended that unless a clear distinction had been made between the "essence" and "energy" in God, one could not distinguish also between "generation" and "creation."[24] And once again this was emphasized, somewhat later, by St. Mark of Ephesus.[25] It was a true Athanasian motive, and his arguments again came to the fore.

Now, the question arises: Is the distinction between "Being" and "Acting" in God, or, in other terms, between the Divine "Essence" and "Energy," a genuine and ontological distinction—*in re ipsa;* or is it merely a mental or logical distinction, as it were, κατ᾽ ἐπίνοιαν, which should not be interpreted objectively, lest the Simplicity of the Divine Being is compromised.[26] There cannot be the slightest doubt that for St. Athanasius it was a real and ontological

difference. Otherwise his main argument against the Arians
would have been invalidated and destroyed. Indeed, the
mystery remains. The very Being of God is "incomprehensible" for the human intellect: this was the common conviction of the Greek Fathers in the Fourth century—the
Cappadocians, St. John Chrysostom, and others. And yet
there is always ample room for understanding. Not only do
we distinguish between "Being" and "Will"; but it is not
the same thing, even for God, "to be" and "to act." This
was the deepest conviction of St. Athanasius.

The Patristic Age and Eschatology: An Introduction

I

FOUR "LAST THINGS" are traditionally listed: Death, Judgment, Heaven, and Hell. These four are "the last things of man." And there are four "last things" of mankind: the Last Day, the Resurrection of the Flesh, the Final Judgment, and the End of the World.[1] The major item, however, is missing in this listing, namely "the Last Adam," Christ Himself, and His Body, the Church. For indeed Eschatology is not just one particular section of the Christian theological system, but rather its basis and foundation, its guiding and inspiring principle, or, as it were, the climate of the whole of Christian thinking. Christianity is essentially eschatological, and the Church is an "eschatological community," since she is the New Testament, the ultimate and the final, and, consequently, "the last."[2] Christ Himself is the last Adam because He is "the New Man" (Ignatius, *Ephes.* 20. 1). The Christian perspective is intrinsically eschatological. "The

This article originally appeared in *Studia Patristica*, Vol. II, ed. Kurt Aland and F. L. Cross (Berlin: Akademie Verlag, 1956), 235-250. Reprinted by permission of the author.

Old has passed away. Behold, the New has come." It was precisely "in these last days" that God of the Fathers had ultimately acted, once for all, once for ever. The "end" had come, God's design of human salvation had been consummated (John 19.28, 30: τετέλεσται). Yet, this ultimate action was just a new beginning. The greater things were yet to come. The "Last Adam" was coming again. "And let him who heareth say, Come." The Kingdom had been inaugurated, but it did not yet come in its full power and glory. Or, rather, the Kingdom was still to come,—the King had come already. The Church was still *in via,* and Christians were still "pilgrims" and strangers in "this world." This tension between "the Past" and "the Coming" was essential for the Christian message from the very beginning. There were always these two basic terms of reference: the Gospel and the Second Advent. The story of Salvation was still in progress. But more than a "promise" had been granted unto the Church. Or, rather, "the Promise of the Father" was the Holy Spirit, which did come and was abiding in the Church for ever. The Kingdom of the Spirit had been already inaugurated. Thus, the Church was living in two dimensions at once. St. Augustine describes this basic duality of the Christian situation in a remarkable passage of his "Commentary" on the Gospel of St. John, interpreting the XXIst chapter. "There are two states of life that are known to the Church, preached and commended to herself from heaven, whereof one is of faith, the other of sight. One—in the temporal sojourn in a foreign land, the other in the eternity of the (heavenly) abode. One—on the way, the other—in the fatherland. One—in active work, the other—in the wages of contemplation . . . The one is anxious with the care of conquering, the other is secure in the peace of victory . . . The whole of the one is passed here to the end of this world, and then finds its termination. The other is deferred for its completion till after the end of this world, but has no end in the world to come" (*in Johan. tr.* 124.5). Yet, it is

essentially the same Church that has this dual life, *duas vitas.*
This duality is signified in the Gospel story by two names:
Peter and John.

II

Christianity was recently described as an "experience of
novelty," a *"Neuheitserlebnis."* And this "novelty" was
ultimate and absolute. It was the Mystery of the Incarnation.
Incarnation was interpreted by the Fathers not as a meta-
physical miracle, but primarily as the solution of an existential
predicament in which mankind was hopelessly imprisoned,
i.e. as the Redemptive act of God. It was "for us men and
for our salvation" that the Son of God came down, and
was made man.[3] Redemption has been accomplished, once
for all. The union, or "communion," with God has been
re-established, and the power of becoming children of God
has been granted to men, through faith. Christ Jesus is the
only Mediator and Advocate, and His sacrifice on the Cross,
in ara crucis, was "a full, perfect, and sufficient sacrifice,
oblation, and satisfaction." The human situation has been radically changed, and the status of man also. Man was re-
adopted as the son of God in Christ Jesus, the Only Begotten
Son of God Incarnate, crucified and risen. The catholic
doctrine of the Incarnation, elaborated by the Fathers, from
St. Irenaeus to St. John of Damascus, emphasizes first of all
this aspect of finality and uniqueness, of accomplishment and
achievement. The Son of God "was made man" for ever.
The Son of God, "One of the Holy Trinity," is man, by the
virtue of the Incarnation, for ever and ever. The Hypostatic
Union is a permanent accomplishment. And the victory of
the Cross is a final victory. Again, the Resurrection of the
Lord is the beginning of the general resurrection. But precisely for these reasons the "History of Salvation" should
go and is going on. The doctrine of Christ finds its fulness

and completion in the doctrine of the Church, i.e. of "the Whole Christ,"—*totus Christus, caput et corpus,* to use the glorious phrase of St. Augustine. And this immediately introduces the historical duration. The Church is a growing body, till she comes to "mature manhood," εἰς ἄνδρα τέλειον. In the Church the Incarnate is unfailingly "present." It was precisely this awareness of His abiding presence that necessitated the orientation towards the future. It was in the Church, and through the Church, that God was still pursuing His redemptive purpose, through Jesus Christ, the Lord. Again, the Church was a missionary body, sent into the world to proclaim and to propagate the Kingdom, and the "whole creation" was expected to share or to participate in that ultimate "re-novation," which was already inaugurated by the Incarnate Lord, and in Him. History was theologically vindicated precisely by this missionary concern of the Church. On the other hand, history, i.e. the "History of Salvation," could not be regarded as an endless process. The "End of times" and the "Consummation" were faithfully anticipated. "The End" was clearly predicted in the Scriptures, as the Early Christians read them. The goal was indeed "beyond history," but history was inwardly regulated and organized precisely by this super-historical and transcendent goal, by a watchful expectation of the Coming Lord. Only an ultimate and final "con-summation," an ultimate and final re-integration or "re-capitulation" could have given meaning to the flux of happenings and events, to the duration of time itself. The strong corporate feeling compelled the Early Christians to look for an ultimate and inclusive integration of the Redemptive process in the Kingdom to come. This was plainly stated already by Origen. *"Omne ergo corpus Ecclesiae redimendum sperat Apostolus, nec putat posse quae perfecta sunt dari singulis quibusdam membris, nisi universum corpus in unum fuerit congregatum"* (*in Rom.* VII. 5). History goes on because the Body has not yet been completed. "The fulness of the Body" implies and presupposes a re-integration of history, including the Old dispensation, i.e. "the end." Or, in the phrase of St. John Chrysostom, "then is the Head filled up, then is the Body rendered perfect, when we are all together, all knit together and united" (*in Ephes. hom.* III, *ad* I. 23). *Erit unus Christus, amans seipsum* (St. Augustine, *in Ps.* 26, *sermo* 2, n. 23). The other reason for looking forward, to a future consummation, was the firm and fervent belief in the Resurrection of the dead. In its own way it was to be a "re-integration" of history. Christ is risen indeed, and the sting of death has been taken away. The power of death was radically broken, and Life Eternal manifested and disclosed, *in Christo.* The "last enemy," however, is still active in the world, although death does not "reign" in the world any more. The victory of the Risen Christ is not yet fully disclosed. Only in the General Resurrection will Christ's redemptive triumph be fully actualized. *"Expectandum nobis etiam et corporis ver est"* (Minucius Felix, *Octavius,* 34). This was the common conviction of the Patristic age, from Athenagoras and St. Irenaeus and up to St. John of Damascus. St. Athanasius was most emphatic on this point, and St. Gregory of Nyssa also. Christ had to die in order to abrogate death and corruption by His death. Indeed, death was that "last enemy" which he had to destroy in order to redeem man out of corruption. This was one of the main arguments of St. Athanasius in his *De Incarnatione.* "In order to accept death He had a body" (*de incarn.* 21). And St. Gregory of Nyssa says the same: "if one inquires into the mystery, he will say rather, not that death happened to Him as a consequence of birth, but that birth itself was assumed on the account of death" (*orat. cat.* 32). Or in the sharp phrase of Tertullian: *Christus mori missus, nasci quoque necessario habuit, ut mori posset* (*de carne Christi,* 6). The bodily Resurrection of man was one of the main aims of Redemption. The coming and general Resurrection will not be just a "re-statement" to the previous condition. This would have been rather an "immortalization of death," as St. Maximus sharply pointed out (*epist.* 7). The coming Resurrection was conceived rather as a new creative act of God, as an integral and comprehensive "re-novation" of the whole Creation. "Behold, I make all things new." In the phrase of St. Gregory of Nazianzus, it was to be the third and final "transformation" of human life ("μετάστασις"), completing and superseding the two previous, the Old and the New testaments, a concluding eschatological σεισμός (*orat. theol.* V. 25).

III

The new vision of human destiny, in the light of Christ, could not be accurately and adequately expressed in the terms of the current philosophies of that time. A new set of concepts had to be elaborated before the Christian belief could be fully articulated and developed into a coherent system of theological propositions. The problem was not that of adjustment, but rather of a radical change of the basic habits of mind. Greek Philosophy was dominated by the ideas of permanence and recurrence. In spite of the great variety of trends, a common pattern can be detected in all systems. This was a vision of an "eternal" Cosmos. Everything which was worthy of existence had to have actually existed in the most perfect manner before all time, and nothing could be added to this accomplished fulness. No basic change was possible, and no real "novelty" could ever emerge. The whole, the Cosmos, was perfect and complete, and nothing could be perfected or completed. There could be but a disclosure of the pre-existing fulness. Aristotle made this point with a complete frankness. "What is 'of necessity' coincides with what is 'always', since that which 'must be' cannot possibly 'not-be'. Hence a thing is eternal if its 'being' is necessary; and if it is eternal, its 'being' is necessary. And if, therefore, the 'coming-to-be' of a thing is

necessary, its 'coming-to-be' is eternal; and if eternal, necessary. It follows that the 'coming-to-be' of anything, if it is
absolutely necessary, must be cyclical, i.e. must return upon
itself . . . It is in circular movement therefore, and in cyclical
'coming-to-be', that the 'absolutely necessary' is to be found"
(*de gen. et corr.* II. 2, 338a). The argument is perfectly
clear. If there is any "sufficient reason" for a certain thing
to exist ("necessity"), this reason must be "eternal," i.e.
there can be no reason whatever, why this thing should not
have existed "from eternity," since otherwise the reason for
its existence could not have been "sufficient" or "necessary."
And consequently "being" is simply "necessary." No increase
in "being" is conceivable. Nothing truly real can be "in-
novated." The true reality is always "behind" ("from eternity"), and never "ahead." Accordingly, the Cosmos is a
periodical being, and there will be no end of cosmic "re-
volutions." The highest symbol of reality is exactly the
recurrent circle. The cosmic reality, of which man was but a
part, was conceived as a permanent cyclical process, enacted,
as it were, in an infinite series of self-reproducing instalments,
of self-reiterating circles. Only the circle is perfect.[4] Obviously,
there was no room for any real "eschatology" in such a
scheme. Greek Philosophy indeed was always concerned
rather with the "first principles" than with the "last things."
The whole conception was obviously based on astronomical
experience. Indeed, the celestial movements were periodical
and recurrent. The whole course of rotation would be accomplished in a certain period ("the Great Year"), and then
will come a "repetition," a new and identical cycle or circle.
There was no "pro-gress" in time, but only eternal returns, a
"cyclophoria."[5] Time itself was in this scheme but a rotation,
a periodical reiteration of itself. As Plato put it in the
Timaeus, time "imitates" eternity, and rolls on according
to the laws of numbers (38a, b), and in this sense it can be
called "a mobile image of eternity" (37 d). In itself, time
is rather a lower or reduced mode of existence. This idea of

the periodical succession of identical worlds seems to be traditional in Greek Philosophy. The Pythagoreans seem to have been the first to profess an exact repetition. With Aristotle this periodical conception of the Universe took a strict scientific shape and was elaborated into a coherent system of Physics. Later on this idea of periodical returns was taken up by the Stoics. They professed the belief in the periodical dissolution and "rebirth" of all things, παλιγγενεσία, and then every minute detail will be exactly reproduced. This return was what the Stoics used to call the "Universal Restoration," ἀποκατάστασις τῶν πάντων. And this was obviously an astronomical term.[6] There was a kind of a cosmic *perpetuum mobile,* and all individual existences were hopelessly or inextricably involved in this cosmic rotation, in these cosmic rhythms and "astral courses" (this was precisely what the Greeks used to call "destiny" or fate, ἡ εἱμαρμένη, *vis positionis astrorum*). The Universe itself was always numerically the same, and its laws were immutable and invariable and each next world therefore will exactly resemble the earlier ones in all particulars. There was no room for history in this scheme. "Cyclical motion and the transmigration of souls is not history. It was a history built on the pattern of astronomy, it was indeed itself a kind of astronomy."[7] Already Origen protested most vigorously against this system of cosmic bondage. "If this be true, then free will is destroyed" (*contra Celsum,* IV. 67 etc.; cf. V. 20-21). Oscar Cullmann, in his renowned book, *Christus und die Zeit,* has well depicted the radical divergence between the "circular" concept of time in Greek thought and the "linear" concept in the Bible and in Christian doctrine. The ancient Fathers were fully aware of this divergence. *Circuitus illi jam explosi sunt,* exclaims St. Augustine. Let us fellow Christ, "the right way," and turn our mind away from the vain circular maze of the impious.—*Viam rectam sequentes quae nobis est Christus. Eo duce et salvatore, a vano et inepto impiorum circuitu iter fidei mentemque avertamus* (*de Civ. Dei,* XII. 20).—Now, this circular conception of the Universe, as "a periodical being," was closely connected with the initial conviction of the Greeks that the Universe, the Cosmos, was "eternal," i.e. had no beginning, and therefore was also "immortal," i.e. could have no end. The Cosmos itself was, in this sense, "Divine." Therefore, the radical refutation of the cyclical conception was possible only in the context of a coherent doctrine of Creation. Christian Eschatology does inextricably depend upon an adequate doctrine of Creation. And it was at this point that Christian thought encountered major difficulties.[8] Origen was probably the first to attempt a systematic formulation of the doctrine of Creation. But he was, from the outset, strongly handicapped by the "hellenistic" habits of his mind. Belief in Creation was for him an integral article of the Apostolic faith. But from the absolute "perfection" of God he felt himself compelled to deduce the "eternity" of the world. Otherwise, he thought, it would be necessary to admit some changes in God Himself. In Origen's conception, the Cosmos is a kind of an eternal companion of God. The Aristotelian character of his reasoning at this point is obvious. Next, Origen had to admit "cycles" and a sort of rotation, although he plainly rejected the iterative character of the sucessive "cycles." There was an unresolved inconsistency in his system. The "eternity" of the world implied an infinite number of "cycles" in the past, but Origen was firmly convinced that this series of "cycles" was to come to an end, and therefore there had to be but a finite number of "cycles" in the future. Now, this is plainly inconsistent. On the other hand, Origen was compelled to interpret the final "con-summation" as a "re-turn" to the initial situation, "before all times." In any case, history was for him, as it were, unproductive, and all that might be "added" to the preexistent reality had to be simply omitted in the ultimate summing up, as an accidental alloy or vain accretion. The fulness of Creation had been realized by the creative *fiat* "in eternity"

once for all. The process of history could have for him but
a "symbolic" meaning. It was more or less transparent for
these eternal values. All links in the chain could be interpreted as signs of a higher reality. Ultimately, all such signs
and symbols will pass away, although it was difficult to see
why the infinite series of "cycles" should ever end. Nevertheless, all signs have their own function in history. Events,
as temporal happenings, have no permanent significance.
The only valid interpretation of them is "symbolical." This
basic assumption led Origen into insuperable difficulties in
Christology. Could the Incarnation itself be regarded as a
permanent achievement, or rather was it no more than an
"episode" in history, to be surpassed in "eternity"? Moreover, "manhood" itself, as a particular mode of existence,
was to be interpreted precisely as an "episode," like all
differentiation of beings. It did not belong to the original
plan of Creation and originated in the general disintegration
of the Fall. Therefore, it was bound to disappear, when the
whole of Creation is restored to its initial integrity, when
the primordial world of pure spirits is re-stated in its original
splendor. History simply has nothing to contribute to this
ultimate "apocatastasis."—Now, it is easy to dismiss this
kind of Eschatology as an obvious case of "acute Hellenization." The true historical situation, however, was much
more complex. Origen was wrestling with a real problem.
His "aberrations" were in fact the birth-pangs of the Christian
mind. His own system was an abortive birth. Or, to change
the metaphor, his failures themselves were to become sign-
posts on the road to a more satisfactory synthesis. It was in
the struggle with Arianism that the Fathers were compelled
to a clear conception of "Creation," as distinguished from
other forms of "becoming" and "being." The contribution
of St. Athanasius was decisive at this point. St. Augustine,
from another point of view, was wrestling with the same
problem, and his discovery that Time itself had to be
regarded as a creature was one of the most relevant achieve-

ments of Christian thought. This discovery liberated this thought from the heavy heritage of Hellenistic habits. And a safe foundation was laid for the Christian theology of History.

IV

No comprehensive integration of human existence is possible without the Resurrection of the dead. The unity of mankind can be achieved only if the dead rise. This was perhaps the most striking novelty in the original Christian message. The preaching of the Resurrection as well as the preaching of the Cross was foolishness and a stumbling-block to the Gentiles. The Christian belief in a coming Resurrection could only confuse and embarrass the Greeks. It would mean for them simply that the present imprisonment in the flesh will be renewed again and forever. The expectation of a bodily resurrection would befit rather an earthworm, suggested Celsus, and he jeered in the name of common sense. He nicknamed Christians "a flesh-loving crew," φιλο-σώματον γένος, and treated the Docetists with far greater sympathy and understanding (apud Origen, *contra Celsum,* V. 14; VII. 36, 39). Porphyrius, in his *"Life of Plotinus,"* tells that Plotinus, it seemed, "was ashamed to be in the flesh," and with this statement he begins his biography. "And in such a frame of mind he refused to speak either of his ancestors or parents, or of his fatherland. He would not sit for a sculptor or painter." "It was absurd to make a permanent image of this perishable frame. It was already enough that we should bear it now" (*Life of Plotinus,* 1). This philosophical asceticism of Plotinus should be distinguished from Oriental dualism, Gnostic or Manichean. Plotinus himself wrote very strongly "against Gnostics." Yet, it was rather a difference of motives and methods. The practical issue in both cases was one and the same—a "flight" or "retreat" from this corporeal world, an "escape" from the body. Plotinus himself suggested the following simile. Two men live in the same house. One of them blames the builder and his handiwork because it is made of inanimate wood and stone. The other praises the wisdom of the architect because the building is so skillfully constructed. For Plotinus this world was not evil, it was the "image" or reflection of the world above, and probably the best of images. Still, one had to aspire beyond all images, from the image to the prototype. One should cherish not the copy, but the pattern (V. 8.8). "He knows that when the time comes, he will go out and will no longer have any need of a house." It is to say that the soul was to be liberated from the ties of the body, to be disrobed, and then only it could ascend to its proper sphere (II. 9. 15). "The true awakening is the true resurrection from the body, and not with the body," ἀπὸ σώματος, οὐ μετὰ σώματος ἀνάστασις,—since the body is by nature opposite to the soul (τὸ ἀλλότριον). A bodily resurrection would be just a passage from one "sleep" to another (III. 6. 6). The polemical turn of these phrases is obvious. The concept of the bodily resurrection was quite alien and unwelcome to the Greek mind. The Christian attitude was just the opposite. "Not that we would be unclothed, but that we would be clothed, so that what is mortal may be swallowed up by life" (2 *Cor.* 5.4). St. Paul was pleading for an ἀπολύτρωσις τοῦ σώματος (*Rom.* 8.23).* As St. John Chrysostom commented on these passages, one should clearly distinguish the body itself and "corruption." The body is God's creation, although it had been corrupted. The "strange thing" which must be put off is not the body, but corruption (*de resurr. mortuor.* 6). There was a flagrant "conflict in anthropology" between the Christian message and Greek wisdom. A new anthropology had to be elaborated in order to commend the Christian hope of Resurrection to the Gentiles. In the last resort it was Aristotle and not Plato who could offer help to Christian philosophers. In the philosophical interpretation of its eschatological hope, Christian theology from the very beginning clings to Aristotle.[10] Such a biased preference may appear to be unexpected and strange. For, strictly speaking, in Aristotle there was no room for any "after-death" destiny of man. In his interpretation man was entirely an earthly being. Nothing really human passes beyond the grave. Man is mortal through and through. His singular being is not a person and does not survive death. But yet in this weakness of Aristotle was his strength. He had a real understanding of the unity of human existence. Man was to him, first of all, an individual being, a living unit. Man was one just in his duality, as an "animated body," and two elements in him exist only together, in a concrete and indivisible correlation. Soul and body, for Aristotle they are not even two elements, which are combined or connected with each other, but rather simply two aspects of the same concrete reality. "Soul and body together constitute the animal. Now it needs no proof that the soul cannot be separated from the body" (*de anima,* 413a). Once the functional unity of the soul and body has been broken by death, no "organism" is there any more, the corpse is no more a body, and a dead man can hardly be called man at all (*meteor.* IV. 12, 389b: νεκρὸς ἄνθρωπος ὁμώνυμος; cf. *de part. anim.* 641a). No "transmigration" of souls to other bodies was possible for Aristotle. Each soul abides in its "own" body, which it creates and forms, and each body has its "own" soul, as its vital principle, *"eidos"* or form. This anthropology easily lends itself to a biological simplification when man is almost completely equated with any other living being. Such indeed was the interpretation of many followers of the Stagirite, including the famous Alexander of Aphrodisias. Aristotle himself has hardly escaped these inherent dangers of his conception. Of course, man was for him an "intelligent being," and the faculty of thinking was his distinctive mark. But the doctrine of νοῦς does not fit very well into the general frame of Aristotelian psychology, and probably is a survival of his early Platonism. It was possible to adapt the Aristotelian conception for Christian purposes, and this was just what was done by the Fathers, but Aristotle himself obviously "was not a Moslem mystic, nor a Christian theologian."[11] The real failure of Aristotle was not in his "naturalism," but in that he could not admit any permanence of the individual. But this was rather a common failure of Greek philosophy. Beyond time Greek thought visualized only the "typical," and nothing truly personal. Hegel suggested, in his *Aesthetics,* that Sculpture gives the true key to the whole of Greek mentality.[12] Recently, a Russian scholar, A. Th. Lossev, pointed out that the whole of Greek philosophy was just "a sculptural symbolism." He was thinking especially of Platonism, but his suggestion has a wider relevance. "Against a dark background, as a result of an interplay of light and shadow, there stands out a blind, colorless, cold, marble and divinely beautiful, proud and majestic body, a statue. And the world is such a statue, and gods are statues; the city-state also, and the heroes, and the myths, and ideas; all conceal underneath them this original sculptural intuition . . . There is no personality, no eyes, no spiritual individuality. There is a 'something', but not a 'someone', an individualized 'it', but no living person with his proper name . . . There is no one at all. There are bodies, and there are ideas. The spiritual character of ideas is killed by the body, but the warmth of the body is restrained by the abstract idea. There are here beautiful, but cold and blissfully indifferent statues."[13] And yet Aristotle did feel and understand the individual more than anyone else in his tradition. He provided Christian philosophers with all the elements out of which an adequate conception of personality could be built up. His strength was just in his understanding of the empirical wholeness of human existence. Aristotle's conception was radically transformed in this Christian adaptation, for new perspectives were opened, and all the terms were given a new significance. And yet one cannot fail to acknowledge the Aristotelian origin of the main anthropological ideas in early Christian theology. Such a christening of Aristotelianism we find already in Origen, to a certain extent in St. Methodius of Olympus as well, and later in St. Gregory of Nyssa, who in his thrilling *De Anima et Resurrectione* attempted a daring synthesis of Origen and Methodius. The break between the "Intellect," impersonal and "eternal," and the soul, individual but mortal, was overcome and healed in the new self-consciousness of a spiritual personality. The idea of personality itself was probably the greatest Christian contribution to philosophy. And then the tragedy of death could be visualized in its true dimension. For Plato and Platonists death was just a welcome release out of the bodily bondage, "a flight to the fatherland." For Aristotle and his followers it was a natural end of earthly existence, a sad but inevitable end, "and nothing is thought to be any longer either good or bad for the dead" (*ethic. Nicom.* III. 6, III. 5a). For Christians it was a catastrophe, a frustration of human existence, a reduction to a sub-human state, abnormal and rooted in the sinful condition of mankind, out of which one is now liberated by the victory of Christ. The task of Christian theologians was now to relate the hope of Resurrection to the new conception of man. It is interesting to observe that the problem was clearly seen and stated in the first theological essay on the Resurrection which we possess. In his brief treatise *De resurrectione mortuorum,* Athenagoras of Athens begins with the plain statement that "God gave independent being and life neither to the nature of the soul itself, nor to the nature of the body separately, but rather to men, composed of soul and body." There would no longer be a man, if the completeness of this structure were broken, for then the identity of the individual would be broken also. "And if there is no resurrection, human

nature is no longer human" (*de resurr. mort.* 13, 15).
Aristotle concluded from the mortality of the body to the
mortality of the soul, which was but the vital power of the
body. Both go down together. Athenagoras, on the contrary,
infers the resurrection of the body from the immortality of
the reasonable soul. Both are kept together."[14] Thus, a safe
foundation was laid for further elaboration.

V

The purpose of this brief paper was not to give a complete summary of the eschatological thought and teaching of
the Fathers. It was rather an attempt to emphasize the main
themes and the main problems with which the Fathers
had to wrestle. Again, it was also an attempt to show how
deeply and closely all eschatological topics are related to
the core of the Christian message and faith, to the Redemption of man by the Incarnate and Risen Lord. Only in this
wider perspective, in the total context of Christian doctrine,
can one fully and faithfully understand all the variations
of Patristic thought. The eschatological hope is rooted in
the faith, and cannot be understood except in this context.
The Fathers never attempted a systematic exposition of
Eschatology, in a narrow and technical sense. But they were
fully aware of that inner logic which had to lead from
the belief in Christ the Redeemer to the hope for the age to
come: the end of the world, the final consummation, the
resurrection of the dead, and life everlasting.

St. John Chrysostom:
The Prophet of Charity

CHRYSOSTOM was a powerful preacher. He was fond of preaching, and regarded preaching as the duty of a Christian minister. Priesthood is authority, but it is authority of word and conviction. This is the distinctive mark of Christian power. Kings compel, and pastors convince. The former act by orders, the latter by exhortations. Pastors appeal to human freedom, to human will and call for decisions. As Chrysostom used to say himself, "We have to accomplish the salvation of men by word, meekness, and exhortation." The whole meaning of human life for Chrysostom was in that it was, and had to be, a life in freedom, and therefore a life of service. In his preaching he spoke persistently about freedom and decision. Freedom was for him an image of God in man. Christ came, as Chrysostom used to remind, precisely to heal the will of man. God always acts in such a way as not to destroy our own freedom. God Himself acts by calls and exhortations, not by compulsion. He shows the right way, calls and invites, and warns against the dangers of wickedness, but does not

This article originally appeared in *St. Vladimir's Seminary Quarterly*, IV, Nos. 3/4 (1955), 37-42. Reprinted by permission of the author.

constrain. Christian pastors must act accordingly. By temperament, Chrysostom was rather a maximalist, sharp and rigoristic, but he was always against compulsion, even in the struggle with heretics. Christians are forbidden, he used to insist, to apply violence even for good aims: "Our warfare does not make the living dead, but rather makes the dead to live, because it is conducted in the spirit of meekness and humility. I persecute by word, not by acts. I persecute heresy, not heretics. It is mine more to be persecuted, than to persecute. So Christ was victorious as a Crucified, and not as a crucifier." The strength of Christianity was for him in humility and toleration, not in power. One had to be strict about oneself, and meek to the others.

Yet, Chrysostom was in no sense a sentimental optimist. His diagnosis of the human situation was stern and grim. He lived in a time when the Church was suddenly invaded by crowds of nominal converts. He had an impression that he was preaching to the dead. He watched the lack of charity and the complacent injustice and saw them almost in an apocalyptic perspective: "We have quenched the zeal, and the body of Christ is dead." He had an impression that he was speaking to people for whom Christianity was just a conventional fashion, an empty form, a manner and little more: "Among the thousands one can hardly find more than a hundred of them who are being saved, and even about that I am doubtful." He was rather embarrassed by the great number of alleged Christians: "an extra food for fire."

Prosperity was for him a danger, the worst kind of persecution, worse than an open persecution. Nobody sees dangers. Prosperity breeds carelessness. Men fall asleep, and the devil kills the sleepy. Chrysostom was disturbed especially by an open and deliberate lowering of standards and requirements, even among the clergy. Salt was losing its savour. He reacted to this not only by a word of rebuke and reprimand, but by deeds of charity and love. He was desperately concerned with the renewal of society, with the healing of social ills. He was preaching and practising charity, founding hospitals and orphanages, helping the poor and destitute. He wanted to recover the spirit of practising love. He wanted more activity and commitment among Christians. Christianity for him was precisely "the Way," as it had been sometimes described in Apostolic times, and Christ Himself was "the Way." Chrysostom was always against all compromises, against the policy of appeasement and adjustment. He was a prophet of an integral Christianity.

Chrysostom was mainly a preacher of morality, but his ethics was deeply rooted in the faith. He used to interpret Scripture to his flocks, and his favorite writer was St. Paul. It was in his epistles that one could see this organic connection between faith and life. Chrysostom had his favorite dogmatic theme, to which he would constantly return—first of all, the theme of the Church, closely linked to the doctrine of Redemption, being the sacrifice of the High-Priest Christ; the Church is the new being, the life in Christ, and the life of Christ in men. Secondly, the theme of Eucharist, a sacrament and a sacrifice. It is but fair to call Chrysostom, as he was actually called, "the teacher of Eucharist," *doctor eucharisticus*. Both themes were linked together. It was in the Eucharist, and through it, that the Church could be alive.

Chrysostom was a witness of the living faith, and for that reason his voice was so eagerly listened to, both in the East and in the West; but for him, the faith was a norm of life, and not just a theory. Dogmas must be practised. Chrysostom was preaching the Gospel of Salvation, the good tidings of the new life. He was not a preacher of independent ethics. He preached Christ, and Him crucified and risen, the Lamb and the High Priest. Right life was for him the only efficient test of right beliefs. Faith is accomplished in the deeds, the deeds of charity and love. Without love faith, contemplation, and the vision of the mysteries of God are impossible. Chrysostom was watching the desperate struggle for truth in the society of his own days. He was always concerned with living soults; he was speaking to men, to living persons. He was always addressing a flock, for which he felt responsibility. He was always discussing concrete cases and situations.

One of his constant and favorite subjects was that of wealth and misery. The theme was imposed or dictated by the setting in which Chrysostom had to work. He had to face the life in great and overcrowded cities, with all the tensions between the rich and the poor. He simply could not evade social problems without detaching Christianity from life, but social problems were for him emphatically religious and ethical problems. He was not primarily a social reformer, even if he had his own plans for Christian society. He was concerned with the ways of Christians in the world, with their duties, with their vocation.

In his sermons we find, first of all, a penetrating analysis of the social situation. He finds too much injustice, coldness, indifference, and suffering and sorrow in the society of his days. And he sees well to what extent it is connected with the *acquisitive* character of the contemporary society, with the *acquisitive* spirit of life. This *acquisitive* spirit breeds inequality, and therefore injustice. He is not only upset by fruitless luxury of life; he is apprehensive of wealth as a standing temptation. Wealth seduces the rich. Wealth itself has no value. It is a guise, under which the real face of man is concealed, but those who hold possessions come to cherish them, and are deceived; they come to value them and rely on them. All possessions, not only the large ones, are dangerous, in so far as man learns to rely upon what is, by its very nature, something passing and unreal.

Chrysostom is very evangelical at this point. Treasures must be gathered in heaven, and not on earth, and all earthly treasures are unreal and doomed to corruption. "A love for wealth is abnormal," says Chrysostom. It is just a burden for the soul, and a dangerous burden. It enslaves the soul; it distracts it from the service to God. The Christian spirit is a spirit of renunciation, and wealth ties man to inanimate things. The *acquisitive* spirit distorts the vision, perverts the perspective. Chrysostom is closely following the injunctions of the Sermon on the Mount. "Do not be anxious for your life, what you shall eat, nor for your body, what you shall put on..." Life is greater than clothing or food, but it is anxiety which is the prevailing temper of the *acquisitive* society.

Christians are called to renounce all possessions and to follow Christ in full confidence and trust. Possessions can be justified only by their use: feed the hungry, help the poor, and give everything to the needy. Here is the main tension, and the main conflict, between the spirit of the Church and the mood of the worldly society. The cruel injustice of actual life is the bleeding wound of this society. In a world of sorrow and need, all possessions are wrong— they are just proofs of coldness, and symptoms of little faith. Chrysostom goes so far as to denounce even the splendor of the temples. "The Church," he says, "is a triumphant company of angels, and not a shop of a silversmith. The Church claims human souls, and only for the sake of the souls does God accept any other gifts. The cup which Christ offered to the disciples at the Last Supper was not made of gold. Yet it was precious above all measure. If you want to honor Christ, do it when you see Him naked, in the person of the poor. No use, if you bring silk and precious metals to the temple, and leave Christ to suffer cold and nakedness in the outside. No use, if the temple is full of golden vessels, but Christ himself is starving. You make golden chalices, but fail to offer cups of cold water to the needy. Christ, as a homeless stranger, is wandering around and begging, and instead of receiving Him you make decorations."

Chrysostom was afraid that everything kept aside was in a sense stolen from the poor. One cannot be rich, except at the cost of keeping others poor. The root of wealth is always in some injustice. Yet, poverty was not for Chrysostom just a virtue by itself. Poverty meant for him first of all need and want, and suffering and pain. For this reason Christ can be found among the poor, and he comes to us in the guise of a beggar, and not in that of a rich man. Poverty is a blessing only when it is cheerfully accepted for Christ's sake. The poor have less anxiety than the rich and are more independent—or at least may be. Chrysostom was fully aware that poverty can be tempting too, not only as a burden, but as an incentive of envy or despair. For that very reason he wanted to fight poverty, in order not only to ease the suffering, but to remove temptations also.

Chrysostom was always concerned with ethical issues. He had his own vision of a just society, and the first prerequisite was, in his opinion, equality. It is the first claim of any genuine love. But Chrysostom would go much further. He felt that there was but one owner of all things in the world—God Himself, the Maker of all. Strictly speaking, no private property should exist at all. Everything belongs to God. Everything is loaned rather than given by God in trust to man, for God's purposes. Chrysostom would add: Everything is God's except the good deeds of man—it is the only thing that man can own. As everything belongs to God, our common Master, everything is given for common use. Is it not true even of worldly things? Cities, market-places, streets—are they not a common possession? God's economy is of the same kind. Water, air, sun and moon, and the rest of creation, are intended for common use. Quarrels begin usually when people attempt to appropriate things which, by their very nature, were not intended for the private possession of some, to the exclusion of others.

Chrysostom had serious doubts about private property. Does not strife begin when the cold distinction between "mine" and "thine" is first introduced? Chrysostom was concerned not so much with the results, as with causes—with the orientation of the will. Where is man going to gather his treasures? Chrysostom was after justice in defense of human dignity. Was not every man created in God's image? Did God not wish salvation and conversion of every single man, regardless of his position in life, and even regardless of his behavior in the past? All are called to repentance, and all can repent. There was, however, no neglect of material things in his preaching. Material goods come also from God, and they are not bad in themselves. What is bad, is only the unjust use of goods, to the profit of some, while others are left starving. The answer is in love. Love is not selfish, "is not ambitious, is not self-seeking." Chrysostom was looking back to the primitive Church. "Observe the increase of piety. They cast away their riches, and rejoiced, and had great gladness, for greater were the riches they received without labor. None reproached, none envied, none grudged; no pride, no contempt. No talk of 'mine' and 'thine.' Hence gladness waited at their table; no one seemed to eat of his own, or another's. Neither did they consider their brethren's property foreign to themselves; it was a property of the Master; nor again deemed they ought their own, all was the brethren's." How was this possible, Chrysostom asks: By the inspiration of love, in recognition of the unfathomable love of God.

In no sense was Chrysostom preaching "communism." The pattern itself may be deceitful and misleading as any other. The real thing is the spirit. What Chrysostom was preaching in the cities, monks were fervently practising in their communities, professing by deeds that God was the only Master and owner of everything. Chrysostom did not regard monastic life just as an advanced course for the select, but rather as a normal *evangelical* pattern intended for all Christian. At this point he was in full agreement with the main tradition of the early Church, from St. Basil and St. Augustine up to St. Theodore of Studium in the later times. But the strength of monasticism is not in the pattern

itself, but in the spirit of dedication, in the choice of a
"higher calling." Was this calling only for the few? Chrysostom was always suspicious of inequality. Was it not
dangerous to discriminate between the "strong" and the
"weak"? Who could judge and decide in advance? Chrysostom was always thinking about real men. There was some
kind of individualism inherent in his approach to people,
but he valued *unanimity* most highly—the spirit of solidarity,
of common care and responsibility, the spirit of service. No
person can grow in virtue, unless he serves his brethren.
For that reason he always emphasized charity. Those who
fail *to do* charity will be left outside the bridal chamber
of Christ. It is not enough, he says, to lift our hands to
heaven—stretch them to the needy, and then you will be
heard by the Father. He points out that, according to the
Parable of the Last Judgment, the only question which will
be asked then is that about charity. But again it was not just
a moralism with him. His ethics had an obvious mystical
depth. The true altar is the body of men itself. It is not
enough to worship at the altars. There is another altar made
of living souls, and this altar is Christ Himself, His Body.
The sacrifice of righteousness and mercy should be offered
on this altar too, if our offerings are to be acceptable in
God's sight. The deeds of charity had to be inspired by the
ultimate dedication and devotion to Christ, who came into
the world to relieve all want, and sorrow, and pain.

Chrysostom did not believe in abstract schemes; he had
a fiery faith in the creative power of Christian love. It was
for that reason that he became the teacher and prophet for
all ages in the Church. In his youth he spent some few
years in the desert, but would not stay there. For him
monastic solitude was just a training period. He returned
to the world to proclaim the power of the Gospel. He was
a missionary by vocation; he had an apostolic and evangelistic
zeal. He wanted to share his inspiration with his brethren.
He wanted to work for the establishment of God's Kingdom.

He prayed for such things in common life so that nobody would need to retire to the wilderness in search for perfection, because there would be the same opportunity in the cities. He wanted to reform the city itself, and for that purpose he chose for himself the way of priesthood and apostolate.

Was this a utopian dream? Was it possible to reshape the world, and to overrule the wordliness of the world? Was Chrysostom successful in his mission? His life was stormy and hard, it was a life of endurance and martyrdom. He was persecuted and rejected not by the heathen, but by false brethren, and died homeless as a prisoner in exile. All he was given to endure he accepted in the spirit of joy, as from the hand of Christ, Who was Himself rejected and executed. The Church gratefully recognized that witness and solemnly acclaimed Chrysostom as one of the "ecumenical teachers" for all ages to come.

There is some unusual flavor of modernity in the writings of Chrysostom. His world was like ours, a world of tensions, a world of unresolved problems in all walks of life. His advice may appeal to our age no less than it did to his own. But his main advice is a call to integral Christianity, in which faith and charity, belief and practice, are organically linked in an unconditional surrender of man to God's overwhelming love, in an unconditional trust in His mercy, in an unconditional committment to His service, through Jesus Christ, our Lord.

The Anthropomorphites
in the Egyptian Desert

Part I

IN HIS TENTH *"Conference"* John Cassian tells the story of a certain Sarapion, a monk of high distinction: *antiquissimae distinctionis atque in actuali disciplina per omnia consummatus*. By inadvertence, however, he lapsed into the errors of the "Anthropomorphites." It was a great scandal in the community. All efforts were made to restore Sarapion to the right way. It appears that the main issue involved was that of certain devotional practices. But some points of exegesis were also implied. At that time, a certain Photinus, a deacon from Cappadocia and a man of profound learning, was staying with the brethren. His testimony was sought concerning the meaning of the scriptural phrase: man was created *"in the image and likeness of God."* In an eloquent and elaborate speech, Photinus explained that in the East "all leaders of the churches" used to interpret this phrase "spiritually"—*non secundum humilem litterae sonum, sed*

This article originally appeared in *Akten des XI Internationalen Byzantinistenkongresses* (Munich: Verlag C. H. Beck, 1958), 154-159. Reprinted by permission of the author.

spiritualiter. Finally, Sarapion was persuaded to discontinue his erroneous practices in worship. Yet he was sorely distressed by the new method. He felt himself utterly confounded and frustrated, when, as it is stated, "the anthropomorphic image of the Godhead, which he used to set before him in prayer, was removed from his heart." In great despair, prostrating himself on the ground, weeping and groaning, he complained: "they have taken my God from me, and I have now none to behold, and whom to worship and address I know not"—*tulerunt a me Deum meum, et quem nunc teneam non habeo vel quem adorem aut interpellem jam nescio* (*Coll.* X. 3, p. 288-289 Petschenig).

What is the meaning of this striking episode? What were, in fact, those "anthropomorphite" practices to which the unfortunate Sarapion had been addicted, and which he was dissuaded from employing? What was the point of his distress and confusion?

Our information about the disputes in the Desert, between the "Origenists" and the alleged "Anthropomorphites," is scarce and biased. Indeed, it comes mainly from the "Origenistic" side. Cassian himself was strongly prejudiced in his description of monastic Egypt. His great treatises, the *"Institutions"* and the *"Conferences,"* were written in order to present a particular doctrine of spirituality, "Origenistic" and Evagrian. The story in Socrates (VI. 7) and Sozomen (VIII. 11-12) was derived probably from the oral reports, and also gossip, circulated in Constantinople by the refugees from Egypt, including the Tall Brothers, and also by Theophilus and his group (cf. Palladius, *Dialogus,* VII). These reports, of course, were tendentiously unfair to the "Anthropomorphites." Indeed, the name itself was a polemical slogan, a derogatory label, invented in the heat of the strife and used as a demagogical weapon. As Owen Chadwick has said recently, "in Egypt 'anthropomorphite' is a malicious term applied by their Origenistic opponents to the literalist Egyptian majority."[1] Its purpose was not to define a group properly, but to discredit it in advance. Indeed, the "Anthropomorphite" monks in the Desert in no sense were a "sect." They had no relation whatever to the heretical sect of Audians, which had spread in Mesopotamia and Syria and by the time of John Cassian was already in steady decay (see Epiphanius, *Haeres.* LXX). Nor should the "literalism" of the alleged "Anthropomorphites" be attributed to their "ignorance" and "simplicity." We are told, in the sources available, about rude and rustic monks who, misled by their crude understanding of certain passages of the Scripture, came to conceive of God in material shape. This aspect of the controversy is grossly misrepresented in our sources. No doubt, "simple" and rustic people were numerous in the monastic ranks, especially among those of Coptic origin, hardly touched at all by any Greek learning. And certain abuses, indeed, might have crept into their practices. But the actual problem was much deeper and more complex than that. The "Anthropomorphites" could quote in their support an old and venerable tradition, which could not be summarily discarded by the charge of "ignorance."

The story of Sarapion, in fact, is an integral part of that great treatise on Prayer which Cassian presents in his ninth and tenth *"Conferences,"* on behalf of the Abbot Isaac. The "Origenistic" character of this treatise is obvious, and close parallels in Origen's writings can be easily found to every point of the discourse. There are stages and grades in spiritual growth. There is an ascension from earthly things to the heavenly. There is an alternative between beholding Jesus "still in His humility and in the flesh"—*humilem adhuc et carneum*—and contemplating Him in His Divine glory and majesty. The former attitude is described as a kind of "Judaic weakness"—*quodammodo Iudaica infirmitate detenti*. At this point II Cor. 5. 16 is quoted: "Those cannot see Jesus coming in His Kingdom who are still kept in a state of Jewish weakness, and cannot say with the Apostle: 'and if we have known Christ after the flesh, yet now we know Him so no more.' But only those can look with purest eyes on His Godhead, who rise with Him from low and earthly works and thoughts and go apart in the lofty mountain of solitude, which is free from the disturbance of all earthly thoughts and troubles." The main emphasis in the argument is precisely at this point: "no more in the flesh" (*Coll.* I. 6, 291-292 P). Accordingly, not only all "images" of the Godhead must be eliminated from prayer (*nullam divinitatis effigiem* —"which it is a sin even to mention"), but "one should not admit any memory of something said, or any kind of a deed, or an outline of any character"—*ne ullam quidem in se memoriam dicti cujusque vel facti speciem seu formam cujuslibet characteri admittet* (X. 5, p. 291 P). The phrase is by no means clear. It refers primarily, of course, to the *katharsis* of the mind, which must be ever cleansed from the flux of fleeting thoughts and "images,"—and this, indeed, was Cassian's permanent concern in the whole system of spiritual discipline. But more than that was obviously implied in these strictures. No *memoria dicti cujusque,* and no *species facti,*—these injunctions, if carried out strictly and consistently, would exclude from prayer, especially at its climax, also any reference to, and any link with, the scriptural "image" of Christ Jesus, His own *dicta* and *facta,* His saving *oikonomia* "in the flesh." *No more in the flesh* . . . This seems to have been the root of Sarapion's perplexity, which could not be easily solved or calmed down by any exegetical arguments. "They have taken away my God from me," he complained. Presumably, he was urged to abstain from using in his devotions any mental image of "Jesus after the flesh," as he was accustomed to do previously in order to fix his attention in prayer and to know "whom to adore." Such practice of his was, from the strict "Origenistic" point of view, just a "Judaic weakness," a mark of imperfection. But to dismiss this "anthropomorphic" image of the Saviour meant for Sarapion to lose ground in prayer. "Whom should I invoke now?"—*quem interpellem nescio.* Indeed, no crude "anthropomorphism" was involved at this point. The basic alternative in the argument of Abbot Isaac was between the *infirmitas Judaica* and the *jam non*. The main question seems to have been about the Christological orientation in prayer. To what extent, and in what manner, should prayer be constantly anchored in the "memory" of the historic Jesus, of Jesus "in the flesh"? In what manner, and to what extent, should this historic "image" be permissibly "transcended" in devotional practice and exercise? And this was, indeed, the crucial problem of "Origenistic" spirituality, beginning with Origen himself.

Now, Origen himself never denied that "history" had to be *the starting point,* both in theology and in devotion. But it had to be no more than a starting point. And one inevitably moves away from the start more and more, while one really progresses. The past events, even the events of the Gospel story, must be left behind in this process of spiritual climbing—to the mountain of solitude. These "images" must be transcended in the new "spiritual" vision. One must not look back any more, but steadily forward, to the glorious things to come. The ultimate goal of contemplation, according to Origen, is the knowledge of the Father,—indeed, through the knowledge of the Son. But His historic *oikonomia,* in "the flesh," must be transcended at this point. In spite of all his ardent love for the Crucified Jesus, and all his emphasis on the mystery of the Incarnation, on the higher stages of contemplation Origen claims to move beyond the Incarnation, in order that the Divine glory of the Son would not be obscured by His *oikonomia.*[2] In this sense, the "Christ-mysticism" was for Origen just a stage on the road toward the "God-mysticism." *"Die Christusmystik ist also Durchgangsstadium zur Gottesmystik,"* as Walter Voelker has well stated.[3] And here lies the major danger of "Origenism." This danger is especially acute in the realm of devotion. "Origenism" tends towards a certain "de-christologization" of worship. Devotion is no more focussed on the historic *oikonomia* of salvation. This tendency is obvious in John Cassian. As Owen Chadwick rightly observes, Cassian is so much concerned with the method of contemplation that he has but little to say about its actual object. "In these monastic books we hear little, surprisingly little, of the Gospel, of the earthly life of Jesus Christ, of the revelation of God."[4] The "simple," the *simpliciores* of Origen, utterly resisted this tendency to move away from the "historic" Gospel. And this was, probably, the true core of the "Anthropomorphite" movement, or rather the "resistance-movement," in the Egyptian Desert. It was a striking example of that conflict between the "faith of the people" and "learned theology" which was one of the distinctive features of Christian life in the third century.[5] This tension continued in the Nicene age. The ultimate mystery of the Christian faith is, indeed, in that "God was manifest *in the flesh.*" The truth of this crucial "manifestation" is in no way contradicted by that other truth that Christ "was received up into glory" (I Tim. 3. 16).

The struggle against the "Anthropomorphites" was initiated already by Origen himself: *qui in Ecclesia positi imaginem corpoream hominis Dei esse imaginem dicunt* (*Comm. in Rom.* 1. 19, MG XIV, c. 870-871). In his commentary on Genesis Origen quotes Melito, as one of those who were committed to this erroneous view. Judging by Origen's rejoinder, we must conclude that Melito's main argument was derived from the fact of corporeal theophanies of the Old Testament and from the "anthropomorphic" phraseology of the Bible (*Selecta in Gen.,* ad 1. 26, quoted by Theodoret, Lomm. VIII. 49-52). There is no text in the extant writings of Melito to support that charge. And it seems highly improbable that Melito was really so crudely "anthropomorphite" as Origen's remarks seem to suggest. He was probably close to that view which has been so emphatically expounded by St. Irenaeus.[6] According to Origen, that man which was created "in the image of God" was not a "bodily man": *hunc sane hominem . . . non intelli-gimus corporalem.* There is no "image of God" in the body, but only in the soul of man. Only the "inner man" was made "in the image": *interior homo noster est, invisibilis, et incorporalis, et incorruptus atque immortalis.* Otherwise, one might be tempted to attribute corporeal features to God himself, as has been actually done by certain carnal men: *carnales isti homines qui intellectum divinitatis ignorant.* Indeed, the "image" in which man has been created was the Son of God, our Saviour, who is "the firstborn of every creature" (*In Genes. hom.* 1. 13, p. 15-18 Baehrens). For Origen it only meant that all intellectual or "logical" beings were made in the shape of the Divine Logos.[7] The same idea has been quite differently elaborated by St. Irenaeus. Here we have a clear opposition of two different views and approaches. According to St. Irenaeus, man was indeed shaped in the image of the Word. But Irenaeus refers here to the Word Incarnate. Man was created in the image of the Incarnate Word, as it were, by anticipation, or proleptically. Accordingly, the bodily figment is also included in the "image": *caro quae est plasmata secundum imaginem Dei . . . imaginem habens in plasmate.* The whole man is created in the "image of God" (*Adv. haeres.* V. 6. 1). "In the times long past, it was said that man was created after the image of God, but it was not yet manifested. For the Word was as yet invisible, after whose image man was created. Wherefore also man has easily lost the similitude. When, however, the Word of God became flesh, He confirmed both these: for He showed forth the true image, since He became Himself what was His image; and He re-established the similitude after a sure manner, by assimilating man to the invisible Father through the means of the visible Word" (*Adv. haeres.* V. 16. 2). This text is of capital importance. The "image of God" in man has been fully manifested precisely through the Incarnation, in the exemplary manhood of the Incarnate God. In his catechetical treatise, St. Irenaeus is quite formal and precise. "He gave his frame the outline of His own form in order that even the visible appearance should be Godlike —for it was as an image of God that man was fashioned and set on earth" (*Demonstr.* II, p. 54 Smith's translation). "And the 'image' is the Son of God, in whose image man was made. And therefore He was manifested in the last times to show that the image was like unto Himself" (*Demonstr.* 22, p. 61 Smith). The concept of "image" has in St. Irenaeus an obvious *"somatic"* connotation,—"a strongly physical emphasis," in the phrase of David Cairns.[8] This emphasis is not accidental for Irenaeus. It is directly related to his basic idea of recapitulation. Indeed, the Word Incarnate, the God-Man, is the center of his theological vision and scheme. This emphasis encourages the use of "visible" and *"somatic"* images in theological thought and language, without committing Christians to any "anthropomorphite" conception of Divinity. The "image" is in the total structure of man; "likeness" is confined to his spiritual sphere.[9]

The "Anthropomorphite" monks stood in a venerable tradition. The conflict in the Desert was not just a clash between the "ignorant" and the "learned." It was the conflict between the two traditions: Evangelical realism and "Origenistic" symbolism.

Theophilus of Alexandria
and Apa Aphou of Pemdje

The Anthropomorphites in the Egyptian Desert

Part II

I

THE "LIFE OF BLESSED APHOU," an Egyptian hermit and eventually Bishop of Pemdje, or Oxyrhynchus, was published for the first time by Eugene Revillout in 1883 from a Turin manuscript. Revillout was aware of the historical value of this hagiographical document and intended to discuss it in detail. But his essay was never completed. He only printed the Coptic text (in Sahidic), with a brief preface.[1] The "Life" was republished again in 1886 by Francesco Rossi, from the same Turin manuscript, together with an Italian translation, but without any commentary or notes.[2] In the same year V.V. Bolotov published a Russian translation of

From the *Harry Austryn Wolfson Jubilee Volume* (Jerusalem: American Academy for Jewish Research, 1965), Vol. I, pp. 275-310. Reprinted by permission of the author.

Revillout's text, with an extensive introduction. Bolotov stressed the interest of the document. "A modest hagiological document of the Egyptian Church, the 'Life of Blessed Aphou' must occupy, in our opinion, an important place in the history of dogma: it throws a totally new and peculiar light on the Anthropomorphite controversy (which developed later into the Origenistic struggle).... Only now the history of the Anthropomorphites becomes really comprehensible." Bolotov planned a special excursus on this particular topic, but the second part of his article never appeared, and we do not know what this great master had actually to say.[3] The only special study of the "Life" of Aphou is by E. Drioton. He was interested primarily in the story of the Anthropomorphites. In his article Drioton reprinted the relevant part of the Coptic text, following Rossi's edition, and also supplied a French translation.[4] Unfortunately, Drioton was misguided by his gratuitous assumption that Egyptian "Anthropomorphites" were actually Audians, and this assumption marred considerably and distorted his analysis of the text itself.

There is no adequate paleographic description of the Turin papyri, even in the catalogue of Rossi.[5] The date of the manuscripts remains uncertain, and their origin is still rather obscure. Indeed, the same may be said of many other collections. Already Zoëga, in his famous Catalogue of the Borgian collection, complained: *Quibus Aegypti locis quibusve in bibliothecis olim adservati fuerint codices, quorum fragmenta sunt in museo Borgiano, plane ignoratur ... Arabes ex monasteriis (eos) rapuisse videntur vel potius in dirutorum olim monasteriorum ruderibus invenisse... Hujusmodi fasciculi vere chaotici cum subinde ex Aegypto adveherentur mihique ordinandi traderentur.*[6] In fact, the Turin papyri were acquired somewhere by Bernardino Drovetti, the French consul in Egypt, and then purchased for the Turin museum.[7] Amedeo Peyron, the first to handle the manuscripts, soon after they were brought to Turin in 1821, had very little to say. They were in miserable condition, sorely mutilated and even torn to small pieces—*piccolissimi pezzi*. For transportation they were carelessly packed in a box—*quam cum aperuissem infandam vidi ac deploravi papyrorum cladem,* exclaims Peyron. Peyron was able, however, to fit the scattered fragments together, and fixed them on transparent sheets[8] Unfortunately, varnish used for fixation deteriorated with time, the paper grew even more fragile, and the text did not read easily. This was one of Rossi's reasons for precipitating the publication.[9]

Among the papyri—*en tête de la masse de ces papyres*—Revillout found an interesting note, on a separate scrap of paper. It appears that these papers were once deposited by a certain pious lady, whose name is known to God, "in this place of St. John the Baptist," with the intention that prayers should be said for her and for her family. No date is given, and it is not certain at all whether this note refers to the whole collection or only to some particular documents in it. One must recall that the documents came to Turin in a poor and confused state, and in complete disorder. Revillout, however, took for granted that the whole collection, as we know it now, was deposited at St. John's already in the first decades of the fifth century, or, in any case, before the Schism.[10] The Church of St. John in Alexandria is, of course, the famous Serapeum. It was made into a church under Theophilus, and in 398 the relics of St. John the Baptist were transferred to the new *martyrion*. For that reason the church came to be known under the name of St. John. There was a library in this church.[11] Now, it seems that the Turin papyri are of a later date, probably of the seventh century.[12] In this case the dating of Revillout is untenable.

Bolotov contested the early dating for other reasons. Certain documents in the collection seem to be of a later date, as, for instance, a spurious "Life" of St. Athanasius. Again, it is hardly probable that numerous homilies of St. John Chrysostom (authentic or spurious) could be included in an Alexandrinian collection in the times of St. Cyril and Dioscoros. Bolotov suggested that the Drovetti collection was, in fact, a part of a Coptic *Menologion,* or Lectionary, compiled in some monastery. The part preserved covers the months *tout* and *paopi,*—that is, the first months of the liturgical year. The "Life of Blessed Aphou" is to be read on the 21st day of the month *tout,* which corresponds to September 18. Now, Zoëga already has shown that most of the Memphitic (or Bohairic) documents in the Borgian and Vatican collections were actually but *disjecta membra* of a Lectionary, which originated in the monastery of St. Macarius in Scete: *olim pertinuisse videantur ad lectionarium, quod secundum menses diesque digestum adservabatur in monasterio S. Macarii in Scetis.*[13] Bolotov suggested that a similar Lectionary, or *Menologion,* existed also in Sahidic. In its content and composition it seems to have differed considerably from the Macarian version. In any case, the names of Aphou and some others do not occur at all in the later *Synaxaria* of the Coptic Church in Arabic.[14] At any rate, particular documents in the *Menologion* can easily be of quite different dates, including some early material. But the whole collection, the *Menologion* as such, could hardly have been completed by 444 or 451, as Revillout contended.[15]

Thus, the date of each particular document must be examined separately. The date of the collection may only provide the ultimate *terminus ante quem.* And, in our case, when precisely this date is doubtful and uncertain, it is rather irrelevant.

Now, the "Life of Blessed Aphou" was written some time after his death, but hardly by a close contemporary, although still at a time when memories of the saint were fresh. The style of the writer is both naive and pathetic, but plain and sober, without legendary adornments and without any emphasis on the miraculous, which are so characteristic of later Coptic hagiography. Bolotov regarded the "Life" as generally reliable.[16] Drioton was of the same opinion: *le*

papyrus porte en lui-même un cachet indubitable d'historicité.
Drioton suggested that the unknown hagiographer might
have had at his disposal certain official documents; his
description of the dispute between Aphou and Theophilus
was based probably on an official record taken formally by
an episcopal clerk: *un procès-verbal de quelque notaire
épiscopal.* On the other hand, the writer was unaware of that
complex and controversial situation in which the dispute had
taken place and therefore had no incentive to be tendentious:
he had a "blind accuracy"—*une exactitude aveugle,* as Drioton
puts it.[17] It may be added that his description of Aphou's
episcopate, in the final section of the "Life," has the character
of an historic narrative.

The only safe date in the biography of Aphou is that
of his disputation with Theophilus. It could have taken
place only in 399. At that time Aphou was already an aged
man, a renowned hermit. According to the "Life," three years
later he was made bishop by Theophilus, and his episcopate
seems to have been of considerable duration. He died as an
old man. This would bring us at least into the second decade
of the fifth century. The "Life" seems to have been written
in a day when the turbulent events of the times of Theophilus
had been forgotten in monastic circles. Some time must have
elapsed before the "Life" could be included in a *Menologion.*
Thus, it seems most probable that the whole collection was
completed in the later part of the fifth century.

II

Aphou was conspicuously a simple and rustic man: his
conversation was "with the wild beasts." He did not dwell
with the people and rigorously avoided their company. Only
on the day of Easter he used to appear in the city, at
Oxyrhynchus, "to hear the preaching" in the church. He led
a solitary life, among the beasts, and they were friends to-

gether—the hermit and the beasts. The beasts were even looking after him. In winter time they would gather around him and warm him with their breathing. They would even bring him food. When, later in life, Aphou was nominated by Theophilus for the episcopal office in Oxyrhynchus, he could not be found. People in the city did not know him. They asked local monks about him, and one of the monks happened to have known him before. He suggested that Aphou must be in the wilderness, as "he did not dwell with men, but with the beasts," and warned in advance that Aphou, surely, would run away if he was told the reason for which he was sought. Finally, Aphou was caught in the net which hunters had set for the beasts. So much we learn from the "Life of Blessed Aphou." The picture is at once coarse and idyllic.

An interesting episode is included in the *Narratio Ezechielis monachi de vita magistri sui Pauli*. The Coptic text was published already by Zoëga with a Latin paraphrase, from a Borgian manuscript, and was republished once more by Amélineau, who also supplied a French translation.[18] Apa Paul of Tamwah (or Thmoui) was notorious for his ascetical excesses, of an almost suicidal character. He dwelt on the Mount of Antinoe. In his later years Paul was intimately associated with Apa Bishai (=Psois), one of the earliest settlers in Scete and the founder of one of the main monasteries there.[19] Ezechiel, a close disciple of Apa Paul, wrote a description of their common journey in the desert, in the course of which they met Aphou. Amélineau was inclined to disavow the narrative as a fiction, *un livre de pure imagination*. The name of Ezechiel was just a disguise, and the story was compiled much later. Amélineau admitted, however, that certain features in the story were of real interest for the history of ideas.[20] Now, whatever may be said about the literary form of the narrative, there is no valid reason to deny its realistic core. The journey in the desert may be a literary device, a means to chain together various *dicta* and episodes, but *dicta* and episodes may still be genuine and authentic. At the present we are concerned only with one episode in the story of Ezechiel, the meeting of Apa Paul with Apa Aphou. We have here a close parallel to the "Life."

> We travelled southward from Mount Terab until we came to Mount Terotashans, south of Kos. We found some antelopes down in the valley, and in their midst was a monk. My father went forward, greeted him, and said to him, "What is your name?" He said, "My name is Aphou. Remember me, my father, Apa Paul, and may the Lord bring my life to a good finish." My father said to him, "How many years have you been in this place?" He said, "Fifty-four years." My father then said, "Who placed the scheme upon you?" He said, "Apa Antonios of Scete." My father said to him, "How have you lived, travelling with these antelopes?" He said, "My nourishment and that of these antelopes is the same nourishment, namely the plants of the field and these vegetables." My father said to him, "Do you not freeze in the winter or roast in the summer?" He said to him, "When it is winter, I sleep in the midst of these antelopes, and they warm me with the vapor which is in their mouth. When it is summer, they gather together and stand and make shade for me, so that the heat should not bother me." My father said to him, "Truly are you given the epithet: Apa Aphou the Antelope." At that moment a voice came to us saying, "This is his name unto all the rest of the eternities of the earth." We were amazed at what had happened so suddenly and we greeted him. Then we left.[21]

Aphou was not the only one in the Egyptian desert to practise this peculiar form of ascetical estrangement, ξενι-τεία. Hermits dwelling with the beasts in the wilderness are mentioned often in hagiographical documents of that time.²² Now, Wilhelm Bousset contended that all these stories were but legends or novels. The paradisiac hermits, wandering with the beasts, existed only in poetical imagination, not in real life: "nur in der Gestalt legendarischer Erzählungen und nicht in greifbarer Wirklichkeit." The monks of Scete were more sound and sober in their ascetical endeavor and did not approve of wandering monks.²³ This peculiar and rough manner of asceticism—"das tierartige Umherschweifen in der Wüste," in the phrase of Bousset,—originated probably in Syria and Mesopotamia, and for that area it is so well attested in the authentic sources that no reasonable doubts can be raised about its historicity. Sozomen speaks of hermits in Syria and in the adjacent part of Persia which were called βοσκοί, because of their manner of life: they had no houses and dwelt constantly on the mountains. "At the usual hours of meals, they each took a sickle, and went to the mountains to cut some grass on the mountains, as though they were flocks in pasture—καθάπερ νεμόμενοι." Sozomen enumerates by names those who have chosen this kind of "philosophy" (VI, 33). The primary meaning of the word βοσκός was herdsman or shepherd. But in this connection it was used rather in the sense of βοσκόμενος νεμόμενος.²⁴ In Palestine also there were numerous ascetics who practiced this or a similar way of life. There were those who dwelt in mountains, dens, and caves of the earth, and others used to live with the beasts—σύνοικοι θηρίοις γενόμενοι. Again, some others led even a harder life—νέμονται δὲ τὴν γῆν, βοσκοὺς καλοῦσι... ὥστε τῷ χρόνῳ καὶ θηρίοις συναφομοιοῦσθαι (Evagrius Schol., *hist. eccl.*, I, 21).

There are good reasons to assume that the same rigid and radical method of ascetical retirement was practiced also in Egypt. It is curious to know that Apa Aphou was not the only one to be given the nickname "the Antelope." According to John Cassian, the same nickname was given also to Apa Paphnutius, who was, in any case, a historical personality. The passage must be quoted in full. *Coll.* III. I). *Ubi rursum tanto fervore etiam ipsorum anachoretarum virtutes superans desiderio et intentione jugis ac divinae illius theoriae cunctorum devinabat aspectus, vastiora et inaccessibilia solitudinis penetrans loca multoque in eis tempore delitescens, ut ab ipsis quoque anachoretis difficulter ac rarissime deprehensus angelorum cotidiano consortio delectari ac perfrui crederetur, atque ei merito virtutis hujus ab ipsis inditum fuerit Bubali cognomentum.* The last sentence is rather puzzling: what is the link between the *consortium angelorum* and *Bubali cognomentum?* Obviously, there must be another reason for this peculiar nickname. Paphnutius used to retire in the *inaccessibilia solitudinis loca,* beyond the reach of hermits themselves. Would it be too much to suggest that there he was dwelling with the beasts?—in this case the *cognomentum* would be well motivated. It should be added at this point that the story of a journey in the wilderness, known as the "Life and Conversation" of Apa Onouphrius, in which "naked hermits" were encountered, is attributed to Paphnutius. On the other hand, Apa Paphnutius of Scete was the only leader there who, according to John Cassian, opposed the monks revolting against Theophilus in connection with his Epistle of 399 against the Anthropomorphites.

In fact, the basic principles of the anchorites was: φεῦγε τοὺς ἀνθρώπους καὶ σώζῃ (*Apophthegmata*, Arsenius I, Cotelerius, *Ecclesiae Graecae Monumenta*, I, p. 353). Retirement and renunciation was usually justified by Biblical examples: the images of Elijah and other prophets, of St. John the Baptist, and even of the Apostles were often recalled and their names quoted.[25] The Epistle to the Hebrews could be also recalled. The way of the anchorites was the way of prophets and apostles. It was precisely in this manner that Apa Aphou used to explain his strange and peculiar mode of life. He was asked by people, in his later years, when he was already bishop, about the reasons of his peculiar life. In reply he simply quoted Scripture. Is it not said in the

Gospel about Christ himself that He was in the wilderness
"with the wild beasts" (Mk 1:13)? Did not the blessed
David say about himself: "I was as a beast before Thee"
(Ps. 73:22)? Did not Isaiah, by the Lord's command, walk
naked and barefoot (Is. 20:2)? Now, if Christ himself and
His great saints had so condescended and humbled themselves, it was much more imperative for him to do the
same—a poor and weak man.

A simple and rustic man, Aphou was a man of genuine
piety, of resolute will, and of penetrating mind. According
to the "Life" Theophilus was much impressed by Aphou:
he appeared before him as a "common man," an ἰδιώτης,
but his speech was that of a wise man. In his later years,
when he was made bishop—indeed, against his own will,
Aphou displayed an unusual pastoral wisdom and zeal. The
image depicted in the "Life of Blessed Aphou" is quite
impressive. Aphou was an active and efficient bishop, although he accepted this charge reluctantly. He still maintained his peculiar habits. He did not reside in the city, but
in a "monastery" outside—in this connection the word
"monastery" means obviously just a solitary cell, which was
actually the primary meaning of this word.[26] Only on week-
ends did he appear in the city. On Saturdays he used to
gather people into the church and instruct them the whole
day. Then he would spend the night in prayer and psalmody,
till the time of celebration. And after the service he used to
continue instruction till the close of the day. Then, in the
evening he would retire to his own place, till the next week-
end. In this way he endeavored to combine his *anachoresis*
with the episcopal duties. It should be kept in mind that
Oxyrhynchus was at that time a very peculiar city. According
to Rufinus, there *multo plura monasteria quam domus vide-
bantur* (*Hist. monach.*, ch. V,—of course, in this text *monas-
terium* denotes the solitary cells; cf. the Greek text, ed.
Festugière, *Subsidia Hagiographica*, 34 [1961], 41-43). The
city was rather a monastic city: *sed nec portae ipsae, nec turres*

*civitatis, aut ullus omnino angulus ejus, monachorum habita-
tionibus vacat, quique per omnem partem civitatis, die ac
nocte hymnos ac laudes Deo referentes, urbem totam quasi
unam Dei ecclesiam faciunt.* And it was a large city: according to Rufinus, there were 20,000 virgins and 10,000 monks.[27]

Aphou was especially concerned with the poor and the
needy, and also with all those who have suffered from injustice. He organized the material life of his church, by ap-
pointing a special officer for this task, in such a way that
he always had means to help the needy, and he almost
abolished poverty in his flock altogether.[28] He enforced strict
discipline in the church: no woman was allowed to receive
communion if she appeared in a colored dress or wearing
jewels. Aphou was concerned not only with the offended
but also with the offenders, as they were transgressing
the law of God and were in peril of damnation. He was quite
strict about the order of the divine service. From his candi-
dates for ordination he used to require a solid knowledge
of Scripture, and examined them himself. Occasionally he had
raptures, and in this manner used to learn what was going
on in the city. His last admonition to his clergy, already on
his death-bed, was not to seek high positions. He could hardly
himself preserve that which he had achieved as a hermit,
when he became bishop, and, while being bishop, he did not
achieve anything. Obviously, it is not just an idealized portrait,
but a picture of a living person, with distinctive individual
features.

There is an interesting pericope concerning Aphou in the
alphabetic *Apophthegmata*, a close parallel to that last
admonition of his which is recorded in the "Life."[29] As a
hermit, Aphou led a severe life. He wanted to continue the
same after he had become bishop, but was unable to do so
—οὐκ ἴσχυσε. In despair, he prostrated himself before God
and asked, whether it was because of his episcopacy that
grace had departed from him: μὴ ἄρα διὰ τὴν ἐπισκοπὴν
ἀπῆλθεν ἡ χάρις ἀπ' ἐμοῦ. No, was the answer in a

revelation. But, when he was in the desert, and there was no
man—μὴ ὄντος ἀνθρώπου—God was helping him: ὁ
Θεὸς ἀντελαμβάνετο. Now, when he is in the world,
people are taking care of him (Cotelerius, pp. 398-399; cf.
Verba Seniorum, XV. 13, ML LXXIII, c. 956). The emphasis
is here on the antithesis: ἔρημος and κόσμος. This episode
is quoted, without the name of Aphou, by St. Isaac of
Nineveh, and this shows its popularity. The context in which
the quotation appears in St. Isaac helps to grasp its full
meaning. It appears in the "Treatise in Questions and
Answers," concerning the life of those who dwell in the
wilderness, or in solitude. The question is asked: why are
"visions and revelations" sometimes given to certain people,
while to others they are not given at all, although they may
have labored more. Now, visions and visitations are granted
often to those who on account of their fervent zeal have fled
from the world, "abandoning it entirely in despair and retiring
from any part inhabited by men, following God, naked,
without hope or help from anything visible, assailed by the
fear of desolation or surrounded by the peril of death from
hunger or illness or any other evil whatever, and near to
dejection." On the other hand, "as long as a man receives
consolation from his fellowmen or from any of these visible
things, such (heavenly) consolation does not happen to
him." This is the answer; and then follow the illustrations.
The second is the story of Aphou (but the name is not
given). "Another witness to this is he who led a solitary
life in reclusion, *and often tasted of consolations granted by
grace, and divine care often became visible to him in manifest
apperception;* but when he came *near the inhabited world*
and sought these things as usual, *he did not find them.* He
besought God that the truth concerning this matter might
become known to him, saying: perhaps, my Lord, grace has
been withdrawn from me on account of my episcopal rank?
It was said to him: No. But then, *there was the desert,* there

were no men, and God provided for thee. Now, there is *the inhabited world,* and men provide for thee."[30]

In this context the pericope of the *Apophthegmata* comes into a clearer light. The "grace" which had been granted to Aphou in the wilderness was actually a *charisma,* or rather *charismata*—of visions and consolations. The term "grace" is ambiguous in this context, meaning at once "help" and "consolation." With Divine help Aphou was able, in the wilderness, to afford his rigid σκληραγωγία. But now it became impossible—"in the inhabited world," in a community of men. Aphou was a charismatic, a πνευματικός, but charismatics must dwell in solitude, or in the desert and not "in the world." It is interesting to note that the author of the "Life" of Aphou mentions his "ecstasies" only in passing. He is much more interested in his pastoral exploits. Was this author a monk himself?

According to the "Life," in his early years Aphou lived "in obedience" with certain chosen and faithful people—some of them taught by the "disciples of the Apostles." After their death Aphou alone was left, except for one brother, probably a novice, whom he was instructing in the ways to heaven. Thus, originally Aphou lived in a community, and only later chose the solitary life. It is possible, however, that he lived in a company of hermits. It was not unusual at that time that even members of a coenobitical community would retire to the solitary life. There was nothing peculiar in the change. Unfortunately, at this very point the Coptic text is deficient: there is a lacuna of an indefinite length. But we have additional information in the "Life of Apa Paul": Aphou was made monk by Apa Antonius of Scete and stayed in the desert for fifty-four years.

Now, at this very point Drioton makes a hasty conclusion that it was an Audian community in which Aphou had been reared. His argument is strained and peculiar, vague and shaky.[31] First, he contends that teachers of Aphou are so "mysteriously" designated in the "Life" as to give an im-

pression that they were a "separate" group: "ces hommes
que le papyrus désigne si mysterieusement donnent bien
l'impression d'être des séparés." In fact, there is simply
nothing "mysterious" in the text at all. The phrasing is
rather trivial and conventional: Aphou came from the company of venerable and "faithful" masters. These masters
themselves were instructed by the "Apostolic disciples." This
phrase may seem, at the first glance, rather peculiar. For
Drioton it is a conspicuous Audian link: "un trait bien
Audien." In this connection Drioton recalls the Audian claim
to follow the "Apostolic tradition" concerning the Paschal
practices. He admits himself, however, that actually there is
no slightest hint in the "Life" of Aphou (which is, indeed,
the only document in which Aphou's teachers are mentioned)
of any peculiar Paschal usages. It is evident, on the contrary,
that Aphou himself followed the regular calendar of the
Church of Alexandria. Moreover, in the "Life" there is no
reference to any Apostolic *tradition*. It is only stated that
Aphou's own masters were instructed by the *disciples* of
the Apostles, the *mathetai*. The question arises as to what
connotation this term has had, or may have had, in the
ecclesiastical or monastic idiom of the fourth century. And
it is not difficult to find it out.

In fact, early monasticism, in Egypt and elsewhere, always
claimed to have followed the Apostolic pattern, and the
term "apostolic" was used, widely and persistently, to denote
ascetical endeavor—renunciation, poverty, the wandering life,
and the like. The term was applied especially to hermits.
The retreat from the world itself was regarded as an
apostolic action, as an imitation of the disciples who left
everything and followed Christ (cf. Luke 5:11—ἀφέντες
πάντα). This idea is plainly implied in the great "Life of
Anthony," although the term itself is not used.[32] Eusebius
reports that Origen emphatically insisted on the evangelical
command of poverty—not to possess anything (VI, 3, 10).
Speaking of the Therapeutai, Eusebius uses the term: ἀπο-

στολικοὶ ἄνδρες, precisely because they were committed to ascetical practices (II, 17, 2). Richard Reitzenstein already has shown that for Eusebius the term "apostolic life" had a definite and established meaning: it meant asceticism.[33] And asceticism also implied a pneumatic endowment. In the phrase of Reitzenstein, "der vollkommene Asket ist ἐμπνευσθεὶς ὑπὸ 'Ιησοῦ ὡς οἱ ἀπόστολοι, er ist der ἀνὴρ ἀποστολικός."[34] Hermits in particular are the Apostolic people, and their life is apostolic. It was a commonplace in the literature of the fourth and fifth centuries.[35] Two examples will suffice at this point. Speaking of the persecutions under Valens, Socrates mentions the Novatian bishop Agelius: "he had led *an apostolic life*—βίον ἀποστολικὸν βιούς—because he always walked barefoot, and used but one coat, observing the injunctions of the Gospel" (IV, 9). Epiphanius uses the term in the same sense: ἀποταξάμενοι καὶ ἀποστολικὸν βίον βιοῦντες. Renunciation and "apostolic life" are equated. Actually Epiphanius was discussing the encratite sect of Apostolics: this name emphasizes their commitment to the Apostolic pattern of life. Epiphanius sharply exposes their exclusiveness and intolerance, but admits that the pattern of renunciation is truly apostolic. Apostles had no possessions: ἀκτήμονες ὑπάρχοντες. And the Saviour himself, while in the flesh never acquired anything earthly: οὐδὲν ἀπὸ τῆς γῆς ἐκτήσατο (*Panar.*, haeres. XLI, al. LXI, c. 3, 4).

It is safe to conclude that the expression "the disciples of the Apostles" is used in the "Life of Blessed Aphou" only to denote their strict ascetical manner of life. They were ἀποστολικοὶ ἄνδρες. Surely, there is nothing *"bien Audien"* in the phrase, and the whole argument of Drioton is based on a sheer misunderstanding.

Finally, Drioton calls attention to the fact that the community of Aphou's teachers probably came to its end approximately at the time in which, according to Epiphanius, Audian communities declined. It is a lame argument: a mere coincidence in time does not prove anything, neither identity nor even connection. Moreover, there is no evidence that the Audian movement ever expanded to Egypt. It is significant that no enemy of the Egyptian "Anthropomorphites" ever suggested that they had any sectarian connection, even in the heat of strife, although, of course, it would have been a good argument in the struggle. Drioton simply begins with the assumption that Audians were the only source from which "Anthropomorphite" convictions could have come. He does not consider the possibility that the allegedly "Anthropomorphite" arguments could be derived from some other source. Drioton is compelled to admit that Aphou's own position was much more qualified than that of the historic Audians. And yet he finds his position to be "heretical," although it is not clear what exactly he regards as heretical in the exposition given in the "Life."

To sum up, Drioton's arguments cannot substantiate his claim that Aphou came from the Audian background, that his teachers were but "authentic adherents of a disappearing sect"—"les adhérents authentiques d'un schisme finissant." One cannot but regret that Drioton put his unwarranted assumption into the very title of his otherwise competent and interesting article: "La discussion d'un moine anthropomorphite audien. . . ." This assumption so blinded Drioton that he failed to grasp the true subject of this "discussion" and to discern its actual theme and its internal structure.

III

The theological discussion between Apa Aphou and Archbishop Theophilus is the crucial and most significant part of the "Life." Let us, first of all, quote the relevant part of the document in full.[36]

And it came to pass, then, that, while yet abiding

with the wild beasts, he went out for the preaching
of Holy Easter. And he heard an expression
(λέξις) which was not in accord with the knowledge of the Holy Spirit, so that he was much
troubled by that discourse. And, indeed, all those
who heard it were afflicted and troubled. But the
angel of the Lord commanded the blessed Aphou
not to disregard the word, saying to him: "Thou
art ordered by the Lord to go to Alexandria to set
this word aright." And that word was as follows:
the preacher, as if he were exalting the glory of
God in his address, had recalled the weakness of
man and had said: *"It is not the image of God
which we men bear."*

When he heard that, the blessed Aphou was filled
with the Holy Spirit and departed for the city of
Alexandria, wearing a wornout tunic. Blessed
Aphou stood at the bishop's gate for three days,
and no one let him in, for they took him for a
common man (ἰδιώτης). Then one of the clerics
took notice of him, observing his patience and
perceived that he was a man of God. He entered
within and informed the archbishop, saying, "Behold, a poor man is at the gate and says that he
wishes to meet you, but we have not dared to take
him to you, for he has not suitable clothing upon
him." But immediately, as though he had been im-
pelled by God, the archbishop ordered that they
bring him to him. And when the latter was before
him, he asked him to state his case. He answered:
"May my Lord bishop bear the word of his servant
with love and patience (ἐν ἀγάπη καὶ ἀνοχῇ)."
He said to him: "Speak." Blessed Aphou replied: "I
know of your soul's kindness (χρηστότητα) and
that you are a thoughtful man. That is the reason
for my approaching your highness. I am certain
that you will not contemn the word of piety, even
though it come from such a poor man as I." And

Theophilus, the archbishop, said to him: "How reprobate is he who shall be mad enough to reject God's word for the sake of a trifle."

Aphou answered him: "Let my Lord command that the original (ἴσον) of the sermon be read to me, wherein I heard the sentence (λέξις) that was not in agreement with the Scriptures inspired by God. Personally, I did not believe (οὐ πιστεύω) that it had come from you, but I thought that the clerk (συγγραφεὺς) had committed a scribal error, regarding which a goodly number of pious people blunder to the point of being greatly troubled."[37] Then Apa Theophilus, the archbishop, gave an order. The original (ἴσον) of the sermon was brought to him. When the reading had begun, that phrase was reached. Then Apa Aphou bowed down, saying: "This sentence like that is not correct; I, on the other hand, will maintain that it is in the image of God that all men have been created." The Archbishop replied: "How is it that you alone have spoken against this reading, and that there has not been anyone in agreement with you?" Apa Aphou said: "But indeed I am sure that you will be in agreement with me and will not argue with me."

The Archbishop said: "How could you say of an Ethiopian that he is the image of God, or of a leper, or of a cripple, or of a blind man?"

Blessed Aphou replied: "If you proclaim that in such fashion, you will be denying that which He said, namely, 'Let us make man in our likeness and in our image' (Gen. 1:26)."

The Archbishop replied: "Far be it! but I believe that Adam alone was created in His likeness and image, but that his children whom he begot after him do not resemble him." Apa Aphou replied, saying: "Moreover, after God had established the covenant with Noah following the flood, He said to him: 'whoever sheds human blood, his own will be shed in return, for man had been created in the image of God' (Gen. 9:6)."

The Archbishop said: "I hesitate to say of an ailing man or . . . that he bears the image of God, Who is impassible and self-sufficient, while (the former) squats outside and performs his necessities (παρα-σκευάζει—cf. I Sam. 24:4, LXX). How could you think of him (as being one) with God, the true light whom nothing can surpass?"

Aphou said to him: "If you mention this too, one may say of the body of Christ that it is not what you say it is. For the Jews will claim: 'How do you take a bit of bread which the earth had so laboriously produced, and then believe and say that this is the body of the Lord?' " The Archbishop said to him: "That is not the case, for it is truly bread before we elevate it above the altar (θυσιαστή-ριον); only after we have elevated it above the altar and have invoked God upon them, does the bread become the body of Christ and the cup become the blood, according as He said to His disciples: 'Take ye and eat, this is my body and my blood'. And then do we believe." Apa Aphou said to him: "Just as it is necessary to have faith in that, it is necessary to have faith . . . that man has been created . . . in the likeness (and) image (of) God. For He Who said, 'I am the bread which is come from heaven', is also He Who said, 'whoever will shed human blood, his own will be shed in return, for man has been created in the image of God'. Because of the glory of God's greatness, whoever. . . capable of arranging that something. . . to him. . . his. . . (will establish) it. . . and because of the weakness of man's insignificance according to the natural frailty of which we are aware. If we think, for example, of a king who will give orders and a likeness (εἰκὼν) will be painted, and all will proclaim that it is the image of the king, but at the same time all know that it is wood and colors, for it does not raise its nose (head), like man, nor are its ears like those of the king's countenance, nor does it speak like the king. And all these weaknesses which belong to it nobody remembers out of respect for the king's judgment, because he has proclaimed: 'it is my image'. On the contrary, if anyone dare deny it (ἀρνεῖν), on the plea that it is not the king's image, he will be executed (killed) for having slighted it. Furthermore, the authorities are mustered concerning it and give praise to bits of wood and to colors, out of respect to the king. Now, if such things happen to an image which has no spirit, neither does it stir, being... delusive (ἀντίθετος), how much more, then, (to) man, in whom abides the Spirit of God, and who is active and honored above all the animals which are upon the earth; but because of the diversity of elements and colors . . . and of weaknesses which in us are... for us on account of our salvation; for it is not possible for any one of these latter to slight the glory which God has given us, according to the word of Paul: 'As for man, it is not proper that he cover his head (because he is the image and glory of God)' (I Cor. 11:7)."

When he heard these words, the blessed Archbishop arose and bent his head, saying: "This is fitting that instruction come from those who search in solitude, for, as for us, the reasonings of our hearts are mixed in us, to the point that we err completely in ignorance."

And immediately he wrote within all the country,

retracting that phrase, saying: "It is erroneous and proceeds from my lack of intelligence in this respect."

It is not difficult to put this episode in a proper chronological setting. The preaching which Aphou attended on Easter day was, obviously, the reading of that Festal "Epistle" of Theophilus, which, according to Sozomen, so strongly offended and irritated the Desert monks. In this epistle, says Sozomen, Theophilus "took occasion to state that God ought to be regarded as incorporeal, and alien to human form" (VIII. 11). To the same effect he preached himself in his church (cf. also Socrates, VI. 7). This Festal Epistle of Theophilus—for the year 399—is not preserved. Yet, Gennadius gives an extensive resumé of it: *sed et Adversum Anthropomorphitas haereticos, qui dicunt Deum humana figura et membris constare, disputatione longissima confutans, et divinarum Scripturarum testimoniis arguens et convincens, ostendit Deum incorruptibilem et incorporeum juxta fidem Patrum credendum, nec ullis omnino membrorum lineamentis compositum, et ob id nihil ei in creaturis simile per substantiam, neque cuiquam incorruptibilitatem suae dedisse naturae, sed esse omnes intellectuales naturas corporeas, omnes corruptibiles, omnes mutabiles, ut ille solus corruptibilitati et mutabilitati non subjacet, "qui solus habet immortalitatem"* (*de scriptoribus ecclesiasticis*, XXXIV, p. 74 Richardson). The same Epistle is mentioned by John Cassian. *Coll.* X. 2: *Theophili praedictae urbis episcopi solemnes epistulae commearunt, quibus cum denuntiatione paschali ineptam quoque Anthropomorphitarum haeresim longa disputatione disseruit eamque copioso sermone destruxit.* Cassian then proceeds to the description of the commotion produced in monastic circles by this sharp and heavy epistle, especially *in heremo Scitii:* in no monastery there, except one, was this epistle permitted to be read, publicly or privately: *legi- aut recitari.* The Archbishop himself was suspected and condemned—*velut haeresi gravissima depravatus:* he contradicted the Holy Scripture—*impugnare sanctae scripturae sententiam videretur.* Was it not written that man was created in the image of God?

The meeting between Aphou and Theophilus took place, surely, *before* that tumultuous intervention of angry monks which is so vividly described both by Socrates and Sozomen.[38] Indeed, it is difficult to conceive that such a peaceful interview as is described in the "Life of Blessed Aphou" could have taken place at a time when a hectic controversy was already raging everywhere in the monastic colonies of Egypt. Moreover, this interview would have been superfluous after Theophilus had changed his attitude. Again, according to the "Life," Aphou was the first to present objections to Theophilus concerning his "preaching." Aphou's intervention was his individual move, based on a private revelation. At that time Aphou was dwelling, apparently, somewhere in the neighborhood of Oxyrhynchus—he calls himself "a man of Pemdje," which refers rather to his residence than to his origin. It was in Oxyrhynchus that he heard the reading of Theophilus's epistle. Aphou's intervention had no direct connection with that general commotion *in eremo Scitii* of which John Cassian spoke.

There is an obvious discrepancy between our sources. Socrates and Sozomen present the story as that Theophilus was frightened by the monks and then yielded to their pressure—to condemn Origen. The name of Origen does not occur in the "Life" of Aphou. The hagiographer insists that Theophilus was moved by Aphou's arguments and "immediately" retracted his unfortunate statement—"has written to all in the country." It is reasonable to assume that Theophilus had various contacts with individuals before the monastic multitudes arrived. In any case, Aphou is nowhere mentioned in this connection, apart from the "Life." On the other hand, it is highly improbable that the whole episode of the monastic tumult could be completely omitted by a close contemporary of the event. It is more probable that the "Life of Blessed Aphou" was written much later, when the memories of the trouble had faded away, and by a writer who was interested only in the ascetical exploits of his saintly hero and in his pastoral work in the community of Oxyrhynchus. Aphou's visit to Theophilus is presented in the context of his biography, and not in the perspective of the history of his time.

It is both curious and significant that, according to the "Life," Aphou took exception to one particular expression, or a λέξις, in the epistle of Theophilus. In his conversation with the Archbishop he was concerned solely with the concept of God's image in man. He did not develop or defend any "Anthropomorphite" thesis. The sting of his argument was directed against the denial of God's image *in man,* and there was no word whatever about any "human form" *in God.* Aphou only contended that man, even in his present condition and in spite of all his misery and destitution, had to be regarded still as being created in the image of God, and must be, for that reason, respected. Aphou was primarily concerned with man's dignity and honor. Theophilus, on the other hand, was embarrassed by man's misery and depravity: could an Ethiopian or a cripple be regarded as being "in the image of God," he asked.

Theophilus appears to have held the view that the "image of God" had been lost by man in the Fall and that, accordingly, the children of Adam were not (pro)created in the image. It is precisely this opinion which was sharply exposed and refuted by Epiphanius, both in his *Ancoratus* and in the *Panarion,* in the section on the Audians. Let us recall that both works were written in the seventies, that is, long before the outbreak of the Origenistic and the Anthropomorphite troubles in Egypt.[39] Epiphanius's own position in this matter was balanced and cautiously qualified. Man was created in the image of God, κατ᾽ εἰκόνα,—this is a Scriptural truth which cannot be doubted or ignored. But one should not

attempt to decide in which part of man this κατ' εἰκόνα
is situated, nor should one restrict this image to one part or
aspect of the human constitution, to the exclusion of others.
One has to confess faithfully the presence of this "image"
in man, lest we despise the Divine grant and appear unfaith-
ful to Him: ἵνα μὴ τὴν χάριν τοῦ Θεοῦ ἀθετήσωμεν
καὶ ἀπιστήσωμεν Θεῷ. What God has said is truth, even
if it escapes our understanding in certain respects: εἰ καὶ
ἐξέφυγε τὴν ἡμῶν ἔννοιαν ἐν ὀλίγοις λόγοις. In any
case, to deny the κατ' εἰκόνα is contrary to Catholic faith
and to the mind of the Holy Church: οὐ πιστὸν οὔτε τῆς
ἁγίας τοῦ Θεοῦ ἐκκλησίας (*Ancoratus*, 55; *Panarion*,
haeres. LXX, al. L, ch. 2). Now, proceeds Epiphanius, there
are many who would attempt to localize the image, either
only in the soul, or in the body alone, or else in the virtues
of man. All these attempts go astray from tradition. The
κατ' εἰκόνα is not exclusively in the soul, nor exclusively
in the body, but it would be wrong to deny that it is also
in the body and in the soul: ἀλλ' οὔτε λέγομεν τὸ σῶμα
μὴ εἶναι κατ' εἰκόνα οὔτε τὴν ψυχήν. In other words,
the "image" is in the whole man: man is created κατ'
εἰκόνα Θεοῦ, and not just one part of man. Finally, there
are also those who concede that God's image was in Adam,
but it was lost when Adam was expelled from Paradise:
ἀπώλεσε. Great is the licentious phantasy of those people,
exclaims Epiphanius: πολλὴ τίς ἐστι τῶν ἀνθρώπων
μυθοποιία. Indeed, we are obliged to believe that τὸ κατ'
εἰκόνα is still in man, and in the whole man: ἐν παντὶ δὲ
μάλιστα καὶ οὐχ ἁπλῶς (ἔν τινι μέρει). But how and
where exactly it resides is known to God alone, Who has
granted it by His grace, κατὰ χάριν. The "image" does not
perish, although it may be polluted and marred by sins. Then
Epiphanius gives his Scriptural references: Gen. 2:6, I Cor.
11:4, Jas. 3:8 (*Panar. LXX*, ch. 3; cf. *Ancor.*, 56, 57). It
should be noted at this point that the same texts (except for
Jas.) were quoted also by Aphou, in his conversation with

Theophilus. Even more significant is the fact that in his *Ancoratus* Epiphanius uses the same Eucharistic analogy which we find in the "Life" of Aphou. The κατ' εἰκόνα is the grant of God, and God must be trusted. The κατ' εἰκόνα can be understood by analogy: ἀπὸ τῶν ὁμοίων. Then comes a brief description of the Institution. Now, says Epiphanius, ὁρῶμεν ὅτι οὐκ ἴσον ἐστὶν οὐδὲ ὅμοιον οὐ τῇ ἐνσάρκῳ εἰκόνι οὐ τῇ ἀοράτῳ Θεότητι οὐ τοῖς χαρακτῆρσι τῶν μελλῶν. But we simply trust the words of Christ (*Ancoratus,* 57).

Epiphanius takes a firm stand: according to Scripture man is created "in the image" of God, and it is against the Catholic rule of faith to doubt or to deny that. But this "image," τὸ κατ' εἰκόνα, is, as it were, a mystery, a gracious gift of God, and this mystery must not be rationalized—it must be apprehended by faith. From this point of view Epiphanius objects both to "Anthropomorphite" literalism in exegesis, and to the vagaries of Origenistic spiritualism. This was the position he maintained at Jerusalem in 394. He stated plainly his argument in his letter to John, which is extant only in the Latin translation of St. Jerome. Among various errors of Origen Epiphanius mentions also this: *ausus est dicere perdidisse imaginem Dei Adam... et illum solum factum esse ad imaginem Dei qui plasmatus esset ex humo et uxorem ejus, eos vero qui conciperentur in utero et non ita nascerentur ut Adam Dei non habere imaginem.* Against this "malicious interpretation"—*maligna interpretatione*—Epiphanius quotes Scripture: an array of texts follows: Gen. 9:4-6; Ps. 38:7; Sap. 2:23; Jas. 3:8-9; I Cor. 11:7. Epiphanius concludes: *nos autem, dilectissime, credimus his quae locutus est Dominus, et scimus quod in cunctis hominibus imago Dei permaneat, ipsique concedimus nosse in qua parte homo ad imaginem Dei conditus est* (Epiph. *ad Iohannem episcopum,* inter *epist. Hieronymi,* LI, 6.15-7.4). It was but natural that John suspected Epiphanius of an "Anthropomorphite" leaning, as Jerome informs us: *volens illum suspectum facere stultissimae haereseos.* Jerome recalls the dramatic clash between John and Epiphanius, and the sermon of John directed against the Bishop of Cyprus. Epiphanius had to restate his position: *cuncta (inquit) quae locutus est collegio frater, aetate filius meus, contra Anthropomorphitarum haeresin, bene et fideliter locutus est, quae mea quoque damnantur voce; sed aequum est, ut quomodo hanc haeresin condemnamus, etiam Origenis perversa dogmata condemnemus* (Hieron., *Contra Iohannem Hierosolymitanum*, cap. II). Although Jerome wrote some years after the events and his treatise is an emotional and venomous invective, we may assume that the position of Epiphanius was stated correctly. It should be added that Theophilus was originally suspicious of Epiphanius too, and "accused him of entertaining low thoughts of God, by supposing Him to have a human form." He reconciled himself and even allied with Epiphanius, but later, after 399, when he changed his position (*Socr.* VI. 10).

Now, let us return to the "Life of Blessed Aphou." Aphou's position in the dispute appears to be very similar to that of Epiphanius. His crucial emphasis is simply this: the reality of the "image" in general is not compromised by its factual inadequacy. An image of the king, which is itself lifeless and material, is still the king's image, the image of a living person, and must be, accordingly, respected. Moreover, man is not a lifeless image, but in him abides the Spirit of God. Again, an official image of the king must be regarded as such on account of the king's declaration, "this is my image." And, in regard to man, this is warranted by God himself, according to the Scriptures. Unfortunately, the text of the "Life" is in this passage corrupt and deficient, but it seems that Aphou had here also a reference to the Incarnation. Aphou's Eucharistic argument was to the same effect: do not trust appearances, but trust the word of God. In the Eucharist we actually see bread, but by faith we behold the Body, and believe it in obedience to the Dominical witness: "this is my Body." In the same way has God declared concerning man: "he is created in My image." In fact, Aphou does not go beyond this statement and does not try to locate the image or to rationalize the mystery. There is nothing specifically "Anthropomorphite" in his exposition. On the other hand, Aphou's reasoning is so close to that of Epiphanius that it may suggest a direct dependence. It is fair to assume that Epiphanius' writings and letters had considerable circulation at that time, and that, if certain people in the Egyptian communities were reading at that time Origen, others read his opponents, of which Epiphanius was the most venerable and conspicuous.

We have to identify now those people denying τὸ κατ' εἰκόνα in man after the Fall whom Epiphanius was so sharply and angrily refuting already in the *Panarion*. He probably had in view Origen and his followers, those especially among the hermits in Egypt. In the section of the *Panarion* on Origen Epiphanius accused him briefly of the contention that Adam had lost the κατ' εἰκόνα (*haeres. LXIV, al. XLIV*, cap. 4). In fact, the thought of Origen was more complex and qualified than a blunt denial. Moreover, one finds in his writings certain passages in which Origen strongly insisted that the "image" simply cannot have been totally lost or effaced and remains even in the soul, in which a "terrestrial image" is, by ignorance or resistance, superimposed over the κατ' εἰκόνα Θεοῦ (*Contra Celsum*, IV. 83; *Homil. in Gen.*, XIII. 3, 4). However, Origen spoke primarily of the "interior man"—the κατ' εἰκόνα was restricted to the νοῦς or the ἡγεμονικόν, and the body was emphatically excluded.[40] In the Greek theology of the fourth century there was an unresolved ambiguity concerning the image of God. One must be very careful at this point: the writers of that time did not claim that man *was an image*, but rather that he was created or shaped *in the image*. Thus, the emphasis was on conformity: an image is a true image when it actually mirrors or reflects adequately that reality of which it is held or expected to be the image. Accordingly, there was always a strong dynamic stress in the concept of the image. The question could not fail to arise, in what sense and to what extent could this dynamic relationship continue or persist when the conformity was conspicuously broken, and fallen man went astray and frustrated his vocation. This ambiguity could be obviated by distinguishing carefully the "image" and the "likeness," or "similitude." But this was never done consistently, nor by all. In fact, the theology of the image was intimately related to the theology of Sin and Redemption, and, again, the theology of Sin was not yet adequately elaborated at that time, either in the East or in the West. There was an obvious tension between different motives in the thought of St. Athanasius, especially in his early period. In the *de Incarnatione* St. Athanasius presents the Fall as a total and radical catastrophe: τὸ μὲν τῶν ἀνθρώπων γένος ἐφθείρετο. Ὁ δὲ λογικὸς καὶ κατ' εἰκόνα γενόμενος ἄνθρωπος ἠφανίζετο (6. I). Fallen man was, as it were, reduced to a sub-human status: ἡ γὰρ παράβασις τῆς ἐντολῆς εἰς τὸ κατὰ φύσιν αὐτοὺς ἐπέστρεφεν, ἵνα ὥσπερ οὐκ ὄντες γεγόνασιν (4. 4). The κατ' εἰκόνα was a grant of grace, and this grant was lost or withdrawn. The κατ' εἰκόνα had to be restored or even re-created: the verbs used by St. Athanasius were: ἀνακαινίζειν and ἀνακτίζειν. According to St. Athanasius, τὸ κατ' εἰκόνα was, as it were, superimposed over the "nature" in man which was intrinsically mutable and fluid—φύσις ῥευστὴ καὶ διαλυομένη. The stability of human composition was insured, in the state of innocence, by its "participation" in the Logos. In the state of estrangement, which was the root of sin, this participation was discontinued.[41] Actually, St. Athanasius wanted to emphasize the depth and radicalness of sin: fallen man is no more man in the full sense, and this is manifested most conspicuously in his actualized mortality, an inherent consequence of the estrangement, the ultimate sting of corruption, on the very verge of annihilation.[42] The same ambiguity remains in the theology of St. Cyril of Alexandria.

In a sense, according to his interpretation, man still is κατ᾽ εἰκόνα, as a "rational" creature endowed with freedom. But other basic aspects or features of the "image," and above all—incorruptibility, were lost, and the "image" itself was distorted or "falsified"—παρεχαράττετο, like a counterfeit coin or seal. Like St. Athanasius, St. Cyril uses the ambiguous word: ἀφανίζειν to characterize the impact of sin on τὸ κατ᾽ εἰκόνα, and it is difficult to detect his proper intention, since the word may mean both a superficial obliteration and total destruction.[43]

It is beyond the scope of the present study to analyze at full length the problem of the κατ᾽ εἰκόνα in the Greek theology of the fourth and following centuries. This brief and rather sketchy survey will suffice, however, for our immediate objective: to explain the position of Theophilus. Obviously, he followed St. Athanasius, just as St. Cyril did later. The brief summary of his controversial epistle given by Gennadius, which we have quoted earlier, is helpful. The emphasis of Theophilus was the same as that of St. Athanasius: the basic contrast between God, Eternal and "Immortal," and man, mutable, corruptible, and unstable, in man's fallen condition. He is no longer "in the image" after the Fall. Moreover, the Alexandrinian Fathers always tended to restrict τὸ κατ᾽ εἰκόνα to the "interior man," to the spiritual aspect of his existence. This was, undoubtedly, an inheritance from Origen.

To sum up: in the conversation between Aphou and Theophilus we have a confrontation of two different conceptions concerning τὸ κατ᾽ εἰκόνα Θεοῦ, that is, concerning the nature and character of "the image of God in man." And we may guess that this was the major issue in that violent conflict which came to be known as the "Anthropomorphite Controversy." No doubt, there were in Egypt also rustic monks who were addicted to literal interpretation of Scriptural images—*simplicitate rustica,* in the phrase of St. Jerome, which refers, however, to the situation in Palestine. But there was a deeper core of theological contention: there was an opposition to the whole tradition of Origen. W. Bousset observed rightly: *"Wenn des Theophilus Bekämpfung des Anthropomorphismus eine so grosse Erregung bei den sketischen Mönchen hervorruft* (Cassian, *Coll.* X), *so handelt es hier eigentlich nicht um das Dogma, sondern um eine Lebensfrage für die von der Gottesschau lebende enthusiastische Frömmigkeit."*[44] The story of Sarapion, told by Cassian (*Coll.* X. 3), is illuminating in this respect.[45]

In the light of the information we can derive from the "Life of Blessed Aphou" we can understand that rather enigmatic phrase with which Theophilus, according to both Socrates and Sozomen, managed to placate the angry monks. "Going to the monks, he in a conciliatory tone thus addressed them: 'In seeing you, I behold the face of God'. The utterance of this saying moderated the fury of these men and they replied: if you really admit that God's countenance is such as ours, anathematize Origen's book" (Socr. VI. 7—οὕτως ὑμᾶς, ἔφη, εἶδον ὡς Θεοῦ πρόσωπον; cf. Sozom. VIII. 11). Indeed, it could be no more than a flattering compliment, as Tillemont has interpreted it.[46] And, of course, it was a Biblical phrase: Gen. 33:10—Jacob meeting Esau—"for therefore I have seen thy face, as though I had seen the face of God." But it does seem to be more than just a compliment. Let us remember now the phrase in the epistle of Theophilus to which Aphou took exception: "It is not the image of God which we men bear." In his rejoinder Aphou insisted that the glory of God could be perceived even in that inadequate image which is man. It seems strange that angry monks be placated by the address of Theophilus, if it was no more than a courteous phrase. In fact, it was just to the point, it was a disguised retraction of his offensive phrase in the controversial epistle that had irritated the monks. It seems that the monks understood it.[47]

According to the "Life" of Aphou, Theophilus was impressed by his arguments, admitted his error, and issued a new encyclical. No such encyclical epistle is known. In his later Festal Epistles, which are preserved only in the Latin translation of Jerome, Theophilus did not discuss the problem of the image at all. They were concerned mainly with the refutation of Origen.[48] But we can trust the "Life" and admit that Theophilus was impressed by Aphou himself. This rustic anchorite was a wise man. Aphou, on his side, praised the humility of Theophilus which allowed him to acknowledge his error. The story may be embellished a bit. Aphou declined the invitation to stay in Alexandria for a longer time and went back to his own place. After three years the see of Pemdje became vacant and Theophilus appointed Aphou, although another candidate had been nominated by the community. There is nothing improbable in that. Already in the time of St. Athanasius it was usual to appoint monks to episcopal position. Theophilus had done this not once. The best known case is, of course, that of Dioscurus, one of the Tall Brothers, whom he made bishop of Hermopolis.

The "Life of Blessed Aphou" comes, obviously, from Coptic circles.

The information on the Anthropomorphite Controversy which we derive from Greek and Latin sources is biased and onesided. This is true especially of John Cassian, a "pious journalist," as René Draguet has labelled him.[49] He was on the Origenist side in the conflict. He wrote from the Evagrian point of view: "noi in Cassiano rileggiamo Evagrio," rightly says a modern student of John Cassian.[50] The picture of Egyptian monasticism presented in the *Historia Lausiaca* is also drawn from the Greek point of view, "in the spirit of Evagrius," as Draguet puts it.[51] The case of the "Anthropomorphites" has been polemically misrepresented since that time. The controversy was presented as a clash between the rustic *simpliciores* and the learned. This aspect of the case should not be ignored or denied. But there was much more than that: there was also a clash of theological traditions, and a clash of spiritual conceptions. The "Life" of Aphou helps us to grasp this theological perspective of the controversy, and this constitutes the high historical value of this peculiar hagiological document.

A Postscript

1.   The valuable book by Antoine Guillaumont, *Les 'Kephalaia Gnostica' d'Evagre le Pontique et l'Histoire de l'Origénisme chez les Grecs et les Syriens* (= "Patristica Sorbonensia" 5, Editions du Seuil, Paris, 1962), appeared after the present article had been delivered for publication. Guillaumont has a brief paragraph on the Anthropomorphite controversy (pp. 59-61). He does not believe that the Anthropomorphites of Egypt had any relation to the Audians: "Cette filiation est difficile à établir historiquement. Il parait plus naturel de ne voir dans ce mouvement qu'une réaction spontanée contre la théorie evagrienne de la prière pure—réaction comprehensible de la part de gens simples qui pouvaient craindre que le Dieu de la Bible, qui a fati l'homme à son image, n'ait plus de place dans une piété si haute," p. 61, note 62. Guillaumont quotes my article of 1960 with general approval, but regrets that I have limited myself to the text of Cassian and did not mention Evagrius and his treatise "On Prayer." In fact, my only purpose in that article of mine—a brief communication at the Congress in Munich, sorely restricted in space—was to describe the position of Sarapion and to stress the importance of the conception of the "image of God" in man for the understanding of the whole conflict. On the other hand, Guillaumont refers to the article of Drioton, but does not seem to have appreciated the significance of the "Life of Aphou," le "curieux document," as he labels it (p. 62, note 63).

2.   βούβαλος (or βούβαλις) is *not a buffalo* (as it has been often mistranslated, for instance by Dom E. Pichery, in his edition of the 'Conferences' of Cassian, in the "Sources

Chrétiennes"—*le boeuf sauvage!*), but antelope, *bubalis mauretanica;* see the Lexicon of Liddell-Scott, *sub voce.* In English the word "buffalo" may denote both a kind of African stag or gazelle, and the wild ox (cf. Webster's Dictionary).

The Hagia Sophia Churches

I

THE FIRST TEMPLE in Constantinople dedicated under the name of "Holy Wisdom" was possibly designed by Constantine himself. The building was however completed much later and the "Great Church" was first consecrated only in 360, under Constantius, by an Arian bishop. It is not at all clear when the name "Hagia Sophia" was first given to the church. Socrates says only: "which is now called Sophia" (II, 43). It is quite possible that the "Great Church" in the beginning had no special name, and the name of Sophia came to prominence later; it was probably a current connotation rather than an intentional dedication.

The name, however, by no means was an accident. Some archeologist of old guessed that the name was rather an abstract idea or a Divine attribute, and that Constantine used to dedicate temples to "abstract ideas,"—Wisdom, Power,

"The Hagia Sophia Churches" originally appeared as a résumé of a lecture entitled "Christ, the Wisdom of God, in Byzantine Theology" in *Résumés des Rapports et Communications, Sixième Congrès International d'Études Byzantines* (Paris, 1940), pp. 255-260. Reprinted by permission. This résumé was only an introduction to a larger paper which was to be presented at the Byzantine Congress at Alger in 1939. The Congress, however, did not take place.

Peace. All this is but a misunderstanding. The name of Wisdom is a *biblical* name, and all these three "abstract" names are used in St. Paul, as names of Christ: Sophia [Σοφία], Dynamis [Δύναμις], Eirênê [Εἰρήνη]. Passages in the Old Testament where the Wisdom of God was described as a person (and specially the VIII-th chapter of Proverbs) were from an early date regarded as referring to Christ, the Incarnate Word. We find this in St. Justin. The other suggestion, that Wisdom meant rather the Holy Spirit (the Spirit of Wisdom, of course), found in Theophilus of Antioch and St. Irenaeus, was not used ever by any of the later writers, and the identification of "Sophia-Wisdom" as of one of the names of the Second Person of the Holy Trinity became the common place of Patristic exegesis and theology. Origen regards the name "Wisdom" as the first and principal name of the Son (*Comm. in Ioann.* I. 22). Both "Wisdom" and "Power" are mentionned in the Symbol of St. Gregory of Neo-Caesarea. In the IV-th century both Arians and Orthodox agreed that the Holy Wisdom described in the book of Proverbs was the Son of God. The eighth chapter of Proverbs was one of the principal topics of dispute throughout the whole IV-th century, and certainly the name was known and comprehensible to all and was full of associations. Anyhow it was the name of Christ, and it was but natural to give this name to the "Great Church."

Hagia Sophia was dedicated to Christ under the name of Wisdom. There is no reason whatever to suspect any change of dedication under Justinian. It is obvious that Sophia was commonly regarded as the temple of Christ. It is clearly shown in the famous story of the construction of Justinian's Sophia: "Hagia Sophia," which means the Word of God (ed. Preger, p. 74: καὶ ἔκτοτε ἔλαβε τὴν προσηγορίαν ὁ ναὸς Ἁγία Σοφία, ὁ Λόγος τοῦ Θεοῦ ἑρμηνευόμενος). It is hardly possible to speak of any specified dedication of churches in Justinian's time or even later. A church was usually dedicated simply to Our Lord or to the

Blessed Virgin, or else to the Saints. But it depended upon some peculiar conditions when any special dedication was stressed. The patronal festival was kept on the Anniversary of the dedication. In St. Sophia it was on the 23-rd of December, because the temple was consecrated under Justinian on the 26-th of December and again on the 24-th. Of course Christmas was chosen as the most suitable season. In the office for the Anniversary, as it is described in the Typik of the Great Church published by Dmitrievsky, there is nothing to suggest any special commemoration for the day; it is rather a general office for any Anniversary. And actually it was recommended for this purpose by Symeon of Salonica.

The churches dedicated to Holy Wisdom were quite numerous both in Byzantium and among the Slavs. On many occasions we have a direct proof that they were regarded as dedicated to Christ, the Word and the Wisdom. And there is no reason or hint whatever to suspect that any other dedication of the Sophia-churches was ever known or used in the Byzantine Church. Scholars were misled or confused by the unexpected and rather startling fact that in Russia the patronal festival in the Sophia-churches was kept on Our Lady's days, on the 8-th of September in Kiev (the Nativity of Our Lady) and on the 15-th of August in Novgorod (the Assumption). This seemed to suggest that these famous Cathedrals were dedicated to the Blessed Virgin, and that the name of Wisdom was applied to Her as well. Some scholars were inclined to see in that a special contribution of Russia to the theology of Wisdom. One has to object first that in earlier times the patronal festival both in Novgorod and Kiev was kept on the Anniversary of the dedication, as it is stated in old calendars. And secondly we are very fortunate to have some formal proofs that the patronal festival was transferred to the new dates quite late. In Kiev this occurred not before the restoration of the Hagia Sophia by Peter Mogila or even later. In Novgorod it took place under Archbishop Gennadius about the close of the XV-th century.

But even after that date the Novgorod Sophia was usually called the temple of the Wisdom and Word.

II

There are two distinct manners to represent the Wisdom of God in Byzantine iconography. First, Christ as Wisdom and Word under the image of an Angel (μεγάλης βουλῆς ἄγγελος, Is. IX. 6). Second, the personification of Wisdom, Divine or human, as a virgin. The first scheme is biblical, the second classical, and they are originally quite independent from each other.

The first one is very rare in early monuments. One has to mention the fresco in the catacombs in Karmuz, where the inscription is emphatic: ΣΟΦΙΑ ΙΣ ΧΣ. The representation is badly described and the whole monument not quite clear. One may interpret the image as a representation of Christ in the Old Testament similitude. One may compare it with the early document as "Shepherd" Hermas, in which the Son of God was described as an Angel and almost confused with Michel the Archangel (ὁ ἔνδοξος ἄγγελος). And one can understand easily why this image could not be very popular in early iconography. The main emphasis was rather on the historicity and reality of the presentation of Our Lord, and it was intended to convey to the worshipers the sound dogmatic idea. Symbolical images were rather definitely discouraged. This was the meaning of the 82nd canon of the Council in Trullo. The image of the Angel of the Great Council becomes popular and usual only in later Byzantine iconography, and is found often in Mistra and Athos, but only as an exception are we warranted to believe that the Angel was meant to represent Wisdom. One can mention only one fresco described by Charles Diehl at St. Stefano in Soleto, probably from the late XIV-th century. The angel has a chalice in his hand, which suggests an eucharistic interpretation (see Prov. IX, 2, which is referred to the Eucharist in the office of Good Thursday). But the inscription is plain: Η ΑΓ. ΣΟΦΙΑ Ο ΛΟΓΟΣ. There are some interesting compositions in miniatures. But it is certain that in Byzantine art we never had any canonized scheme for the representation of Divine Wisdom.

The second composition, the personification, can be found first in the miniatures. It is enough to mention the famous Parisin. N. 139 (X-th cent.). But even here the classical motive was possibly amalgamated with the biblical. One can recall the vision of St. Cyril, where Wisdom was seen as a virgin (see Sap. Sal. VIII, 2). In monumental art the composition in Monreale has to be mentioned. All that does not suggest that the image of Wisdom had any special appeal to the Byzantine Christians. But a basis was provided for the further development of the topic in Russian iconography. The famous Novgorod icon of St. Sophia is hardly older than the late XV-th century. It is a peculiar kind of Deisis, where Christ is represented as Wisdom under the image of the Angel, and the Blessed Virgin and St. John the Baptist standing at His sides. The icon belongs to a very interesting series of the new Russian compositions of the XV-th and XVI-th centuries and is a new interpretation of some traditional Byzantine motives.

II
ASPECTS OF RUSSIAN CHURCH HISTORY

Russian Missions:
An Historical Sketch

I

IN A CERTAIN SENSE the whole history of Russia is a process of colonization, the peopling of a country or the settling of inhabitants in different parts of it. In this movement the Church took a creative part and not only did she follow the people but often she led them. Strangely enough, she led them even at the time when she seemed to be deserting them by withdrawing from the outer material world into the world of the spirit, for it frequently happened that the ascetics and hermits were the pioneers on the rough and half-wild virgin soil in the north and north-east of Russia. For them the dense forests served as a desert, but they were followed by the world from which they wished to escape and so they had to depart from their settlements and get away still farther, cutting into the very depths of the primeval forests. Thus the ascetic retreat from the world attracted, as it were, the advance of the world; a process which historians call monastic colonization.

"Russian Missions: An Historical Sketch" appeared in *The Christian East*, Vol. XIV, No. 1 (1933), pp. 30-41. Reprinted by permission of the author.

This was an important factor and moment in the social history of the Russian people, and at the same time it was a missionary process, that is, a geographical propagation and extension of the Church. The baptism of Russia cannot be looked upon as a single fact; it was rather an extensive process spread over centuries, a process of Christian occupation of new lands and territories. For a long time the Russian Church was in a state of constant movement, wandering about, practically leading a nomadic life and always entering into the lands of the unbaptized either simultaneously with the State or often before it. Up to the last the Russian Church was like an island in the midst of a pagan sea, and even inside Russia itself she was always a missionary Church. Missionary work, that is the calling of unbelievers to the faith, was a part of her daily life.

It was from Byzantium that the Russian Church received the request of carrying on this missionary work and to this end it adapted Byzantine methods.

This meant putting in the forefront the use of the vernacular or local dialects in preaching. In other words, it was evangelization as a way of awakening the new peoples to a Christian life, and at the same time it was an adaptation to a tradition of culture, but without any negation or suppression of national differences and peculiarities. By this means the Slavonic people, enlightened and baptized by the Byzantine missionaries, were drawn into the vortex of Byzantine civilization and yet did not lose their Slavonic features. (The history of the Georgian Church should be mentioned in this connection.)

Translation as a method of missionary influence is a major premise of Byzantine missionary work, and that method was adopted by the Russian civilizers and missionaries from the very beginning. In this respect the personality of St. Stephen of Perm, the civilizer of Zirian and a friend of St. Sergius (d. 1396), is most brilliant and expressive. Of his own accord he undertook a missionary journey through the district of Perm. He not only preached but even officiated in the vernacular, with which purpose in view he had to translate the holy scriptures and Church books, and to do this it was first necessary to work out a Zirian alphabet which he probably based upon the local Runic signs.

St. Stephen's idea was to create a local "Perm" Church in which all the spiritual forces of the newly civilized people would have revealed themselves and received their consecration. His immediate successors in the see of Perm were inspired by the same ideal, which, however, was not attained, his Zirian Orthodox Church being finally absorbed by the Russian Orthodox Church. It is indeed possible that St. Stephen wanted to give the Zirians somewhat more than they really needed or were able to absorb and retain. Not all peoples possess their own culture, or indeed can possess it, and that "can" or "cannot" is a bare historical fact. Not every people or tribe has its own spiritual words, its own creative style for biological and spiritual expressions and phenomena of different grades. These facts present great difficulties for missionary work and a missionary must possess great tact and sensitiveness in order to learn and find the right way.

In any case, however, it was the missionary ideal of St. Stephen of Perm that continued to be a typical guide in the Russian Church till quite recently. The Gospel was preached and divine service performed in many tongues.

Particularly noteworthy is the creation of an Orthodox Church for the Tartars with their own native clergy in the Kazan region. But the most brilliant example of that missionary nationalism is the creation of a Japanese Church, which grew up and still remains as one of the dioceses of the Russian patriarchate.

Missionary work must start first of all with translation, as it is always necessary to begin in the vernacular. The Gospel must be translated and reduced to writing, or at any rate related in the tongue of the country; but as the work goes on questions arise. Is it necessary to translate the whole Bible and the whole cycle of Church books as well as to work out in each tongue the theological terminology which is necessary for the translation of dogmatic formulæ? The difficulty here lies in the fact that many of the tongues are still undeveloped and insufficiently flexible and rich in their vocabulary to be used in mystical and sacred quotations. The missionaries often have not only to invent an alphabet but, as it were, to invent and work out the tongue itself. Another difficulty arises in translating into languages of non-Christian civilizations, for there are many old associations and a lack is felt of words to express the new conceptions because the old words have too many old connotations. In any case a missionary must have a great philological gift and sensitiveness; a loving and lively sense of the tongue; a desire and power to penetrate into the foreign soul and understand it; that is to say, one has in a certain sense to have the faculty of sympathetic reincarnation.

The same is, no doubt, required from every pastor and teacher in general, but the claim on these qualities in missionary work is especially acute. Very often missionaries have to create and build up the civilization of the natives, for it is often impossible to draw the line between evangelical doctrines and everyday life. Too often it is necessary to change or even to break up the whole structure or mode of life which has become too closely amalgamated with the pagan past and too firmly a part of daily life. Sometimes it is necessary to isolate the neophytes from their own people, often for the sake of their own safety. Again, for them to benefit from the preaching of the Gospel, it is important to enlarge the mental outlook of a flock that is being sought for, so as to arouse and elevate its requirements, and this again is only possible by bringing them into touch with a higher civilization which has already taken root. It is generally only by the acceptance of this higher civilization that the hidden forces of a newly enlightened people can be awakened. In experiments in real life one cannot draw a line between religious and worldly things. According to the inner logic of missionary work itself a missionary ought to enter into the daily life of his people. It is not wrong that a missionary should be involved in worldly business and cares; this is only wrong if he loses the true perspective of the Gospel and yields himself up to the spirit of the world. It is inevitable for the mission to come face to face with the State, *i.e.* to co-operate with it, or at least to work alongside the State's compulsory and organizing institutions, but it is difficult to say which is more difficult, to co-operate or to struggle. Help and facilities from the State generally rather complicate the inner work of a missionary. The application of direct force is not so dangerous, but the strength and power of the State unwittingly overawe, and superiority of culture attracts, with the result that the genuine simplicity of a Christian conversion and its growth is hampered and the *tempo* of missionary work becomes too rapid. Sometimes the mission inevitably enters into controversy with the State; for it may happen that the interest of the State demands delay in the Christianizing movement among younger nations; or sometimes, on the contrary, baptism acquires for the empire the means of forcing them into a central civilized political union. In the case of local dialects, too, the methods of evangelization may appear injurious from the point of view of the State. To find a way through all these difficulties and conflicts in the process of creating the Christian life is only possible by creative inspiration and sagacity.

II

The concrete tasks of Russian missionary activity were defined by the growth of the Empire. At first it was the evangelization of an inhabited country, above all of a Slavonic population. Then the movement spread into the region of the Finnish tribes. Strictly speaking, the conversion of the smaller Finnish tribes has never been completed. The influence of pagan inertia remained strong up to the last and was responsible for the fact of masses falling back to paganism after the Russian Revolution. In this respect the North-East of European Russia may be taken as an example. The religion of these Finnish tribes may be defined as animism with a strongly developed belief in magic and sorcery; in this sorcery and still more in the sorcerers themselves lie the chief causes of pagan stability.

In the sixteenth century the Russian Church came face to face with Islam, and especially in the time of Ivan the Terrible, after his conquests and annexation of the Tartar kingdoms along the river Volga. The meeting with Islam was rather hostile. It is true that many Tartar races accepted baptism at once, but on the whole the mass of the Tartars remained faithful to the traditions of their fathers, and it was only for the sake of preserving their national characteristics that the principle of toleration was advanced against any intrusion of the Orthodox mission into the secluded world of the Tartars. The right course of making missionary influence felt was found here only when the ideal of Tartar Orthodoxy was brought forward openly and fearlessly. But one has to bear in mind that the presence of a Russian mission amongst the local Moslems was only one of the incidents of the great world struggle of Christianity with Islam, and that it was always affected by the broad religious and political perspective. The regions along the river Volga remained the experimental fields for missionary work up to the last. Here the old paganism was still preserved amongst the natives, and all this country overlooked Asia with its religious zeal and inertia.

Here the Orthodox mission for the first time came into touch with the Lamaism of the Kalmuck who migrated to the province of Saratov at the end of the seventeenth century. In the eighteenth century the circumstances of missionary

activities were not, in general, favorable: the State inter-
fered too powerfully with the affairs of the mission, pursuing its own interests, that is to say, getting the maximum
benefit for itself from the people. Often enough, indeed,
the State put obstacles in the way of the missionary work,
especially among Moslems, and generally speaking the
eighteenth century was a difficult period in the history of
the Russian Church, which was somewhat restrained by the
supervision of the State and weakened materially by the
secularization of her property. Only a few held fast at the
period of general indifference and spiritual backwardness.
The advance started again only at the beginning of the nineteenth century. This delay is very important to note. With
it are bound up the chief difficulties of the mission of the
nineteenth century. A new tradition began and was established.

As a matter of fact it was only at the beginning of this
nineteenth century that the mission commenced its development in the provinces along the river Volga. This was above
all due to the activities of the Bible Society and its branches.
In the first decade of the nineteenth century the New Testament was published in the following translations: Nogay,
Tartar, Tchuvash, Morduates, Tcheremiss, Kalmuck, Zirian,
Votiak and Korel. It must, however, be noted that these
translations are far from being always satisfactory and reliable.

At that same time native schools were opened and teaching was commenced in the local dialects. Special courses were
organized in ecclesiastical seminaries for the training of
teachers and the more serious study of the native environment and the work to be undertaken by the mission were
organized in the Kazan Ecclesiastical Academy (founded in
1842). Here a special section of missionary training was
opened in 1854. In the year 1867 the missionary brotherhood
of St. Gouri was also started, which occupied itself with
the external and internal arrangements of the mission and

especially with the publishing work and the starting of schools. In 1833 it was generally recognized in principle that the performance of divine services in the local tongues was admissible and desirable. A whole series of brotherhoods came into being in other dioceses and a network of native schools began to spread abroad. The missionary struggle with Islam was particularly difficult because of the well-developed network of Moslem schools and the great zeal of the Moslem clergy. In order to succeed it was generally necessary for the missionaries to break up the primitive form of life and to work out new and independent ways of social life for the neophytes.

One must point out yet another object of missionary activities within the boundaries of European Russia, the enlightenment of the Eskimo who led a nomadic life on marshy plains in the Government of Archangel. Since the twenties of the nineteenth century the whole New Testament and catechism had been translated into the Eskimo tongue, and a grammar and dictionary were compiled (Mission of Archimandrite Veniamin Smirnov).

The missionary activities in Siberia were still more intricate. There they had to preach to pagan Shamanists predominantly small Finnish tribes) and to the Moslems, and, above all, to the Lamaists, and one must strictly distinguish these different spheres of missionary work and the varied methods that they required.

The great extent of territory and the roughness of the climate fully explain the comparative slowness of regular Church and even governmental organization. Small and isolated oases sprang up in the midst of an empty, and, for a long time, inimical world.

At the beginning of the eighteenth century one should draw attention to the activities, full of inspiration (particularly amongst the Finnish tribes) of Phylophei Leshchinski, the missionary who was twice Bishop of Tobolsk, and between these appointments became a monk. In spite of this he carried on the missionary work, personally exposing his life to great risks. He made several journeys to preach the Gospel to the Ostiaks and Voguls, etc. To consolidate the results, he opened schools and organized churches, though for a long time the newly opened churches could only be served by visiting chaplains. The new parishes were at enormous distances from each other, and consequently the chief centers, monasteries and cathedral cities, were of great importance, these providing the constant stream of active workers. It is particularly necessary to note also the missionary expeditions (in the middle of the eighteenth century) to Kamschatka, whence Christianity spread across the islands to the Alaskan shores of North America.

In the eighteenth century, also, there sprang up an Orthodox mission in China, at Peking, principally on behalf of the Russian prisoners of war who had settled there, but also for the purpose of collecting information. But, generally speaking, missionary work in the eighteenth century was very insignificant. Its revival in Siberia begins only in the nineteenth century, and once more we must emphasize the rather unfriendly attitude adopted by the State towards the Orthodox mission. In the eighteenth century, preaching to the Kirgeeses was forbidden, and conversions to Islam were, if anything, patronized. At the beginning of the nineteenth century the Lamaian hierarchy was recognized by the State. The spiritual awakening which followed conversion and baptism troubled the local representatives of the government. The raising of the tone of life meant that the pulse was quickened and strengthened, and that appeared to be troublesome. In the eighteenth century the too zealous missionaries were moved farther on, to places where there was no one to convert. But at last, in the nineteenth century, several outstanding and permanent missionary centers arose in Siberia, amongst which the Altai mission deserves above all to be noted. It was started in 1830 at the initiative of Evgeni Kazantzev, at that time Archbishop of Tobolsk, and at the head of it was placed the Archimandrite Makarios Gloukarev. Archimandrite Makarios was a remarkable man, of great spiritual earnestness and very profound, but rather exalted by eschatological interests and those Utopian ideas which were characteristic, even in the West, at the beginning of the nineteenth century. Undoubtedly a mystic, and the translator of eastern and western mystics (*e.g.,* St. Teresa of of Spain), he knew how to find common expression with others and to sympathize even with the Quakers. He himself led a very rigid, ascetic and evangelical life, and Metropolitan Philaret, who knew him intimately and loved him, called him a "romantic missionary." And, indeed, Makarios introduced into his missionary work a literally romantic zeal and ardor. He looked upon his missionary calling with sincere humility and he tried to arrange it on the principles of a strict communalism. "Let it be our rule that we should possess everything in common, money, food, clothes, books and everything else, and let this be a means of facilitating our inspiration towards unanimity." It is an apostolic rather than a monastic ideal. Makarios had few assistants, but with them he succeeded in achieving unanimity. He did not hurry to baptize, and during the thirteen years of his work he converted only about 650 persons. In his work he laid great stress on the "call to faith." He endeavored to attain spiritual regeneration and to awaken sincere and sparkling faith in sleeping souls. He preached Christ crucified, and great stress was laid on re-education and the achievement of moral ideals. In accordance with his ideas a sisterhood of widows and young women was attached to the mission.

Makarios himself was much occupied with translations, and at one time he was preoccupied with the idea of translating the Bible (especially from the Hebrew), but his work was disapproved by the central authority, and to this resistance he attached great importance. He worked out a general missionary scheme which was called *"Some notes on the means for an intensive propagation of the Christian Faith amongst*

Jews, Moslems and heathen in the Russian Empire" (1839). For those destined to missionary work he considered it necessary to establish in Kazan an educational missionary center, a monastery-school for which a more elaborate scheme for ecclesiastical and ethnographic education was to have been worked out.

The full significance of Fr. Makarios' enterprise can only be appreciated when the harsh and rugged nature of the region of the Altai is borne in mind, and the poverty of the mission as well (up to 1857 its budget was only 571 roubles a year).

After Makarios the Altai mission continued to flourish, particularly under the management of Father Vladimir Petrov, who later on became a bishop in the Altai, and died Archbishop of Kazan. Still later another Makarios worked there, who in the time of the Great War was Metropolitan of Moscow. Less valuable work was done by the Obdorsk and Surgut missions in the same diocese of Tobolsk.

In course of time the missionary duties were distributed amongst the parish clergy, and they had to face the work unaided by special missionary institutions. This step was somewhat untimely and indiscreet. The missionary advance ought to have continued constant and persistent in view of the general low standard of life, and the absorbing influence of environment.

The second bright page in the history of the Siberian mission opens with the activities of Archbishop Nilus in Eastern Siberia (Irkutsk 1838 to 1853, depicted in Leskov's famous novel *On the Edge of the World*) and in particular of Innokenti Veniaminov, later Metropolitan of Moscow after the death of Philaret.

Archbishop Nilus took an interest in mission work while Bishop of Viatka, even before he was appointed to Siberia. In Irkutsk and the Trans-Baikal region it was necessary to preach to the Buriats who belonged to the Lamaian faith. Nilus worked a great deal on the translation of Church books into the Mongol-Buriat language and still carried on that work after his reappointment to Yaroslavl'. Innokenti Veniaminov commenced his work on the Aleutian Islands, which at that time belonged to Russia. Here he preached to the Koloshes and the Aleutes for about fifteen years. He studied local dialects, compiled a grammar and a dictionary and began to make translations; he also left us a description of the country and the ways of life there. According to his scheme made in 1840, the mission at that time in the Russian possessions in North America was legally organized and placed under the management of the Bishop of Kamschatka. Innokenti was appointed to the bishop's throne, and for twenty-eight years he worked in this new country, new and yet his by birthright. His diocese covered enormous distances, and most of his time was spent in travelling. His assistants translated the Church books into the Yakut and Tungus tongues.

Mission work against the Lamaian faith in the Trans-Baikal Country was most difficult; yet many improvements were made there by Parpheni Popov, the Archbishop of Irkutsk, and later on by the Archbishop Veniamin Blagonravov. The mission in China never could attain any noticeable growth, though a great work was done in translation, and the mission at Peking was the general center of sinological studies for a long time. The mission workers were in consequence more prominent for their scientific than for their apostolic achievements. China is in general a very difficult country and unfavorable for missionary work.

In a very different way the life of the Russian mission in Japan was progressing. Of course, it was very much owing to the personal qualities and exploits of the first of the Russian missionaries Nikolai Kazatkin, who, later on, became Archbishop of Japan, or rather its apostle in the true sense of the word. He began his work in 1861, soon after Japan opened her doors to Europeans and prior to the declaration of toleration. Yet the mission began to grow very quickly.

Again the method of translation was adopted and many years were spent in the translation of the Christian service books, and a net of Orthodox parishes spread gradually all over Japan.

In the history of the Japanese Orthodox Church one is struck by the astonishing simplicity and strength of the immediate corporate Church feeling. Parish life goes on very actively and intensively. Diocesan meetings with the parishioners participating are organized every year. The work of the catechists goes on slowly and steadily and the cultural level of Japanese Orthodoxy is sufficiently high for it to spread also among educated people. For many years an ecclesiastical seminary existed in Tokyo, and the Japanese Church has long ago become an independent diocese with complete internal status and management and is canonically a member of the Moscow patriarchate.

III

Missionary work does not lend itself well to schemes of management and organization issued from the center. It is, above all, the work of pastoral creative power and inspiration. Therefore it depends much more upon the personality of the individuals who are the active workers than upon plans and programmes, and that is why the history of a mission is bound up closely with names. Therefore, too, missionary work often progresses spasmodically and stops altogether at intervals. And yet it is very important that the personal initiative should find an encouraging response, sympathy and facilities in the whole Church body. Therefore when in 1865 the Orthodox Missionary Society was inaugurated this was considered an event of great importance. Its work, however, became really effective only after its reorganization in 1869, when Innokenti, at that time Metropolitan of Moscow, be-

came its president and its activities became more interwoven
with the metropolitan see.

The missionary society had its branches in the centers
of work and took the financial cares of the mission and its
parishes upon itself. Yet there was another important task
which required organized help, the scientific and scholastic
training of the missionaries who were in need of good knowledge and understanding of the environment in which they
would have to work. It was necessary to know the language
of the people, their history and their ways of living, all leading on to an understanding of the soul. It was necessary to
see how to approach that soul with the word of Christ's
truth, and for this, knowledge of a language and folklore
is not alone sufficient. The specific blending of an apostolic
divine light and the *pathos* of a stranger's philosophy is
essential and these qualities are more easily to be found in
natives.

The necessity for a high ecclesiastical missionary school
was not realized at once. Only in 1854 was a special missionary section opened in the Kazan Ecclesiastical Academy,
and it was left there even after reforms had been introduced
in ecclesiastical schools in general in 1870. A specific teaching
of missionary subjects had already begun in 1845 with the
participation of the professors of the Kazan University, but
as a matter of fact the studies were concentrated exclusively
on languages.

Names such as Sabloukov, Ilminsky, Bobrovnikov, are
important and unforgettable in the history of the Kazan
Academy. Sabloukov was a man self-taught in Arabic
and Tartar philology. By hard work, fired by scientific
enthusiasm and a natural love of work, he attained to profound erudition not only in the languages themselves but in
history and archaeology as well. His translation of the Koran
is especially well known. Not all the books written by him
were published; many of them perished in a fire at his home.
His teaching in the Academy and his participation in all

missionary undertakings amongst the Tartars meant very much.

Still more important was the work of Ilminsky, who arranged his work of preaching to the Tartars in systematic order. Ilminsky was adverse to the method of polemics. He tried to work out a scheme of preaching for the purpose of conversion. He not only had scholastic and theoretic training, but understood intimately the life and ways of the local Tartars. He visited their villages and lived amongst them for some time in order to penetrate intimately into their manner of life. He also in 1851-3 travelled in the east with many stops along the way, making long stops at Cairo, Lebanon and Constantinople. As the outcome of this practical acquaintance with the mass of the people he came to a very important conclusion with regard to translations. He insisted on the necessity of these being made in the living conversational Tartar language and not in the literary language, and this was of the utmost importance. In the first place the literary language of the Tartars was laden with Arabic and Persian words and had a general flavor of Islam, and by the use of colloquial speech it was possible to escape that hidden Moslem taint. Secondly, the translation into a colloquial tongue requires great creative powers and intensity on the part of the translator and this was exactly what Ilminsky wanted. He was aiming at the formation of a specific Christian Tartar language in opposition to an Islamic one and saw in this an important step in the matter of preaching. The language itself was not to him something already developed and stationary, it was a living spiritual element which it was possible to transmute and transfigure. With this was connected a scheme for working out a whole network of Christian Tartar schools with the teaching carried on in the tongue of the people. Thirdly, there was in view the democratization of the mission, which spread far and wide among the masses, avoiding the book-learned and the aristocrats. Ilminsky's scheme was a complete system for the Christian transformation of the Tartars, yet without the least trace of any Russification. A note should also be made about the Arabic letters which he changed into Russian, as being more convenient, since he saw in the Arabic alphabet the presence of Moslem culture while that of Russia bore the symbols of Christianity. He did not believe in the fruitfulness of any preaching unless done in the people's own tongue. "Christianity as a living principle should work as a leaven in the thoughts and feelings and after having taken shape in men of advanced minds it should come from and through them to others. We believe that the evangelical word of our Saviour Jesus Christ, having become incarnate, so to speak, in the living tongue of the Tartars and through it having associated itself most sincerely with their deepest thoughts and religious consciousness, would produce the Christian revival of this tribe." Nevertheless, Ilminsky's scheme did not spring into being at once nor without some opposition both in the Kazan district and in Turkestan.

A net-work of schools, with a seminary as a center at Kazan, was organized and Ilminsky was appointed director of the seminary. Yet the most important work was still translating. This required great creative power and for it Ilminsky found help amongst the baptized Tartars. Furthermore, the introduction of divine service in the Tartar language proved one of the most effective missionary methods. Of Ilminsky's assistants and followers should be mentioned such persons as the Archpriest Malov, Ostrooumov, and the Tartar Timofeiev. The principles laid down by Ilminsky were also applied to other spheres of missionary enterprise among the natives. In connection with the study of anti-Lamaian controversies, there were no such outstanding organizers in the Kazan Academy as this man.

A. A. Bobrovnikov was a great authority on the Mongol-Buriat dialect and he compiled the first successful Mongol-Kalmuck grammar of that period. A native of the Irkutsk district and the son of a missionary, he felt, when mingling with the Buriats, an intimate nearness to this Mongol people. His book studies were supplemented by his scientific expeditions. Yet he was not a man of initiative and could not find the true methods of translating though he did expose some faults of the previous literary translations. In spite of all its incompleteness the work done by the Kazan Academy was of great importance for the help given to the missionaries to penetrate into the souls of non-Europeans, and it has not even yet been fully appreciated or used to the uttermost.

IV

Russian missionary work amongst the foreign tribes was put an end to forcibly. The Gospel of Christ on Russian soil became an impossibility and as a consequence a return to former beliefs took place especially among the Shamaist tribes in the districts of the river Volga and in Siberia, though at one time for some reason a partial freedom was enjoyed by Islam.

It is not given to us to foresee the future or to make guesses with regard to the fate of the Christian Faith among the native tribes of Russia; but we can, and it is necessary that we should, look back, so as to understand and consider well the lessons of the past which bear on the words: "Whosoever shall do and teach them the same shall be called great in the Kingdom of Heaven." (*Matt.* v. 19.)

Western Influences
in Russian Theology

THE QUESTION concerning Western influences on Orthodox Theology is a complex one. This question is still
often raised today, sometimes sharply and with excitement.
According to Metropolitan Antonii Khrapovitskii (d. 1936),
the whole development of Russian Theology since the 17th
century, as taught in the schools, was but a dangerous borrowing from heterodox Western sources. And, for that
reason, according to him, it must be completely disavowed
and eliminated.

> The system of Orthodox theology is still something
> to seek for, and, for that reason, one must identify
> and examine its genuine sources instead of copying
> systems of heretical doctrines, as it has been our
> custom for 200 years.[1]

This paper was first presented to the First Congress of Orthodox Theology
at Athens in 1936.

This article originally appeared as "Westliche Einflüsse in der Russischen
Theologie" in *Kyrios,* II, No. 1 (Berlin, 1937), 1-22 as well as in *Procès-
Verbaux du Premier Congrès de Theologie Orthodoxe* (Athens, 1939).
Reprinted by permission of the author. Translated from the German by
Thomas Bird and Richard Haugh.

Many got the impression that Russian theology had been entirely *disfigured* by Western influences. Thus the conviction arose that a basic and decisive redirection of the whole theological task was necessary, a radical return to the ignored and forgotten sources of genuine and patristic Orthodoxy. This return implies denial and abrogation. There is a bit of truth in such assertions. "The Struggle against the West" in Russian Theology can be justified. There are certainly enough occasions and reasons to justify this attitude. And it is precisely the history of these Western influences and borrowings in Orthodox Theology which has still not been sufficiently explored. One must, by all means, always start with an exact description of the facts.

In this short essay one must be content with a selection of a limited number of facts, the most important, decisive or distinctive ones. For a fuller presentation of the problem I would refer the reader to my book, *Puti russkogo bogosloviia* [*The Ways of Russian Theology*] (Paris: YMCA-Press, vii, 574 pp. [in Russian]).

I

The traditional view of the complete isolation and enclosure of Ancient Russia was discarded long ago. Ancient *"Rus'"* was never fully cut off from the West. And this connection with the West asserted itself not only in the political or economic sphere but also in the sphere of spiritual development, even in the realm of religious culture.[1] Byzantine influence indeed prevailed, but it was by no means the only influence. One must acknowledge a weakening of Byzantine influence already in the 16th century, a *crisis of Russian Byzantinism*. The Western relations of Novgorod were the most conspicuous and continuous. And precisely in the 14th and 15th centuries this city became the religious and cultural center, the center for the entire Russian North and East. Moscow, rapidly rising at that time, was still for the most part culturally dependent upon sources from Novgorod. Books were supplied precisely from this Northern democracy.[3]

At that time, under the stimulus of Archbishop Gennadii, a most responsible work was initiated—the compiling of the first complete Slavic Biblical Codex. The Bible had not been originally translated into Slavic as a uniform and complete book but rather as a collection of liturgical readings based on the order and cycle of the liturgical year—and this translation did not include the whole of the Biblical text; the non-canonical books of the Old Testament were not translated since they are scarcely represented in Eastern lectionaries. The general supervision and execution of the work at Novgorod was officially in the hands of the bishop's archdeacon, Gerasim Popovka. The actual spiritual leader, however, was a Dominican monk named Benjamin, who, according to the words of the chronicler, was "a priest and a monk from the order of St. Dominic, by birth a Slav, by faith a Latin." We do not know much more about him. But one can hardly assume that this Dominican monk from Croatia came to Novgorod just by accident. Apparently he had brought with him some completed Biblical texts. Indeed the influence of the Vulgate is strongly felt in the Biblical Codex of Gennadii, for the Vulgate and *not* Greek manuscripts served as the model for the text. The non-canonical books were included in the Codex according to Latin usage. The Books of Paralipomenon, the third book of Ezra, the Book of Wisdom, and the first two books of Maccabees were translated in entirety from the Latin. One student of "the manuscript tradition of the Slavic Bible" [Prof. I. E. Evseev] characterizes the significance of the Codex of Gennadii as "the turning of the Slavic Bible from the Greek "waterway" to the Latin." And one should not forget that it was precisely "the Gennadii Bible" upon which the first Slavic edition of the Ostrog Bible (1580) was based. At this opportunity the text was, to be sure, once again revised and compared (after printed editions) with the Greek—the entire historical significance of the Ostrog Bible is indeed determined by the fact that it is based on the Greek text—however, the slipping away into the Latin channel was nevertheless not fully overcome. With certain improvements the Ostrog text was reproduced in the "Elizabethan Bible" of 1751—and this is the presently used text.[4] In the "house of the archbishop" Gennadii much was translated from the Latin. During the work on the new liturgical order, the famous book by V. Durantius, *Rationale divinorum officiorum,* was (at least partially) translated, presumably for reference. Judging from the language, it seems the translator was a foreigner, i.e. not a Russian—once again it was probably the monk Benjamin. Also translated from Latin at this time was the "Short Word against Those Who Claim Possession of Holy Things, Moveable or Immoveable, from the Cathedral Churches"—a defense of Church property and of the complete independence of the clerical class, which thereby also possesses the right "to act with the aid of the secular arm." Also well-known is the significant reference of Gennadii to the "Spanish King," about whom the imperial envoys related that he "purified" his land of heretics by state executions.[5]

There is good reason to speak of a "very dominant Catholic atmosphere" surrounding Gennadii [I. E. Evseev]. Russian iconography of the 15th and 16th centuries was also penetrated by Western motives and themes, again coming from Novgorod and Pskov to Moscow where they were contested in certain circles as innovations or perversions: herein lies the historical significance of the well-known "Doubt" of D'jak I. M. Viskovatii concerning the new icons. The Church authorities, however, were in favor of these innovations,

regarding them as something ancient. In any case, Western
influence now asserted itself quite noticeably even in the
sacred art of iconography.[6] "Western" means, in this case,
Latin or Roman. And "the marriage of the Tsar in the
Vatican" was the symbol of the movement toward the West.
Indeed, this marriage signified Moscow's drawing nearer to
the Italy of that time rather than reviving Byzantine traditions. It is characteristic that the Kremlin Cathedrals were
built or rebuilt at that time by Italian craftsmen. And indeed
these new Moscow buildings were, as Herberstein describes
them, expressly *more italico.*[7] Even more characteristic was
the fact that Maxim the Greek, summoned to Moscow from
the monastery of Vatopaedi on Mt. Athos to aid in the
work of translation, could find no one in all of Moscow who
could speak Greek with him. "He speaks Latin and we
translate it into Russian for the scribes"—the translator was
Dmitrii Gerasimov, a former student and assistant of Benjamin.[8] It would indeed be totally false to interpret all these
facts as proof of a Roman sympathy at Novgorod or Moscow.
It was rather a half unconscious assimilation of foreign
spiritual values with the naive conviction that one could still
remain loyal to the native and traditional truth. Thus, simultaneously, a "Western" psychology strangely united itself
with an intolerance toward the West.

II

On the other side of the Moscow border the encounter
with the West was more direct and more intimate. In
Lithuania and in Poland this was at first an encounter with
the *Reformation* and with "Socinianism," and later on with
the *Roman Church,* the Jesuit order and the "Unia." Since
the circumstances surrounding the struggle for the Orthodox
Church were exceedingly complicated and difficult, it was

simply psychologically unavoidable to make certain accommodations with heterodox allies, associates, rivals, and even enemies. At first a Hellenistic orientation was strongly emphasized—as the ideal and goal of Slavo-Greek culture—in the Ostrog Circle and in Lemberg [Lvov] at the home of Prince Ostrozhskii himself. There were many reasons why this goal was abandoned, indeed why it had to be abandoned. Even in the Ostrog Circle the mood was unsteady and the opinions divergent.

The practical wisdom of life pushed one toward the West. In the face of the threat of "Unia," the Orthodox were the obvious, occasionally even the unwilling, "confederates" of the Protestants and "Heterodox." And many were prepared to go even beyond simple religious and practical assistance; in this respect, for example, the attitude of the Orthodox and Calvinists at the Conference and in the "Confederation" at Vilna (before 1599) is quite characteristic. Even Prince K. Ostrozhskii thought it proper to commission the Socinian Motovila to translate the Orthodox refutation of Peter Skarga's book, *On the Greek Apostasy,* a project against which Prince A. M. Kurbskii, the implacable fugitive from Moscow, protested with the greatest indignation. And the Orthodox reply to Skarga's book about the Council of Brest was actually written by a Calvinist—the well-known *"Apokrisis"* was published in 1587 under the name of Christopher Philaletes. There is good reason to presume that the pseudonym actually belonged to the well-known diplomat of that time, Martin Bronevskii, the secretary to King Stephen Batorii, who was deeply involved in the confederation of the Orthodox and the Evangelicals. In the *"Apokrisis"* itself one notices occasionally an obvious similarity with Calvin's *Institutio Christianae religionis.*[8]

There was, however, in all this no conscious betrayal of Orthodox tradition and no real inclination toward Protestantism. More important and more dangerous, however, was

the ever-increasing custom among Russian writers of discussing religious and theological questions within a Western
frame of reference. At this time, however, refuting Latinism
did not mean strengthening Orthodoxy. Especially since even
the arguments of the Reformers were employed in the
polemical discussions of that time, arguments which certainly could not always harmonize with the basic tenets of
Orthodoxy. Historically this admixture of Protestantism was
perhaps unavoidable, but under its influence the "way" of
a Slavic and Hellenic culture became dim and obscure. In
addition to this was the fact that one could no longer rely
upon the Greeks for help. In fact, at that time Greek teachers
usually came from the West where they had studied. Whether
they had studied at Venice, Padua, Rome, or even at Geneva
or Wittenberg—from none of these centers did the Greeks
bring with them the Byzantine heritage or the patristic
legacy. Rather they brought precisely Western innovations.
In the 16th century their sympathies were generally with the
Protestants; later there emerged a slightly covert Latinism.
Thus there was some truth in the malicious, ironic words of
the Uniate Metropolitan Hypatius Pociei, when he wrote to
Patriarch Meletius Pigas that Calvin has replaced Athanasius
in Alexandria, Luther rules in Constantinople, and Zwingli
in Jerusalem.[10] It is sufficient to recall the "Confession" of
Cyril Lukaris, the authenticity of which can no longer be
doubted. This unexpected presentation of Calvinism by the
Orthodox Patriarch can be partially explained as a result of
his studies at Geneva. It can also be partially explained by
the fact that he was in West Russia precisely at the time
of the common struggle against the *"Unia."* Presumably it
was there that he got the idea of a "Confederation" with
the representatives of the Swiss Confession.

The influence of the Reformation in Western Russia
was only temporary. Soon the opposite tendency prevailed—an
enthusiasm for the *Roman pattern.* The significance of this

change is illustrated by the figure of the famous Metropolitan of Kiev, Peter Mogila, whose historical influence was decisive. An entire epoch in the history of the Church and culture of West Russia is, quite rightly, denoted by his name. He and his disciples were openly and decidedly pro-Western. At its root, however, this "Westernism" was really a disguised Romanism. Although Mogila had certainly fought for the legal independence of the Kievan Church and had supported the resistance of the Orthodox Church against the *"Unia,"* there was however on many points no doctrinal difference between him and Rome. For that reason he used Latin sources quite easily and unhesitatingly, assuming that he would rediscover in them true, undistorted Orthodoxy. There was a certain inexplicable discrepancy in the image of Peter Mogila. He led the West Russian Church out of its helplessness and decay from which it had suffered so much since the Council of Brest. Thanks to Mogila, it received a legal status in the Republic of Poland. But the whole structure was at the same time reconstructed in a new and alien spirit—a Latin spirit. The struggle surrounding all Mogila's plans and projects was caused by two opposing views—the Western and the Helleno-Slavic. Peter Mogila also rendered an indubitable but ambiguous service with the establishment of the Kiev Collegium. For it was a Latin school. Not only was it a "Latinization" of language, custom, and theology but it was also a "Latinization" of the entire religious psychology: thus the very soul of the people was once again Latinized. And, oddly enough, all this occurred in the name of the most extremely national and political struggle against Rome and Poland. Because of this, internal independence was indeed lost, relations with the East were sundered; an alien, artificial and borrowed direction was adopted which often enough in the future unfortunately obstructed the pathos of creativity.

Mogila was not alone in his crypto-Romanism. He rather expressed the spirit of his time. The basic and most signifi-

cantly expressive monument of his epoch is the so-called
"Orthodox Confession." It is difficult to assert with any
certainty who the author or editor of this "Catechism" was;
generally it is thought to be Mogila himself, although it was
in fact a collective work of several assistants. It was obviously
composed originally in Latin and in this original draft one
notices a much stronger influence of Latin models than in
the definitive version which underwent a critical revision at
the conferences in Kiev (1640) and in Jassy (1642). The
instances here of borrowing and imitation are actually less
important than the fact that the *Confessio Orthodoxa* in its
entirety was merely an accommodation to, indeed an "adaptation" of Latin materials. In any case, it is more closely connected with the Roman Catholic writings of that time than
with the spiritual life of Orthodoxy or the traditions of the
Eastern Fathers. Particular Roman doctrines—for example,
the doctrine of the primacy of the Pope—are rejected here,
but the general style remains nevertheless Roman. The same
is true of Peter Mogila's *liturgical reform.* His famous *Book
of Ritual* or *Euchologion* (1646) is heavily influenced by the
Ritual of Pope Paul V, from which the introductory explana-
tions of particular rites and ceremonies were taken almost
verbatim.[11] Mogila's *Kiev Collegium* soon became the central
base of this imitative Latinism not only for the Southern
and Western parts of Russia but also for the Muscovite
North. Kievan religious literature of the 17th century was
completely dependent on Latin sources and patterns. It is
sufficient to mention the name of *Stefan Iavorskii,* who later,
under the reign of Peter the Great, went north. His "Rock
of the Faith" [*"Kamen' Very"*] was actually only a "summary," a shortened "compilation" of various Latin works,
mainly of Bellarmine's *Disputationes de controversis christianae fidei.* His book about the coming of the Anti-
Christ is patterned after the book by the Spanish Jesuit
Malvenda.[12] The essence of this Roman pseudo-morphosis lies

in the fact that Scholasticism screened and obstructed Patristics for the Russians. It was a psychological and cultural Latinization rather than a matter of creed.

Nevertheless the scales of doctrine were also shaken. Under Peter the Great theological schools or seminaries were also established throughout Great Russia precisely according to the southern, Kievan model. These schools were thoroughly Latin and their teachers were for a long time recruited from the "institutes" of the Southwest. Even the Slavic-Greek-Latin Academy in Moscow had used Kiev as its model and pattern. This Petrine reform, however, also meant a "Ukrainianization" in the history of ecclesiastical schools. There was, as it were, a migration of South Russians to the north where they were regarded as foreigners for two reasons: their schools were "Latin" and they were themselves "foreigners." In his distinguished book on the theological schools of the 18th century Znamenskii passes the following sharp judgment (see Anm. 1, p. 216): "For the student, all these educators were in the fullest sense of the word— aliens from a foreign land—"Little Russia" was regarded at that time as a foreign land. It had its own peculiar customs and conceptions, and a strange "scholarship." Its language was difficult to understand and sounded odd to the Great Russians. In addition, these teachers never tried at all to adapt themselves to their students or to the country to which they had been called. Rather, they openly despised the Great Russians, considered them savage, and derided them. They found fault with everything which was not similar to their own "Little Russian" ways. They pushed their way of life in the foreground, forcing it on everyone as the proper style of life. This was a time when one could consecrate only "Little Russians" (Ukrainians) as bishops and archimandrites since the government was suspicious of Great Russians, presuming that they were sympathetic with pre-Petrine customs.

The people accepted the establishment of Latin schools

only reluctantly and with great distrust. And only unwillingly did the clergy entrust their children to these schools. And even the students themselves frequently ran away. All this took place not because the clerical estate was addicted to superstition or engrossed in ignorance, but because they considered these schools as something unfamiliar and foreign —as an unwanted Latin-Polish colony in the homeland, as an "institution" which, even from a purely practical point of view, could only appear useless. The "practical mind" regarded "Latin grammar" as of little use as well as the "fine manners" which were cultivated in the seminaries. For the "practical mind" there was absolutely no reason to replace the traditional manner of preparation for the priesthood—at one's own home—with new, unaccustomed and dubious ways. "It still remained to be seen who in general was better prepared for the priesthood: the psalm-reader who, from youth on, had served in the Church, learning in a practical way the readings, the hymns, and the order of services; or, the student of Latin who had merely memorized some Latin vocabulary and inflexions" (Znamenskii). In these Latin schools one began to become almost unaccustomed to Church Slavonic—even the texts of Scripture were usually quoted in Latin. Grammar, rhetoric and poetics were taught in Latin, while Russian rhetoric was taught only on the higher levels. It is understandable that parents sent their children to "these cursed schools of torture" only with mistrust. And the children preferred even the penitentiary to such schools. Indeed the depressive feeling soon developed that one could lose, if not his faith then at least his nationality, in these newly established schools. In general the establishment of the schools was obviously a positive achievement. But the extension of these Latin schools into the territory of Great Russia meant a break in the Church's mentality—a split between theological "learning" and the experience of the Church: one still prayed in Slavonic but thought in Latin.

The same Scriptural words resounded from the floor of the school in international Latin, but resounded from the floor of the Church in the maternal Slavic language. This painful split in the very spiritual mentality itself is perhaps the most tragic result of the Petrine epoch. There developed a certain "duality of faith," in any case a spiritual division, a disunity of the soul.[13] *A Western culture, indeed a Western theology was established.* It was a "school of theology" which of course had no roots in life. Established and grown on an alien foundation, it now became, as it were, a "super-structure" built over an empty spot. Instead of growing on natural foundations, it rested solely on props. *A theology on props—that is the result of the theological Westernization in 18th century Russia.*

III

Theological instruction in the schools still remained Latin in character even when the "Romish" orientation was replaced by that of the Reformation or, more correctly, by the influence of early Protestant scholasticism. And it retained its Latin character even when the influence of Aquinas in philosophy was replaced by the authority of Christian Wolff. The language of instruction remained Latin and both the "structure" of the school and its education remained Western. The Protestant trend is associated first of all with the name and influence of Theophan Prokopovich, the well-known close collaborator of Peter the Great, the latter's advisor and executor in all reforms of ecclesiastical life, and the compiler of the "Spiritual Reglament" [*"Dukhovnyi Reglament"*]. Theophan's theological lectures, given in the Kiev Academy, were published much later in Latin (in Leipzig 1782-1784), but they had circulated earlier in manuscript form and had influenced the new turn in theology. In his dogmatic lectures or "tracts" Theophan followed Western models rather closely

—he seems to depend especially upon Amandus Polanus from Polansdorf and upon the latter's *Syntagma Theologiae Christianae* (1609). He systematically used Johann Gerhard's *Loci communes*. He was, however, not just a compiler even when he followed foreign masters. Well read and knowledgeable of contemporary literature, he was thoroughly in control of his material, handling and adjusting it in his own manner. One point is in any case beyond doubt: he was not just "connected" with Protestant scholasticism of the 17th century; he simply belonged to their tradition. He was not only under the influence of Protestantism, but he was simply a Protestant himself (A. V. Kartashov). His works actually belong to the history of German theology of the Reformation. And if there was not on his books the name of a Russian bishop, it would be most natural to seek the author among the professors of some Evangelical theological faculty. Everything he wrote was permeated by the atmosphere of the Reformation, by the Western spirit. This atmosphere can be traced everywhere—in the entire manner of his thought and expressions. It is not just a man writing under Western influence, but one who is a Western man himself—a foreigner. Theophan looked at Orthodoxy as though he himself were a Westerner. He did not know or experience Orthodoxy from *within*. He was pre-occupied with Western problems and controversies, completely taking the side of the Reformation. The entire pathos of his tracts was directed against Rome and he was never able to extricate himself from the "enchanting sphere" of the polemics of Western confessional theology.[14]

In his well-known book *Stefan Iavorskii and Theophan Prokopovich*, Iurii Samarin wanted to present the clash of Romish and Reformation trends as a moment of an alleged inner *"dialectic of Russian theological thought."* One can hardly speak about any such organic process here. It was simply a confrontation of foreign influences and because of the opposition of these influences Russian theological thought was only narrowed. One cannot speak of any inner spontaneous dialectic. There was rather a forcible *pseudomorphosis* of Orthodox thought. The Orthodox were forced to think in essentially alien categories and to express themselves in foreign concepts. At most theological seminaries and academies the instruction in the second half of the 18th century was based on Western Protestant manuals. Since Latin was used as the common scholarly and instructional language, even the trouble of translation was not necessary. Metropolitan Philaret recalled that he had studied theology at school from the textbook by Hollatz (d. 1713). Certain sections of the textbook were simply dictated in class. Other parts of the course were taken from the manuals by Quenstedt or from I. A. Turretini (d. 1737). But even manuals written by Russians themselves did not deviate much from Western models—this is true of the *Doctrine* written by Theophylakt Gorskii (Leipzig 1784), the *Compendium* by Iakinth Karpinskii (Leipzig 1786), the *Compendium* by Silvester Lebedinskii (1799 and 1805), as well as Irenei Falkovskii's manual (1802!), a manual faithfully based on Theophan Prokopovich. One would seek in vain for any independent thought in all these compendia and tracts. These were books for memorization, presenting a "theology of the school," a ballast of formal school tradition. By habit, certain Protestant doctrines were accepted—their doctrine of Scripture and Tradition, their definition of the Church, and their concept of Justification.

In the second half of the 18th century the powerful stream of *Pietism* was added to the previous influence of Protestant Scholasticism. One only needs to mention the name of Simeon Todorskii (1701-1754), who died as Bishop of Pskov. Previously, however, he had been for a while a teacher at the famous *Waisenhaus* in Halle where he translated Johann Arndt's *Wahres Christentum* into Russian, basing his translation on the 1735 Halle-edition. Most significant in this connection is Platon Levshin (1737-1811), the famous Metropolitan of Moscow under Catherine II, later described so appropriately by the historian of the Academy, S. K. Smirnov, as "to some extent the Peter Mogila of the Moscow Academy." Platon was more of a preacher and catechist than a systematic theologian. But his "catechisms," sermons or "initial instructions in Christian doctrine," delivered in Moscow while he was still in his early years (1757-1758), marked a change in the history of theology itself. His instructional lectures given to the Grand Duke (the future Emperor) Paul were published in 1765 under the title *Orthodox Doctrine or Christian Theology in Summary.* This was the first attempt at a theological system in the Russian language. Nevertheless, this "theological book" was also inevitably translated into Latin for the theological schools. And it was Platon himself who insisted on this, for he also believed that theological instruction in a language other than Latin would be a lowering of scholarly standards. His view was especially remarkable since it came from one who was such a zealous fighter for the "catechization of the people," a popularizer of Christian faith and Christian morals. Even in his old age, before the Patriotic War of 1812, Platon was greatly excited when the plan of using Russian as the instructional language at theological schools was brought up. He vigorously and constantly advised against this. In Platon's Russian writings one clearly sees the complete inadequacy of confused theological definitions and descriptions which he took from his Latin sources. He had much more interest in morals than in the doctrines of faith. Throughout the entire 18th century the doctrines of the Church, of Tradition, of the Sacraments—these remained quite undeveloped.[15]

The Reform of Russian theological schools at the beginning of the reign of Alexander I was not a return to Byzantine or Eastern foundations. The entire reform was concerned more with the spirit of Pietism, of "inner Christianity" rather than with the corporate life of the Church. As previously, instruction remained closely bound up with the patterns of Western schools in which pietistic moralism and a certain inclination toward mysticism was conspicuous at that time. Innerly the schools remained Western. Yet an opposite tendency was taking place which later overcame the split between "school" and "life": *instruction could be given in Russian.* The goal of the new theological "school reform" was to awaken both society and the people, to urge them on to higher spiritual interests, and to stimulate a religious and moral independence. This intention was, of course, organically connected with the entire *Zeitgeist* of that epoch; it was rooted in the mystical inclinations of the epoch, the epoch of the Holy Alliance and the Bible Societies. The "Latin Captivity" could easily be replaced by a German or English "captivity," only in the place of scholasticism there arose the danger of vague mysticism and German Theosophy. From that time on the shadow of German scholarship falls over the whole of Russian theology for quite some time—much to its detriment. Since that time it became a standard practice in Russian theological academies to learn German as the basic language of theology in general.

Despite this, it was a step forward, the beginning of a creative rise. Although much was unsound in this new pseudo-morphosis, it was nevertheless a *sickness unto life and unto growth* and not a sickness unto death or degeneration. Between the two extremes of mystical and philosophical enthusiasm on the one hand, and mistrustful fears on the other, the narrow and precipitous way of Church Theology was gradually discovered. Outstanding in this epoch is the majestic figure of Philaret, Metropolitan of Moscow (1782-1867), perhaps the most significant Russian theologian of earlier times. He too had studied in a Latin school and had grown up under the gentle guidance of Metropolitan Platon in the seminary at Troitsko-Sergievskii Monastery where that mixture of pietism and scholasticism dominated at that time. In his young years he passed through the mystical movement and was also a convinced supporter of the Bible Society. One can also find certain traces of these "Protestant" and "mystical" influences in his later theological works. In general, however, his *Weltanschauung* remained ecclesial. With Philaret begins the real liberation of Russian theology not only from Western influences but from Westernization in general. It occurred in the only way which could have achieved lasting results—that is, by a creative return to Patristic foundations and sources, by a return to the Fathers of the Church—this was the true source of inspiration for Philaret and served as the criterion of his own presentation. Externally Philaret did not immediately break away from the earlier "old-Protestant" traditions of the Russian schools, from the tradition of Prokopovich. There is much in Philaret's own expressions which reflect the influence of Protestant doctrines or which simply reveal a borrowing from Protestant sources. In his *Survey of Theological Scholarship,* prepared in 1814 for the St. Petersburg Academy, he himself refers the reader to Protestant works. That characteristic imprecision or defectiveness of conceptual definitions in his early writings, often pointed out by Philaret's enemies, originated from these Protestant sources—especially striking was his omission of Holy Tradition as an authoritative doctrinal guide, which was not mentioned at all in the first edition of his *Catechism.* However, this omission does not in fact indicate so much an error or inaccuracy of thought, but rather it was a matter of the common habit of that time.

Psychologically the reversion to Scholasticism and to Romanizing moods is thoroughly understandable and explainable in connection with the reforms of the Chief Prokurator of the Holy Synod under Nicholas I, Count Pratasov.

Yet this return to the Romanizing formulations of the 17th and 18th centuries, to the *Orthodox Confession* of Peter Mogila, to the works of St. Dmitrii of Rostov, or to Stefan Iavorskii's *Rock of Faith* proved fruitless because it offered no creative exit from the historical difficulties of Russian theology. The inclination to Protestantism could only be overcome by a return to the historical sources of Eastern Orthodoxy, by a creative restoration of that once existing organic continuity and cultural tradition and not by hasty and scholastic assessments of ready-made "solutions" of Western thought. In this sense Philaret accomplished incomparably more of the actual *"Churchification"* [*"Verkirch-lichung"*] of Russian "school theology" than did Pratasov and his advisors. The *Dogmatics* by Makarii Bulgakov, an eminent historian of the Russian Church and later the Metropolitan of Moscow, remained—despite all its merits—a dead book, a memorial to lifeless scholarship, uninspired by the true spirit of the Church: once again precisely a Western book. The return to a truly genuine and living Christianity was possible only by the *historical path,* not by the path of scholasticism. It is possible only by the living, albeit sometimes contradictory, experience of the history of the Church which contains embryonically the sought-for synthesis, and not by a hasty "systematization" based on alien sources. This "historical method" was the path of Russian theology at the end of the previous century. This method (see, for example, the *Dogmatic Theology* of Bishop Silvester) was the most important achievement of the Russian theological heritage.[16]

IV

In the history of Western Theology of the previous centuries the influence of *German idealistic philosophy* was one of the most significant phenomena, not only in Evangelical circles but also—suffice it to mention the Roman

Catholic school at Tübingen—to a very significant extent in the works of Roman Catholic theology and scholarship, especially in Germany. This influence of German *Idealism* was strong in the Russian theological schools, although here it was more of a philosophical, than theological, concern. The influence of philosophical idealism was almost not at all apparent in the genuine theological literature, genuine in the strictest sense of the term. This is partially explained by the strictness of censorship. We know from the memoirs of contemporaries that many of the Academy professors were inclined to a philosophical interpretation of the *data* of Revelation rather than to a strictly theological interpretation.

The psychological influence of Romanticism and Realism was, in any case, strong. Schelling and Baader, as well as Romantic psychologists such as G. H. Schubert (d. 1860), were very popular among the students of the Academies. Even in the works of Theophan the Recluse, the authoritative interpreter of patristic asceticism, we find certain traces of Schubert's *History of the Soul* [*Geschichte der Seele;* 1830, 4th edition, 1850]. Schubert's book was used as a textbook in the Kiev Academy when Theophan was a student. In any case, the philosophical awakening in Russia began precisely in the theological schools and all the early disciples of philosophical idealism came from theological Academies or Seminaries: Vellanskii from the Kiev Academy, Nadezhdin from Moscow, Galich from the seminary at Sevsk, and Pavlov from the Voronezh Seminary. Later, university professors of philosophy also came from the theological Academies: Sidonskii and M. I. Vladislavlev in St. Petersburg, P. D. Iurkevich and M. M. Troitskii in Moscow (both from the Kiev Academy), Archimandrite Theophan Avsenev, O. Novitskii, S. S. Gogotskii in Kiev, and I. Mikhnevich in the Richelieu Lyceum of Odessa. Professors of philosophy at the Academies were: Th. Golubinskii and V. D. Kudriavtsev at the Moscow Academy, V. N. Karpov, the well-known translator of Plato, and M. I. Karinskii in St. Petersburg. Thus a specific internal tradition of religio-philosophical idealism was created in the Academies. It kept alive a philosophical thirst for knowledge and directed attention to problems of faith. It was precisely from the theological schools that the Russian "love for wisdom" began and Russian theological knowledge was exposed to a speculative testing. One of the *conservative* professors of the Theological Academy outlined at the beginning of this century the task of philosophical Dogmatics: behind every dogma one must search spiritually for that question to which the dogma responds. "This is the analytics of the natural demands of the spirit in relation to various truths." First, one must establish the positive witness of the Church from Scripture and Tradition, "and here a mosaic of texts is never sufficient but only an organic growth of knowledge." Then dogma comes alive and discloses itself in its entire speculative depth— as a divine answer to human questions, as a divine Amen and as a witness of the Church. It appears as a "genuine self-understanding" which is spiritually unthinkable to contradict. Dogmatic theology, when it confronts the questions of the present, must constantly re-create dogmas afresh so that the dark coals of traditional formulas are transformed into the illuminating jewels of true faith.[17] In such a presentation of the speculative problems of theology the philosophical and historical methods go hand in hand. The historical method, for its part, leads back to the speculative confession of the faith of the Holy Fathers.

The influence of philosophy is especially clear in the systematic construction of Russian "secular theologians"— the Slavophiles and Khomiakov, but especially Vladimir Solov'ev and his followers. The close connection between the religio-philosophical *Weltanschauung* and quest of Vladimir Solov'ev with German idealistic philosophy, especially with Schelling, partly with Baader, Schopenhauer, and Ed. von

Hartmann is completely obvious. Solov'ev's system, however, was an attempt to re-shape afresh the dogmas of Christian belief and Tradition in the categories of modern philosophy, a task which had already concerned Khomiakov. From Solov'ev this tradition, taken up by his spiritual followers and successors, passed into the contemporary religio-philosophical tradition. To such an understanding of theological tasks one should oppose another: the task of theology lies not so much in translating the Tradition of faith into contemporary language, into the terms of the most recent philosophy, but lies rather in discovering in the ancient patristic tradition the perennial principles of Christian philosophy; this task lies not in controlling dogma by means of contemporary philosophy but rather in re-shaping philosophy on the experience of faith itself so that the experience of faith would become the source and measure of philosophical views. The weakest side of Solov'ev and his school was precisely this misuse of the speculative process which can enchain, and often even deform, Tradition and the experience of faith. The influence of German philosophy, in any case, organically penetrated Russian theological consciousness.

V

From the foregoing brief and fleeting survey of Western influences in Russian theology the following disquieting and hopeless conclusion seems inevitable: was not and is not Russian theology, in its development—as one critic sharply stated—always a *"wandering theology"*? Was it not peculiarly moveable, changeable, inconsistent and incomprehensible? Such is quite often the conclusion of foreign—especially of Roman Catholic—theologians, who usually get the impression from reading Russian theological works of something uncertain, something indefinable. Impressions and conclusions

of this type are in fact the results of a very dangerous misunderstanding, a kind of optical illusion. Something very
tragic, however, stands behind such an interpretation—a
disastrous schism, a split in Orthodox consciousness, traceable
in the history of Russian theology as a certain *creative confusion,* as a lack of clarity about the road to be followed.
Saddest of all was that this peculiar split was between piety
and theology, between theological erudition and spirituality,
between theological schools and Church life.

This new theological *scholarship* came to Russia from
the West. It remained an alien accretion in Russia much too
long. It continued to use a special language, foreign to the
people, a language which was neither that of common life
nor of prayer. It remained an alien body in the structure of
the Church, developing into artificial and totally estranged
forms. It was and it remained "school scholarship." As such
it transformed itself into a text for instruction and all too
often ceased seeking the truth and the profession of the
faith. Theological thought gradually digressed from hearing
the rhythm of the Church's heart and thereby lost the "way"
to this heart. It did not understand the necessity of awakening
attention as participation in the wider circles of the Church
community and of the people. It looked at them rather with
distrust, jealousy, and enmity. There were, in fact, reasons
for this. They lay in the prejudice against an imported and
self-sufficient scholarship which was not even rooted in the
reality of religious experience or in life, a prejudice against
a theology which had ceased to express and bear witness to
the faith of the Church. To this extent it can be justly
characterized as a "wandering theology." Herein lies the
entire problem of Russian religious existence: in the depths
and the intimacy of Church experience the *Faith* is kept
and preserved undistorted. In the quiet acquiescence to God,
in the style of prayer, in its monasticism the Russian soul
preserved the old, strict, patristic style; it lived in a fully

undisturbed and undivided fulness of *Sobornost'* and Tradition. In this spirituality and depth of prayer the ancient Faith still remained "the apostolic, patristic Faith,"—the faith of ancient, Eastern, and Byzantine Orthodoxy. But *"thought"* had separated itself, had torn itself away from these spiritual depths, returning only too late to the realization of its unholy deviation. The wanderings of *thought,* however, could not and did not destroy the authenticity of faith: Orthodoxy remained, nevertheless, unchanged. One serious danger exists, however, in that theological pseudo-morphosis, when natural language is lost and theology becomes alien and strange. Most dangerous was the fact that theological problematics lost their proximity to life and that the Truth of God became a school exercise limited to specialists and professionals. N. P. Gillarov-Platonov gives a very characteristic example of such an alienation of school from life in his extraordinarily captivating memoirs:

> The semi-Protestant interpretation of Tradition was then quite common in the schools. Even the catechism of Philaret had no section on Tradition. The Theology of Ternovskii did not discuss it either. The handwritten text from which I taught, when I was already forty, was also silent on this subject. The age of Prokopovich still lingered on . . . This situation was not just restricted to the subject of Tradition . . . The doctrine of Justification was also presented in conformity with Latin books . . . While Moscow more or less wandered in the footsteps of Prokopovich, a reaction took place in St. Petersburg, the result of the theology of A. N. Murav'ev . . . It is particularly noteworthy that professional theologians remained quite indifferent to the innovations in the obviously important dogma of Tradition (Tradition as a second and independent source of Faith). They began to write and teach in the

new manner as if they had always done so . . . The
reader may think this is an unusual lack of faith
on the part of these religious persons. But what
appears at first glance a peculiar indifference was
really no lack of faith. It rather indicated that the
formulae of Western theology had no "living" content for the Eastern Church. In the West these
questions belong to the essence of various confes-
sions and are burning issues. In the East, however,
these questions were in general not raised at all.
Informative in this regard is the exchange of letters
in the 16th century between Patriarch Jeremiah
of Constantinople and the Tübingen theologians.
The latter asked him for his views on the issues
which constituted the essence of the strife between
Rome and Luther—for example, the issue of faith
and works. The Patriarch, however, answered
casually and superficially; he could not understand
the full context of these questions precisely because
these questions had arisen from the religious speculations in the Western Church, the latter being involved in these problems because of a peculiarity
of its own historical development.[18]

In these observations there is much truth, especially from
a psychological point of view. The danger lay not so much
in the errors as in the separation of theological thought and
its scholarship from the people.

*Western influences in Russian theology must be over-
come.* This concerns, first of all, the inorganic *"Western
style."* This process actually began long ago in the Russian
schools—precisely at the time of Philaret and in connection
with the revival of asceticism in Russian monasteries. It is
sufficient to recall the school of *Staretz* Paisii Velichkovskii
and especially the hermitage of Optino. Orthodox theology
can ultimately restore the independence from Western

influences only through a *spiritual return to patristic sources* and foundations. To return to the Fathers does not mean to retreat from the present or from history; it is not a retreat from modernity or from the field of battle. It means much more—it is not only a preservation and protection of patristic experience but also the very discovery of this experience and the bringing of this experience into life. On the other hand, independence from the West must not degenerate into an alienation which becomes simply opposed to the West. For a complete break with the West does not give a true and authentic liberation. Presently Orthodoxy can and must no longer circumvent or hush up the issue. This, however, means that Orthodoxy must encounter the West creatively and spiritually. The dependence and imitation of the past cannot be considered *an encounter.* An *encounter* only really occurs in the freedom and equality of love. It is not sufficient merely to repeat Western answers, to play one Western answer off against another. But rather we must precisely recognize, experience, and penetrate these Western questions, we must familiarize ourselves with the entire dramatic problematic of Western religious thought.

VI

Orthodox Theology's path of overcoming the Western "scandal" does not lie in rejecting or even overthrowing Western results. The path, rather, lies in overcoming and surmounting them in a *new creative activity.* Only a creative return to the unique and ancient depths will serve Orthodox thought as the authentic "antidote" against the open and hidden—or even yet unknown—aspects of "Western poisoning." Orthodox Theology is summoned to answer Western questions from the depths of the unbroken Orthodox experience and to confront the movements of Western thought with the unchanged *truth* of *patristic Orthodoxy.*

Translated from the German by
THOMAS BIRD and RICHARD HAUGH

The Ways of Russian Theology

I

THE HISTORY of Russian culture is marked throughout with crises, intermittent occurrences, fits of disillusionment or enthusiasms, betrayals or ruptures. It shuns a continuous and integral coherence. Its fabric is entangled, rumpled, frayed. "Most characteristic of Russian history are its scissions and breaks of continuity" (Nicolas Berdyaev). It displays foreign influences rather than its own creativity. There are many more contradictions and incompatibilities in the soul of the Russian people than the Slavophiles or the Populists [*narodniki*] were ready to admit. The traditional *mores* keep strange company with a revolutionary spirit. P. Kireevski has rightly observed that the very *being* of Russia evolved on several levels. This is also true of the intimate being, the inner, subtle structure of the popular soul. The latter has ever been living simultaneously in several eras or different ages. In it, psychic forms which cannot be measured, hailing from diverse epochs, combine and inter-

Translated from "Les Voies de la Theologie Russe," in *Dieu Vivant*, 13 (Paris, 1949), 39-62. Translated from the French by Georges A. Barrois. Printed by permission of the author.

penetrate. This does not mean that they constitute a synthesis. In fact, a synthesis did not succeed. This complexity of the popular soul is caused by the weakness of an excessive impressionability and an exaggerated sensitiveness. The Russian soul has a dangerous tendency, a treacherous inclination toward those transformations or those cultural metempsychoses of which Dostoevski spoke in his discourse on Pushkin. Or in the words of Alexander Blok:

> We perceive every thing,
> The sharp mind of France,
> And the somber genius of the Germans
> [*The Scythians*]

This gift of being a sonorous and universal echo is, all in all, fatal and ambiguous, since sensitiveness and lively reactions make the concentration of the spirit very difficult. By roaming freely through ages and cultures, man runs the risk of not finding himself. The soul is unsettled and becomes lost under wave after wave of impressions and historical experiences. The soul seems to have lost the capacity for returning into itself, attracted and distracted as it is by too many things, which detain it elsewhere. Thus it acquires nomadic habits, it gets used to living in ruins or in encampments. The Russian soul is oblivious of its ancestry. It is customary to quote its propensity for dreaming, its feminine suppleness. Now this is not false. But the trouble does not derive from the fact that the fundamental element, plastic and highly fusible, of the Russian people, was not reinforced nor armored with "logoi," that it did not crystallize into cultural action. There is no way of measuring or exhaustively explaining the Russian *temptation* merely by naturalistically contrasting "nature" with "culture." This temptation arises from within the culture itself. Generally speaking, the "popular soul" is less a biological quantity than a historical, created value. It is made and it grows through history. The

Russian "element" is by no means an "innate reaction to its being," the natural, inborn "original chaos," which does not bear any fruit yet, which the light of the spirit has not yet brightened and enlightened. It is rather the new secondary chaos, that of sin and disintegration, of the fall, the revolt, the hardening of a darkened and blinded soul. The Russian soul is not stricken by original sin only, it is not poisoned only by an inherent Dionysiac strain. More than that, it bears the burden of its historic sins, whether conscious or unconscious: "A dismal swamp of shameful thoughts wells up within me..." The true cause of this evil lies not in the fluidity of the primordial element of the people, but rather in the infidelity and the fickleness of its love. Only love is the true *fora* for synthesis and unity, and the Russian soul has not been steady and devoted in this ultimate love. Too often was it swayed through mystical unstableness. Russians have become far too much used to suffer at fatal crossroads or at the parting of ways, "not daring to carry the scepter of the Beast nor the light burden of Christ..." The Russian soul feels even passionately drawn toward such crossings. It does not have the steadfastness necessary for choice, nor the willpower for taking responsibilities. It appears, in some undefinable way, too "artistic," too loose-jointed. It expands, it extends, it languishes, lets itself be overcome as ensnared by a charm. But being under a spell is not synonymous with being in love, not any more than amorous friendship or infatuation are synonymous with love. Only sacrificial love, voluntary love, makes one strong, not the fits of passion, nor the mediumnistic attraction of a secret affinity. Now the Russian soul lacked precisely that spirit of sacrifice and self-denial in the presence of Truth, of the ultimate humility in loving. It divides itself and meanders through its attachments. *Logical conscience,* being sincerity and responsibility in the act of knowing, wakes up late in the Russian soul.

Two temptations keep it spellbound; on the one hand,

the temptation of the holy life: it is the temptation of Old
Russia, of the "Old Believers," the optimism of a Christian
order established on the historic soil, followed, as if it were
by a shadow, with the apocalyptic negation in the schism
[*raskol*]. On the other hand, the temptation of pietistic
consolation, which is the temptation of the new "intelligentsia," whether the occidentalist or the populist. It is also
a temptation *sui generis* of the spiritual life, the charm of a
spiritual *Gemütlichkeit*. History is not assumed in a creative
way, as superior high feat, as pilgrimage, as impersonal
forces, even unconscious and elemental, on "organic pro-
cesses," on the "power of the earth," as though history would
evolve, as if it would *just happen,* rather than being *self-
creative.* "Historicism" is no defense against "pietism," for
it remains a point of view of the intellect. The category of
responsibility is missing, in spite of historical sensitiveness,
receptivity, and keenness of observation. This irresponsibility
of the national spirit is most conspicuous in the evolution of
Russian thought. And here is the essence of our cultural
tragedy. It is a Christian, not an *antique,* tragedy; the tragedy
of voluntary sin, of a freedom which ceases to be clear-sighted;
it is not the tragedy of a blind fate, nor of the primordial
darkness; it is the tragedy of divided love, of mystical
infidelity, that of spiritual servitude and of demoniac possession. Therefore it reaches its dénouement in a paroxysm of
red madness, of God's denial, of war against God, of fall.
And it is impossible to tear oneself loose from this whirl
of passion except by penitence, vigil, concentration, spirituality, and the return of the soul. The way out is not found
in culture, in society, but in asceticism, beyond the "internal
desert" of the spirit which returns.

II

One perceives a certain embarrassment of the creative

spirit in the history of Russian theology. The main neuralgic point is the strange divorce between theology and piety, between erudition and meditative prayer, between the school and Church life; a separation and a schism between the "intelligentsia" and the "people," in the very bosom of the Church. Let it suffice to recall at this point that this estrangement has been harmful to both parties. The Athonite disturbances (1912-1913), caused by controversies about the Divine Name and the "Prayer of Jesus," are a typical illustration.

Theological scholarship was borrowed from the West. Too long did it remain foreign with us. It even persisted in using a particular language (which was neither that of everyday life, nor of prayer). Theology remained an enclave within the organism of the Church. As it developed in an artificial milieu and in isolation, it became and remained a school discipline, more and more a matter that is taught, less and less a quest for truth or a profession of faith. Theological thought gradually lost its faculty to apply itself to the live pulsations of the Church. It could not any more find the way to its heart. It attracted neither the attention nor the sympathy of large social and popular circles of the Church. Theology, in the best circumstances, seemed useless. But often incomprehension worsened into umbrageous mistrust, even ill-will. Consequently numerous believers acquired the unfortunate habit of doing without theology altogether, and replaced it, some with canons, some others with prayers, with ancient traditions, with ritual, with the lyricism of the soul. This gave rise to an obscure sort of abstinence, to a refusal of knowledge, we might say to theological *aphasia,* to uncalled for "a-dogmatism" or even to agnosticism under pretence of piety; in a word, to a renewal of the heresy of the "antisophoi," "gnosimachoi."

The sin consisted not only in the fact that spiritual riches remained buried and deliberately unused; this "gnosimachia,"

threatened even the soundness of the spirit. In the practice
of devotion, private as well as liturgical, there always lurks
the danger of "psychological subjectivism," the temptation
to receive or to offer the psychic for the spiritual. It can
take the appearance of ritual or canonical formalism, or else
of an enticing sensibility. It is nonetheless a temptation. The
theological spirit alone—humble, straightforward, vigilant,
experience—may preserve us from such temptations. Neither
the traditional rites nor the canons are a sufficient safeguard.
The soul lets itself be carried away by the lure and the
appeal of its own plight. In such a psychological climate,
the mistrust with regard to theology became doubly harmful.
Research lacked ground. Without a theological criterion, the
Russian soul was so unstable, so exposed to temptations!. . .
Since Peter I, "piety" had been, so to speak, driven back
toward the lower strata of the society. The break between
the "intelligentsia" and the "people" had occurred precisely
at the level of faith! The higher strata were soon con-
taminated with unbelief and rationalistic libertarianism. Faith
had been preserved in the lower classes most of the time in a
superstitious and "popular" context. Orthodoxy was reduced
to being the confession of "simple folks," of the merchants,
of the peasants. Many began to think that they could not
possibly rally to the Church unless they would make themselves simple, unless they would blend with the people, dig
as deep as the national, historical foundations, and return to
the land. And they confused too often rallying to the Church
with going back to the people. Shortsighted zealots, such as
repentant intellectuals, the rudes and the snobs, concurred in
spreading dangerous prejudices. The Slavophiles carried their
share of responsibility. According to them, the life of the
people itself was a kind of natural catholicity. The com-
mune, the *"mir,"* was an embryo of the Church. Even today
there are too many who regard a certain "populism" as the
necessary mode of true Orthodoxy. The *foi du charbonnier*,
the faith of the old nanny, or of the illiterate churchgoer,

was considered as the model and the most authentic type.
It seemed proper and safer to enquire concerning the essence
of Orthodoxy from the "people" rather than from the
"Fathers." Theology, therefore, was not included in the
structure of "Russian Orthodoxy." In the name of "simple
piety," it is generally acceptable, even today, to use a made
up language, falsely popular, bearing the stamp of com-
punction and piety. This is the most dangerous form of
obscurantism and often the appanage of repentant intellectuals. In such a context, orthodoxy often turns into some
sort of moralizing folklore. "What would Tsar Alexis
Mikhailovich have said, if he had been told that true
orthodoxy, outside of monastic enclosures, was preserved only
among peasants, that it had been dispelled from among the
boyars, the nobles, the prominent merchants of the capital,
the officials, and a great many representatives of the small
bourgeoisie? In its time, the Church was founded upon the
better people of the land, not upon the obscure masses of
the countryside, which retains to this day so many uncertain
beliefs, pagan survivals, and among which the schism had
soon grown deep roots." (S. Trubetskoy)

The entire falsity of religious "populism" is clearly
shown by the fact that contrition can never be an "organic"
process, although it restores or initiates the spiritual integrity
of the soul. For repentance is always a *crisis,* that is to say,
a judgment. The only means for truly rallying to the Church
is a severe asceticism, and not a return to the people, to the
rudiments, and to the simple unity of the origins. Not the
folklore, the popular traditions of daily life, but fasting and
penitence. There is no reverting to native primitivism, but
one has to enter into history, by the assimilation of ecumenical
and catholic traditions. "Christianity in Russia, like everywhere else, has ceased to be a popular religion in essence.
The people, the simple folk, for the most part, ebb toward
half-intellectualism, materialism, socialism; they experience a
first-taste infatuation for Marxism, Darwinism, etc. On the

contrary, the intellectuals, from the upper, cultured strata of society return to Christian faith. The old-style Orthodoxy, folklore and peasantish, has come to an end; it cannot be brought back to life. We make infinitely higher demands on Christianity, be it ever so mediocre. The Christianity of the humble peasant woman is today a myth; she has become nihilistic and atheist. The believer of today is the philosopher, the man of culture" (Nicolas Berdiaev).

There is in the Russian spirit a fatal *schizothymia*. On the one hand, a craving for knowledge, an intellectual restlessness, an Aristotelian spirit of inquiry. On the other hand a dry and cold passion for simplification. Two wills oppose each other; more exactly, the will is split asunder in twain. We hear often about Russian obscurantism. Now, rare are those who perceive its truly tragic depth. The movement is extremely complex; I say "movement," for it should not be confused with numbness or drowsiness of the rational will; we have to deal with a most active attitude, a positive stand, by no means a passivity. Most diverse elements concur in tying a desperate knot. In the last analysis, what is called "obscurantism" is a *mistrust with regard to culture*. The *stubborn suspicion* of many toward theological science is only a particular case of whatever poisons the Russian genius. Historically, this "obscurantism" was born as a restlessness and vigilance in the presence of a borrowed science, allegedly self-sufficient, yet without roots in the reality of religious experience and life. It was above all a protest and a defense against a lifeless erudition. Such a protest was liable to turn easily into the flatest utilitarianism, as it often happened, and still happens. However, erudition or intellectualism are not yet real knowledge, and the distrust was not without motives or without grounds. The ultimate reason for distrust was that theology had ceased to express, and to witness to, the faith of the Church. And not without cause did one hold theology as being mistaken. In this lies the essential paradox of our religious history. In the depths and recesses of ecclesiastical experience, faith remained intact. Through its contemplation, prayer, and practice of devotion, the Russian soul keeps the style, ancient and rigorous, of the Fathers, it lives in a total communion. But thought has detached itself from it; too often did the soul retreat from the depths and find itself, quite late, aware of this fatal uprooting. "Obscurantism" was the dialectical warning of this loss of ground. Creative theological thought alone will be able to overcome these adverse circumstances, when theology shall return to the depths of the Church and lighten them from within, when reason shall find its center in the heart, and when the heart shall mature through rational meditation. Only then shall there be an entrance into the understanding of truth.

III

Our crisis of breaking away from Byzantinism in the 16th century was an abandonment of Patristic tradition as well. There was no rupture within spiritual experience; on the contrary Russian piety, if we look back, appears even archaic. But theology had lost the Patristic style and methods. The works of the Fathers became archives, lifeless documents. It is not enough to be acquainted with the texts and to know how to draw from them quotes and arguments. One must possess the theology of the Fathers from within. Intuition is perhaps more important for this than erudition, for intuition alone revives their writings and makes them a *witness*. It is only from within that we can perceive and distinguish what (actually) is a catholic testimony from what would be merely theological opinion, hypothesis, interpretation, or theory. "The Fathers are," Newman observed keenly, "our teachers, but not our confessors or casuists; they are the prophets of great things, not the spiritual directors of individuals" (*Essays,* 11, 371). Reviving the Patristic style is

the very premise of theological renaissance. This does not
mean a restoration, a return to the past, nor a repetition.
"Returning to the Fathers" means, for all intents, to advance,
not to go backwards. What we need is to be faithful to the
spirit, not to the letter of the Fathers, to let ourselves be
kindled at the flame of their fiery inspiration, not to gather
specimens for a herbarium.

There are two types of consciousness; individual and
catholic. "Catholic consciousness" is not collective consciousness, not a kind of "consciousness in general." The ego does
not disappear, nor is it dissolved in the "we." On the contrary, personal consciousness reaches its completion and its
accomplishment in the catholic transfiguration, liberates itself
from its reclusion and alienation, and inhales the integrality
of the other individuals. According to a suggestive formula
of Prince S. Trubetskoy, "it holds in itself the communion with all." This is why it acquires the capacity and
the strength to assimilate and to express the consciousness
and the life of the all. Only in the integral communion of
the Church is this "catholic transfiguration" of consciousness
truly possible. Those who, by reason of their humility in the
presence of the Truth, have received the gift to express this
catholic consciousness of the Church, we call them Fathers
and Doctors, since what they make us hear is not only their
thought or their personal conviction, but moreover the very
witness of the Church, for they speak from the depth of its
catholic fullness. Their theology evolves on the plane of
catholicity, of universal communion. And this is the first
thing we must learn. Through asceticism and concentration,
the theologian must learn to find his bearings *in* the Church:
Cor nostrum sit semper in Ecclesia: We must mature and rise
up to the catholic level, go beyond our narrow subjectivism
and out of our particular retreat. In other words, we must
be engrafted in the Church, in order to grow in it and live
in that mysterious tradition, integral and trans-temporal,
which embraces the sum of all revelations and visions. There,

and there only, is the guaranty of creative work, and not in the seductive affirmation of a prophetic freedom. We need less to worry about freedom than about Truth. Only truth makes free. To believe that "a thought without roots, a schismatic truth, is always freer" would be a dangerous illusion.

Freedom is neither in being rooted in the natural soil, nor in being uprooted; it is found in Truth and in the life of Truth, in the illumination of the Spirit. The Church alone possesses the strength and power of the true, catholic synthesis. In this consists its *potestas magisterii*, the gift and unction of infallibility.

The consciousness of knowing must expand, embrace the fullness of the past, and, at the same time, the continuity of growth into the future. Theological consciousness must become historical. Only on account of its historicity can it possibly be catholic. Indifference for history always leads to a sectarian dryness, to a doctrinaire attitude. Historical sensitiveness is indispensable to the theologian, it is the necessary condition for being in the Church. Whoever is insensitive to history would hardly be a good Christian. Not by mere chance did the decline of ecclesial awareness during the Reformation coincide with a mystical blind spot with regard to history. It is true that the Protestants, in their polemic with Rome on papal innovations, were in fact the creators of "Church history" as a particular discipline, and they contributed more than any others to this ecclesiastical science. Nevertheless the historical phenomenon as such had, in their eyes, lost its religious value and virtue; what they saw in history was merely the genesis of a decadence (it was their purpose to prove this), the object of their research being rather "primitive" Christianity, to wit, something which antecedes the history of the Church. Such is the very point of "modernism." It implies a kind of unbelief toward history; it hails back to positivism and humanism; one begins by thinking that Christian truth cannot be established from history as a starting point, and that it can be affirmed only by "faith." History knows only Jesus of Nazareth; faith alone confesses in Him the Christ. This historical scepticism is overcome in the Church through the catholicity of its experience, far beneath the surface, on which a humanist's glance strays and skids. The Church recognizes and proclaims dogmatic events as facts of history. Theandry is such a fact, and not merely a postulate of the faith. In the Church, history must be for the theologian a perspective that is *real*. To do the task of a theologian in the Church is to work in the element of history. For "ecclesiality" is tradition. The theologian must discover history as a *theanthropic process,* a pass-over from time to the eternity of grace, the becoming and the building of the Body of Christ. Only in history is it possible to know this growth of the Mystical Body, to be convinced of the mystical reality of the Church, and to rid oneself from the temptation which consists in dehydrating Christianity in order to reduce it to an abstract Doctrine or a system of morals. Christianity is whole in history, it concerns history. It is not a revelation in history, but rather an appeal to history, to *historical action and creation*. Everything in the Church is dynamic, everything is in action and in motion since Pentecost until the Great Day. Now such a movement is not a movement away from the past. On the contrary, it is much more to be regarded as its continuous bearing of fruit. Tradition lives and quickens within creation. *Accomplishment* is the fundamental category of history. Theological endeavor is justified only within the perspective of history, in as much as it is a creative ecclesiastical datum.

The historical sensitiveness of Russian thought, the testing of its meditations and of its experiences, are the best token of its expected theological renewal. To be sure, the road of historical reminiscence was travelled too fast, and only on the plane of contemplation. It would not be correct to say that Russian theology, in its creative development, has perceived and assimilated completely or deeply enough the

Fathers and .Byzantium. This, it must still do. It must pass
through the austere schooling of Christian Hellenism. Hellenism, so to speak, assumed a perpetual character in the
Church; it has incorporated itself in the very fabric of the
Church as the *eternal category* of Christian existence. Of
course what is meant here is not that ethnical Hellenism
of modern Hellas or of the Levant, nor Greek phyletism,
which is obsolete and without justification. We are dealing
with Christian antiquity, with the Hellenism of dogma, of
the liturgy, of the icon. In the liturgy, the Hellenic style of
the "piety of the mysteries" enter into the rhythm of the
liturgical *mystagogy* without passing through some sort of
mystical "re-hellenization." Could anyone who is in the
Church be foolish enough to deliberately "de-hellenize" the
services and transpose them into a more "modern" style?
Moreover, Hellenism is something more than a passing
stage—in the Church. Whenever a theologian begins to think
that the "Greek categories" are outmoded, this simply means
that he has stepped out of the rhythm of communion. Theology cannot possibly be catholic except within Hellenism.
Now, Hellenism is ambiguous. An anti-Christian element was
predominant in the ancient mind. Till now, there are many
who take refuge themselves in Hellenism for the express
purpose to rise and fight against Christianity (simply think
of Nietzsche!) But Hellenism was integrated into the Church;
such is the historic meaning of Patristic theology. This
"integration of Hellenism" involved a merciless rupture, the
criterion of which had been the preaching the Gospel, the
historical manifestation of the Incarnate Word. Christian
Hellenism, transfigured as it was, is wholly historical. Patristic
theology is always a "theology of facts," it confronts us with
events, the events of sacred history. All the errors and temptations of a Hellenization forwarded indiscretely—they happened repeatedly in the course of history—cannot possibly
weaken the significance of this fundamental fact: the "good
news" and Christian theology, once and for all, were ex-

pressed from the start in Hellenistic categories. Patristic and catholicity, historicity and Hellenism are the joint aspects of a unique and indivisible datum.

This plea for Hellenism will stir up foreseeable objections. These were formulated more than once, and from several sides. The attempt of A. Ritschl and his school is well known. It aimed at emptying Christian doctrine of all its historical elements, in order to return to a purely "Biblical" foundation. Whenever this process is carried to its logical conclusion, the result is that the whole of Christianity disintegrates into humanitarian morals, in effect a travesty; such a return to the Bible is an illusion. Equally insufficient would be any interpretation of Revelation based exclusively on "semitic" categories, namely the "Law" and the "Prophets."

This approach has seduced many scholars; it is particularly evident in "dialectical theology," in K. Barth, E. Brunner, and others. The New Testament is interpreted in the framework of the Old, at the level of Prophecy, but Prophecy without a consummation, as if the prophecies had not been fulfilled. History is underrated, and the emphasis is placed on the Last Judgment, with the effect of narrowing the full span of Revealed Truth. But Biblical prophecy finds precisely its true realization in Christian Hellenism: *Vetus testamentum in Novo patet.* The New Testament and the Church of the New Testament embrace Jew and Greek in the unity of a new life. The categories of sacred Hebraism have lost their independent meaning. Every attempt at disengaging them or extracting them from the Christian synthesis leads to a relapse into Judaism. The truth of "Hebraism" is included in the Hellenic synthesis. Hellenism was integrated into the Church precisely through the Biblical engrafting. It is impossible, even from a historical point of view, to justify the opposition between "Semitism" and "Hellenism." When German idealism conquered the hearts, some scholars devised to transpose all the dogmatics and even the dogmas from the allegedly obsolete language of Hellenism into the idioms, more intelligible and actual, of the new idealism, in the manner of Hegel, Schelling, Baader, and their like (Khomiakov himself had thought to do that). Similar attempts went on to our days. Could the man of Faustian culture be satisfied with the static code of an ancient Hellenism? All these antiquated words, have they not lost their flavor? The soul itself, was it not so altered, as to lose its faculty of being impressed by all those terms "hopelessly and fatally obsolete?" But why, shall we ask straightway? Would it not be that our contemporaries fail to remember their lineage, and are therefore unable to understand, within themselves, their own past which they have rejected? After all, "modern philosophy and psychology" must first be submitted to a test and a justification, the criterion of which is rooted in the depths of ecclesiastical experience. And there is no common measure between the latter and the methods of Hegel or Kant. Or are we supposed to evaluate the fullness of the Church according to a Kantian standard, or to re-measure it with the yardstick of Lotze or Bergson, even perhaps of Schelling? The very idea is somewhat tragi-comic.

No, what is wanted, is not to translate the old dogmatic formulas into a modern language, but, on the contrary, to return creatively to the "ancient" experience, to re-live it in the depth of our being, and to incorporate our thought in the continuous fabric of ecclesial fullness. All those tentative transpositions or translations have never been anything else but betrayals, that is to say, new interpretations in terms thoroughly *inappropriate*. Their terms always suffered from an incurable particularism. They satisfied less the needs of contemporaries than the fads of the day. Turning away from Christian Hellenism is by no means moving ahead, but backwards, toward the dead ends and the perplexities of the other Hellenism, the one that had not been transfigured, and from which there was no escape but through Patristic integration. German idealism itself was nothing else but a backsliding into pre-Christian idealism. Whoever is unwilling to abide by the Fathers, who fears to be left trailing after "Patristic scholasticism," who strives after progress and presses onward on the secular plane, in vain, is fatally thrown back by the very logic of things and finds himself again in the company of Plato and Aristotle, Plotinus and Philo, that is to say, before Christ. His journey is a futile, outmoded excursion from Jerusalem to Athens.

Other objections against the "plea for Hellenism" come from the opposite side, not from Western philosophy, but form the spirit of the Russian people itself. Would it not be proper to transcribe orthodoxy in the Slavic key, in conformity with the style of this "Slavic soul" recently gained for Christ? A few Slavophiles (for example Orest-Miller), and after them some Populists, conceived of such endeavors. Whatever was Greek was suspected of intellectualism and consequently pronounced superfluous and alien to the exigencies of the Russian heart. "Not by chance did our people assimilate Christianity by starting, not from the Gospel, but from the Prologue; was catechized, not by predication, but by the liturgy, not by theology, but by worship, adoration and reverence for the sacred things." Tareiev has recently questioned Greek "tradition" or influence more frankly than anyone else. Quite logically, he extends to Patristic tradition his rejection of all kinds of Hellenism. "Patristic doctrine is from end to end a gnosticism," he believed. It is proper therefore that theology should proceed along its own track in order to obviate "Byzantine gnosticism." It is necessary to create a "philosophy of the heart." If such a philosophy does not replace dogmatic theology, which is a typical product of Greek intellectualism, it might at least disguise it. Tareiev declaimed with pathos against Greek oppression, against the Byzantine yoke: "Greek gnosticism had fettered religious thought, checked our theological creativity; it hindered the growth of our philosophy of the heart, it caused its root to dry up, it burned its shoots." In fact Tareiev is simply inserting surreptitiously an illusory foundation beneath that sweet and widespread kind of obscurantism which appears whenever one seeks in the ardor of piety as in the "philosophy of the heart" a refuge from all the tribulations of the spirit. We cannot help wondering how a man can so naively withdraw himself from history and from the Christian heritage, with the candor and indifference of those who have forgotten their origins. Russian theology did not suffer from Greek oppression. It suffered, on the contrary, for its imprudence and lightheartedness in breaking up the continuity of the Hellenic and Byzantine traditions. The fact of excluding itself from this succession has cast a lasting spell on the Russian soul and made it barren, for creation is impossible without living traditions. Renouncing the Greek patrimony is actually tantamount to ecclesiastical suicide.

IV

In the order of imitation, our theology went through the principal stages of religious thought in modern Europe, namely: the theology of the Council of Trent, the period of the Baroque, Protestant scholasticism and Protestant orthodoxy, pietism and freemasonry, German idealism and romanticism, the social-christian fermentation in the wake of the French revolution, the decomposition of the Hegelian school, the new critical and historical science, Tübingen and Ritschl, neo-romanticism and symbolism; all these came and left their imprint on the Russian cultural experience. Dependence and imitation, however, did not yet mean an intimate meeting. The latter is achieved only in the freedom and equality of love. It is not sufficient to repeat the ready-made answers of the West; we must rather analyze them and personally experience them, penetrate and appropriate to ourselves all the problematics and the drama of Western religious thought, follow and interpret the most difficult and winding course travelled since the Schism. One cannot possibly enter into a life as it is being created, except through the channel of its problematics, and one must feel and perceive it precisely in its problematic aspect as a quest and as an unrelenting search. Orthodox theology shall not be able to establish its independence from western influences unless it reverts to the Patristic sources and foundations. This does not mean forsaking our time, withdrawing from history, deserting the battlefield. We must not only retain the experience of the Fathers, but moreover develop it while discovering it, and use it in order to create a living work. Likewise, independence with regard to the heterodox West must not degenerate into alienation. Breaking away from the West does not bring about any true liberation. Orthodox thought has to feel the Western difficulties or temptations and bear with them; it may not usurp the right to bypass or brazenly to ignore them. We must, through creative thinking, resume and transmute all this experience of the West, its pangs and its doubts; we must take upon ourselves, as Dostoevsky used to say, "the European anguish," accumulated through centuries of creative history. It is only through such sympathy, such active compassion, that the divided Christian world may possibly find the way to union, welcome the separated brethren and witness their return to unity. We must not merely refute and reject Western pronouncements and errors, but rather overcome them through a new creative activity. This will constitute for Orthodox thought the best possible antidote against the hidden or unknown poisons which affect it. Orthodoxy is called upon to answer the questions of the heterodox from the utmost depth of its continuous catholic experience, and to offer to Western heterodoxy less a refutation than a testimony, even the truth of Orthodoxy.

There has been much concern among us Russians concerning the meaning of the Western evolution. Several found Europe truly a "second fatherland." Could one nevertheless affirm that we really knew the West? There was much more dialectical arbitrariness than correct vision in the current schemes which were applied to the Western process. The picture of an imaginary Europe, as we wished to see it, hid too often the real Europe. The soul of the West manifested itself principally through the arts, chiefly since the end of the nineteenth century, following the renewal of esthetics. The heart had been moved, and sensibility had increased. But *"Einfühlung"* never leads to the core of things, it even precludes feeling all the acuity of religious distress and anxiety. The attitude of "esthetism," generally speaking, does not favor much problem raising; it satisfies itself too easily with an inactive contemplation. More and earlier than any others, the Slavophiles, since Gogol and Dostoevsky, perceived the Christian strain and restlessness of the West. Soloviev was less familiar with the West, less aware of its inconsistencies and contradictions, obsessed as he was with "Christian politics." In fact, he knew very little of the West, besides ultramontanism and German idealism (one should add perhaps Fourier, Swedenborg, the spiritualists and, among the ancient masters, Dante). But Soloviev believed overmuch in the steadiness of the West. He was unaware of the romantic thirst and of the anguish from which Christian souls suffered; this he realized only toward the end of his life. The categories of the "old" Slavophiles were also very narrow. Yet they had some sort of intimate acquaintance with the most secret themes of the West. Moreover still, they were conscious of the kinship and responsibility of the Christians, they had an instinct of brotherly compassion, and an awareness or a premonition of the Orthodox calling in Europe. Soloviev dealt with the nation's calling, the theocratic mission of the Russian Empire, rather than with the mission of Orthodoxy. The "old" Slavophiles disengaged the Russian problems from the European exigencies, from the unsolved or insoluble questions raised by the other half of the one Christian world. The feeling of Christian responsibility did constitute the high truth and great moral strength of the early Slavophiles.

Orthodoxy is called to witnessing. Today more than ever,

the Christian West stands before open prospects, as a living question addressed also to the Orthodox world. In this lies the entire significance of the so-called ecumenical movement. Orthodox theology is called upon to demonstrate that the ecumenical problem cannot possibly be solved unless the Church reaches its fulfilment in the fullness of the catholic tradition, intact and immaculate, yet renewed and always growing. Again, it is impossible to "return" save through a crisis, for the way to Christian restoration is *critical,* not *irenic.* The old "polemic" theology has for a long time lost all internal relation to reality. It was nothing more than a school discipline, edified by means of similar western "manuals." *New theology,* in order to refute errors, must be informed by a *historiosophic exegesis* of the religious tragedy of the West. However, such an exegesis must be tested; we must make it our own, and show that it can undergo *catharsis* in the fullness of ecclesial experience and of Patristic tradition. In the new Orthodox synthesis, the centuries old experience of the West must be taken into consideration and studied with more attention and sympathy than our theologians ever did thus far. This does not mean that we should borrow nor adopt Roman doctrines, and indulge in romanizing mimesis. What I try to say is that Orthodox thought shall, at any rate, find a better source of creative inspiration in the great systems of higher scholasticism, in the experience of the western mystics and in the theology of modern Catholicism, than in German idealism, in the Protestant critique of the past centuries or of the present, or even in contemporary "dialectical theology." The rebirth of the Orthodox world is the necessary condition for the solution of the "ecumenical problem."

The *"encounter"* with the West has also another aspect. During the Middle Ages, the West had given birth to a theological tradition characterized by an extreme complexity and intensity, science, culture, research, action, and controversies. Such a tradition continued, to some extent, even in the epoch of the quarrels and most violent antagonisms of the Reformation. The solidarity in knowledge was not completely lost in the later free-thinking and libertarian age. In a sense, western theology remained one up to our day, being gathered through a feeling of mutual responsibility in the presence of similar weaknesses and errors. Western tradition presided to the birth of Russian theology with regard to its method and contents. We should therefore participate in this same tradition, with freedom, with responsibility, with conscience, openly, and we should by no means abandon it. The Orthodox theologian must not and dares not disengage himself from the universal tide of religious research. It happens that, after the fall of Byzantium, the West alone continued in the theological endeavor. The latter constitutes essentially an ecumenical, catholic problem, but the solution of this problem was sought only in the schism. Here is the fundamental paradox of the history of Christian culture. The West works, while the East keeps silent, or else, and this is worse; the East repeats bits of sentences spoken by the West, but without passing them through the sieve of criticism. The Orthodox theologian is still depending too much on Western support for his own work. Orthodox theology borrows its sources from the West; it reads the Fathers and the acts of the Councils in Western editions, often merely for the sake of example, and it learns the methods and the technique of utilization of sources at the school of the West. We know the past of our Church above all thanks to the efforts of many generations of Western scholars, as far as both the facts and their interpretation are concerned. The fact that the conscience of the West is constantly attentive to the ecclesial reality of history, that it assumes a responsible and heedful attitude toward it, that it never desists from reflecting and meditating on the Christian sources, this fact already is important. Western thought continues to live in that past, thereby compensating, so to speak, the weaknesses of its mystical memory with the liveliness of its recollections. To the western world, the orthodox theologian himself must bring its witness, the witness of the intimate memory of the Church, in order to have it coincide with the results of historical research. It is only that intimate memory of the Church which vitalizes fully the silent witness of the texts.

V

Prophetizing is not the historian's task. Yet the historian must perceive the rhythm and the meaning of events. And eventually events do prophetize. In such cases, the historian must be aware of his own mission in the presence of their entanglements. Who could possibly doubt this? A new aeon has recently begun in the history of the Christian world. It can be labelled as apocalyptical. I do not mean that our task is to decipher with temerity unknown or forbidden terms. But the *apocalyptic theme* appears far too evident in the entire evolution of actual events. For the first time in history, so it seems, the revolt against God and without God is unleashed with unheard of violence. All Russia is aflame with this anti-God fire and exposed to this fatal precipitation. Generation after generation is dragged into this deadly temptation. There is nothing left neutral in the world, no more dealing with ordinary, homely things; everything now is denied, debated, split asunder, and must be wrestled out of the hand of Antichrist, since his claim is universal; he aims at leaving his imprint on all things; all men are faced with the choice: faith *or* unbelief, and this *or* has become a burning issue. "He that is not with me is against me, and he that gathers not..., scatters abroad." The Revolution has revealed a hard and terrifying truth concerning the Russian soul, to wit an abyss of ancient faithlessness and denial, of demoniac possession and of deterioration. This soul is poisoned, subverted, torn to pieces. Being possessed and seduced, beset by doubt and lure, it cannot possibly be healed and recover its strength except through intense catechizing, through the light of Christian reason, through the language of sincerity and truth, through the voice of the Spirit and through its power. The time is come already when the debate concerning the souls of men appears in plain daylight. Now is the time when every question about knowledge and life must truly find and receive its Christian answer, when it must be integrated in the synthesis and plenitude of confession. Now is the time when theology ceases to be a "private affair," to which everyone may freely attend or show no regard, in proportion of his aptitudes, tendencies, or moods. In this time of temptation and judgment, theology becomes again a public thing, a universal catholic mission. It behooves all to take to spiritual arms. Now is already the time when theological silence, uncertainty, inarticulate witness, are tantamount to treason and flight before the enemy. Silence can cause trouble as much as a hasty or elusive answer. Moreover, unto him who keeps silent, his mutism can be poison and mean his downfall, and he becomes an accomplice, as though faith were "a fragile thing, and not so certain."

A "new theological epoch" has begun. Our time is called upon to resume the task of theology. Some may find this affirmation presumptuous, excessive and arbitrary. Was our epoch not placed under the sign of "social Christianity" ever since Lamennais and Morris, perhaps since Saint Simon? In our troubled age, should not Christianity be called to "social endeavors" for the edification of the New City? Is it still in order today to re-direct religious consciousness toward the intellectual problems of theology and to divert it from the actual "social theme" which an irreversible course of events has brought to the fore? To do this seems rather incongruous in view of the conditions which prevail today in Russia. Is not Russia marked for action, rather than contemplation? Are we justified in weakening the militant "activism" through an appeal to reflection and concentration of the soul? "Doing some theology" in our days appears to many among us almost a treason or an escapism. Such objections or doubts manifest a fatal blindness. This is certainly not the time to withdraw from the "social question" precisely when the "scarlet star" of socialism is risen to the firmament of history. However, is not the "social question" first and foremost a spiritual question, a question of conscience and wisdom? Is not the social revolution above all a psychic, confused reversal of the tide? Is not the Russian Revolution a spiritual catastrophe, a collapse of souls, a passionate outburst? Should it not be explained in spiritual terms? The secret of Russia's future lies far less in her social structure or technique, than in the *new man* that they try over there to grow and develop, without God, without faith, without love. As for the question of faith itself, is it not brought back to the fore by an irretrievable course of events, in its rigor, and its ultimate, apocalyptical evidence? Does not all the intimate problematics of the absence of faith, of the struggle against God, impose itself today with extreme acuity? "The spirit, not the flesh, has grown corrupt today, and man knows a hopeless anguish." (Tyutchev)

It is precisely because we are already engaged in the apocalyptic struggle that we are called upon to do work as theologians. Our task is to oppose a responsible and conscious profession of Christian truth to the atheistic and anti-God attitude which surrounds us like a viscosity. There cannot be, there is not, a "neutral" science of God and of Christianity, indifference and abstention are no longer "neutral" also; unbelieving knowledge of Christianity is not objective knowledge, but rather some kind of "anti-theology." There is in it so much passion, at times blind, often obscure and malignant. There is also restlessness and unexpected glimmers; it would be only an "anti-theology." Here again theology is called not only to judge, but also to heal. It is necessary to enter into this world of doubt, illusion and lies, in order to answer doubt as well as reproach. But we must enter into this world with the sign of the Cross in our heart and the name of Jesus in our spirit, because this is a world of mystical wanderings, where everything is fragmentized, decomposed and refracted as if through a set of mirrors. And here again the theologian must bear witness. This situation is not unlike that of the early centuries, when the seeds had been sown and sprouted in a soil not yet transfigured, but which this first sowing sanctified for the first time. By then, those who announced the Good News had to address themselves most of the time to hearts not enlightened, to the obscure and sinful conscience of the "nations" to which they had been sent, and which were sitting in darkness and in the shadow of death. Our contemporary world, atheistic and ridden with unbelief, is it not comparable in a sense with that pre-Christian world, renewed with all the same interweaving of false religious trends, sceptical and anti-God? In the face of such a world, theology must all the more become again a witness. The theological system cannot be a mere product of erudition, it cannot be born of philosophical reflection alone. It needs also the experience of prayer, spiritual concentration, pastoral solicitude. In theology, the good news, the *kerygma*, must be proclaimed. The theologian must speak to living beings, address himself to living hearts, he must be full of attention and love, conscious of his immediate responsibility for the soul of his brother, and particularly for the soul that is still in the dark. In knowledge in general there is and there must be an element, not merely dialectic, but *dia-logical*. He who knows bears witness for the benefit of those who together with him have the knowledge of the truth; he calls upon them to bow and be humble before it, and he should humble himself as well. Humility is particularly necessary to the theologian. He cannot possibly solve today the problems of souls and consciences arising daily in the pastoral-pedagogical domain, but should not brush them aside either. He must answer from within a complete system of thought, by a theological confession. He must experience in himself, as through an intimate suffering, the entire problematic of the soul which believes not and seeks not, the problematic of voluntary ignorance and of ignorance not desired. The time is come when the refusal of theological knowledge becomes a deadly sin, the stigma of self-conceit and lovelessness, of cowardice and maliciousness. Affected plainness seems a demoniac maneuver; distrusting the reason that seeks must be condemned as satanic mischief. "They are stricken with fear, where there is no fear..." It may be appropriate to recall the sharp words of Metropolitan Philaret of Moscow, here, spoken long ago in a time of trial and of evasive attitudes. "It is very true that the gift and the duty to teach are not everybody's lot, and rare are those whom the Church has honored with the name of Theologian. However, it is not permissible to anyone in Christianity to know nothing at all and to remain ignorant. Was not the Lord himself called Master and did he not call his followers disciples? Christians, before they assumed this title, bore the name of disciples. Would these terms be vain or meaningless? And why did the Lord send apostles into the world? It was first and foremost to teach all nations... If you refuse to teach or to learn within Christianity, you are not disciples of Christ and you do not follow Him; the apostles were not sent for you; you are not what all Christians were from the very beginning of Christianity. I do not know what you are, nor what shall become of you." (*Sermons and Discourses,* IV, pp. 151-2; sermon preached in 1841, on the feast of St. Alexis).

VI

The future reveals itself to us under the sign of duty more surely and with greater depth than it would under the sign of expectation and foreboding. The future is not merely something we are looking and waiting for, but rather something we must create. Our vocation has its source precisely in the responsibility of duty. Even though we are not expecting, yet we find in obedience itself the strength to create and the power to beget. The arbitrariness of the will, on the contrary, is a principle of dispersion. Integration in the Church is through prayer, apocalyptic faithfulness, return to the Fathers, a free *encounter* with the West: these, and other similar factors compose the *creative postulate* of Russian theology within the contemporary framework. Here also is the legacy of the past, and our responsibilities, our obligation toward it. Past errors and failures should not disturb us. We have not reached the term of our course, the history of the Church is not over yet, Russia is not yet at the end of the road. The way ahead is still open, even though it is difficult. The rigorous verdict of history must be transformed into a creative appeal, in order that we may achieve what remains to be done. "Through many pains does it behoove one to enter into God's kingdom." Orthodoxy is not a tradition only; it is also a task; not the unknown *x,* but the data of the problem, which we must forthwith work out. It is a germ of life, a seed that sprouts, our duty and our mission.

The Russian way shall be for a long time a double one. For those who have remained, there is the mysterious way of asceticism, of the secret, silent work of acquiring the Spirit. As for those who have left, there is also a way they must travel, since freedom was left to us and also the power for the spiritual activity of witnessing and preaching. It is only through such effort that the past, filled as it is with forebodings and premonitions, shall be justified, in spite of its weaknesses and errors. True historical synthesis consists not merely in interpreting the past, but also in shaping the future by a creative act.

> "Erat ante in operibus fratrum candida, nunc facta est in matyrum cruore purpurea. Floribus ejus nec lilia, nec rosae desunt."
>
> *St. Cyprian*

Translated from the French by
GEORGES A. BARROIS

III
NOTES AND REFERENCES

Notes and References

PATRISTIC THEOLOGY AND THE ETHOS
OF THE ORTHODOX CHURCH

[1]F. Kattenbusch, "Kritische Studien zur Symbolik im Anschluss an einige neuere Werke," in *Theologische Studien und Kritiken,* Jg. 51, 1878, ss. 94-121 and 179-253. Kattenbusch deals with Gass in the first part of his article.

[2]F. Kattenbusch, *Lehrbuch der Vergleichenden Confessionskunde.* Erster Band: Prolegomena und Erster Teil: *Die Orthodoxe Anatolische Kirche* (Freiburg i/Br. 1892; the only volume published).

[3]Nicholas N. Glubokovsky, *Orthodoxy in Its Essence,* in "The Constructive Quarterly," June 1913, p. 296-297.

[4]W. Gass, "Zur Symbolik der Griechischen Kirche," in *Zeitschrift für Kirchengeschichte,* Bd. III, 1879, ss. 329-357.

[5]Cf. Ernst Benz, *Die Ostkirche im Lichte der Protestantischen Geschichtsschreibung von der Reformation bis zur Gegenwart* (München, 1952), ss. 195-201, 206-217.

[6]Louis Bouyer, *Le renouveau des études patristiques,* in "La Vie Intellectuelle." Février 1947, p. 18.

[7]Mabillon, in the Preface to Bernard's *Opera,* n. 23, Migne, *P. L.,* CLXXXII, c. 26, quoted recently in the Encyclical of Pope Pius XII, *Doctor Mellifluus* (1953); English translation of the Encyclical in Thomas Merton, *The Last of the Fathers,* N. Y., 1954.

[8]L. Thomassin, *Dogmata theologica,* vol. I, Praefatio, p. XX.

[9]Kabasilas' treatises are reprinted in Migne, *P. G.,* t. CL. Cf. M. Lot-Borodine, *Un maître de la spiritualité byzantine au XIV* siècle: Nicolas*

Cabasilas (Paris, 1958); on the Jesus Prayer see *La Prière de Jésus,* par un moine de l'Église d'Orient (Éditions de Chevetogne, 1951), and also E. Behr-Sigel, "La Prière à Jésus, ou le Mystère de la spiritualité monastique orthodoxe," in *Dieu Vivant,* No. 8 (1947), pp. 69-94.

[10]L. A. Zander, *The Problems of Ecumenism*—Paper prepared for the Study Department of the WCC, not yet published, but distributed in a mimeographed form.

ST. ATHANASIUS' CONCEPT OF CREATION

[1]See, e.g., J. Baudry, *Le Problème de l'Origine et de l'Éternité du Monde dans la Philosophie grecque de Platon à l'ère chrétienne* (Paris 1931), and also Jacques Chevalier, *La Notion du Nécessaire chez Aristote et chez ses prédécesseurs* (Paris 1915). Cf. my article, "The Idea of Creation in Christian Philosophy," in the *Eastern Churches Quarterly* 8, 1949, Supplementary issue: "Nature and Grace."

[2]Etienne Gilson, *God and Philosophy* (Yale University Press 1941), p. 88.

[3]Etienne Gilson, *L'Esprit de la Philosophie Médiévale*, Deuxième édition revue (Paris 1944), p. 82, n. 1.

[4]St. Justin's *Dialogue with Trypho*, c. 5 and 6. See my Ingersoll lecture for 1950-1951, "The Resurrection of Life," in the *Bulletin of Harvard Divinity School;* cf. J. Lebreton, *Histoire du Dogme de la Trinité*, t. II (Paris 1928., p. 635 ff.

[5]G. L. Prestige, *God in Patristic Thought* (S.P.C.K., 1952 [1936]), p. 123.

[6]V. V. Bolotov, *Origen's Doctrine of Holy Trinity* (St. Petersburg, 1879 [in Russian]), p. 380-381. It is still the best exposition of Origen's Trinitarian doctrine, at no point superseded by later research. One may add only H. Crouzel, *Théologie de l'Image de Dieu chez Origène* (Paris 1956).

[7]J. N. D. Kelly, *Early Christian Creeds* (London 1950), p. 137. Cf. also the comments of Antonio Orbe, S. J., *Hacia la primera teologia de la procesión del Verbo* (Rome 1958 [Estudios Valentinianos], vol. I/1), p. 169, n. 14.

[8]Cf. the exposition of Père Jean Daniélou in his recent course at the Institut Catholique in Paris: Le IIIme Siècle: Clément et Origène, Notes prises au Cours par les Élèves, p. 148-154.

[9]Cf. Orbe, p. 77, 176 ss.

[10]Cf. Orbe, p. 165 ss. and especially the summary, p. 185: "Orígenes discurre siempre vinculando la Subiduría personal de Dios al mundo (inteligible, o quizá también sensible). La generación del Verbo, que hubiera en absoluto bastado a explicar el misterio de la prehistoria del mundo, no adquiere autonomía propia. De seguro su coeternidad con el Padre se halla en Orígenes mejor definida que en ninguno de sus contemporáneos; pero las múltiples coordenadas que de diversos puntos traza el Alejandrino para definir igualmente la eternidad del mundo, comprometen las fronteras entre la necesidad de la generación natural del Verbo y la libertad de la generación intencional del mundo en El. Los límites entre la Paternidad y la Omnipotencia na aparecen claros en el Alejandrino." See also P. Aloysius Lieske, *Die Theologie der Logosmystik bei Origenes* (Münster i/W. 1938), p. 162-208, and Endre v. Ivánka, *Hellenisches und*

Christliches im frühbyzantinischen Geistesleben (Wien 1948), p. 24-27 and passim.

[11]Cf. Crouzel, p. 98ss.

[12]See Orbe, p. 674ss., and especially the section: "Orígenes y los Arrianos."

[13]Cf. Crouzel, p. 90ss.

[14]Cf. Ernst Benz, *Marius Victorinus und die Entwicklung der abend-ländischen Willensmetaphysik* (Stuttgart 1932), p. 329-340.

[15]See the excellent and exhaustive essay of D. A. Lebedev, "St. Alexander of Alexandria and Origen," in the *Trudy Kievskoj Dukhovnoj Akademii* (1915, October/November and December), p. 244-273 and 388-414 [in Russian]; cf. also another article by the same author, "The problem of the Origin of Arianism," in the *Bogoslovskij Vestnik* (1915, May), p. 133-162 (also in Russian).

[16]Only a Syriac version of this important document is preserved. It was published for the first time and retranslated into Greek by Eduard Schwartz, "Zur Geschichte des Athanasius," VI, in *Nachrichten von der Königlichen Gesellschaft der Wissenschaften zu Göttingen* (1905), p. 272-273 (now reprinted in his *Gesammelte Schriften*, Dritter Band (Berlin 1959), pp. 136-143). I am quoting the English translation of Kelly, made from the Greek of Schwartz—*Early Christian Creeds*, p. 209-210. The authenticity of the Antioch Council has been vigorously contested by Harnack and others. The best analysis of all evidence and a convincing defense of the authenticity can be found in a series of articles by D. A. Lebedev: "The Council in Antioch of 324 and its Epistle to Alexander, Bishop of Thessalonike," in *Khristianskoje Chtenije* (1911, July/Aug., 831-858; Sept.), 1008-1023; "On the Problem of the Council in Antioch of 324 and on the Great and Holy Council in Ancyra," in *Trudy Kievskoj Dukhovnoj Akademii* (1914, April. July/August, November; 1915, January); continued in *Bogoslovskij Vestnik* (1915, July/August, p. 482-512). All these articles are in Russian.

[17]See A. Gaudel, *"La théologie du Λόγος chez Saint Athanase,"* in the *Revue des Sciences religieuses* 11, 1931, 1-26; J. B. Berchem, "Le rôle du Verbe dans l'oeuvre de la création et de la sanctification d'après Saint Athanase," in *Angelicum*, 1938, p .201-232 and 515-558; and especially Louis Bouyer, *L'Incarnation et l'Église—Corps du Christ dans la théologie de Saint Athanase* (Paris 1943) ; cf. also Regis Bernard, *L'Image de Dieu d'après St. Athanase* (Paris 1952).—Professor I. V. Popov, of Moscow Theological Academy, in his book, *The Personality and the Doctrine of Saint Augustine* (1917 [in Russian]), gives an excellent survey of the history of the distinction: essence—energy, from Philo to Pseudo-Dionysius, t. I 2, p. 330-356; see also A. I. Brilliantov, *The Influence of the Eastern Theology on the Western in the Works of J. S. Eriugena* [in Russian] St. Petersburg 1898), p. 221 ss.

[18]Cf. Ernst Benz, *op. cit.*, p. 340-342: "Durch die Scheidung von Substanz und Wirkung des Willens ist die engste substantielle Verbindung von Vater und Sohn und zugleich die Begründung der 'creatio ex nihilo' gegeben." The whole paragraph on St. Athanasius in Benz's book is highly stimulating.

[19]Cf. Orbe, *op. cit.*, p. 465s., 692s., 751.

[20]Louis Bouyer, *op. cit.*, p. 47s.: "Le premier élément nouveau du Contra Arianos—et il est considérable—c'est qu'il nous fait contempler la vie divine en Dieu lui-même avant qu'il nous la communique. Cette contemplation est l'inspiration de tout cet ouvrage, car elle inclut les raisons profondes de la distinction radicale entre Dieu et le créé qui ruine par la base les thèses ariennes. La transcendance divine est vraiment absolue parce que Dieu n'a aucun besoin de ses créatures: il possède la vie en lui-même, et cette vie consiste dans les relations qu'il entretient avec son Verbe."

[21]See F. A. Staudenmeier, *Die Christliche Dogmatik*, Bd. III (Freiburg i/Br. 1848).

[22]Cf. Jacques Liébaert, *La doctrine christologique de Saint Cyrille d'Alexandrie avant la querelle nestorienne* (Lille 1951), p. 19-43; Noël Charlier, "Le Thesaurus de Trinitate de Saint Cyrille d'Alexandrie," in the *Revue d'Histoire Ecclésiastique* 45, 1950, 25-81.

[23]Cf. Th. de Regnon, Études de Théologie Positive sur la Sainte Trinité, Troisième Série: Théories Grecques des Processions Divines, Paris 1898, p. 263ss. "Cette fécondité de Dieu, cette procession par voie d'activité substantielle, telle est l'idée maitresse de la théorie grecque au sujet du Fils" (269).

[24]See, for instance, St. Gregory Palamas, Capita physica, theologica etc., 96, *PG* 150, 1181: εἰ...μηδὲν διαφέρει τῆς θείας οὐσίας ἡ θεία ἐνέργεια, καὶ τὸ ποιεῖν, ὃ τῆς ἐνεργείας ἐστί, κατ' οὐδὲν διοίσει τοῦ γεννᾶν καὶ ἐκπορεύειν, ἃ τῆς οὐσίας ἐστίν... καὶ τὰ ποιήματα κατ' οὐδὲν διοίσει τοῦ γεννήματος καὶ τοῦ προβλήματος. Cf. my article, "St. Gregory Palamas and the Tradition of the Fathers," *The Greek Orthodox Theological Review* 2, 1960, 128-130 and in Volume I of *The Collected Works*. Cf. also Jean Meyendorff, *Introduction à l'étude de Grégoire Palamas*, Paris (1959), especially p. 279ss.

[25]See S. Marci Eugenici Ephesini Capita syllogistica, in W. Gaβ, *Die Mystik des Nikolaus Cabasilas* (Greifswald 1849), Appendix II, p. 217: ἔτι εἰ ταὐτὸν οὐσία καὶ ἐνέργεια, ταύτῃ τε καὶ πάντως ἅμα τῷ εἶναι καὶ ἐνεργεῖν τὸν Θεὸν ἀνάγκη· συναΐδιος ἄρα τῷ Θεῷ ἡ κτίσις ἐξ ἀϊδίου ἐνεργοῦντα κατὰ τοὺς Ἕλληνας.

[26]The latter point of view has been recently ably elaborated by Professor Endre v. Ivánka, "Palamismus und Vätertradition," in *L'Église et les Églises, Études et Travaux offerts à Dom Lambert Beaudouin*, vol. II (Chevetogne 1955), p. 29-46. Ivánka's arguments are not convincing; he seems to miss the crucial point. But it has been the common attitude of Western theology, especially in the Roman Church.

THE PATRISTIC AGE AND ESCHATOLOGY:
AN INTRODUCTION

[1]See e.g. Msgr Joseph Pohle, *Eschatology,* Adapted and edited by Arthur Preuss (Herder Book Co., St. Louis, Mo., & London, 1947), p. 2.

[2]See Kittel's *Theologisches Wörterbuch,* vol. III, p. 451/452, s. v. καινός (Behm).

[3]The question whether this redemptive purpose was the only reason or motive of the Incarnation, so that it would not have taken place if man had not sinned, was never raised by the Fathers, with one single exception. The Christian message was from the very beginning the message of Salvation, and Christ was described precisely as the Saviour or Redeemer of mankind and the world, who had redeemed His people from the bondage of sin and corruption. It was assumed that the very meaning of Salvation was that the intimate union between man and God had been restored, and it was inferred therefrom that the Redeemer Himself had to belong to both sides, i.e. had to be at once both Divine and human, for otherwise the broken communion would not have been recovered. This line of reasoning was taken by St. Irenaeus, later by St. Athanasius, and by all the writers of the IVth century, in their struggle against the Arians. Only in St. Maximus the Confessor we find the suggestion that Incarnation belonged to the original plan of Creation and in this sense was independent of the Fall: *quaest. ad Thalassium,* qu. 60, *PG* XC, c. 621; cf. *Ambigua,* XCI, 1097, 1305, 1308 sq. Cf. the remarks of Fr. Hans Urs von Balthasar, *Liturgie Cosmique, Maxime le Confesseur* (Paris, Aubier, 1947), p. 204-205 (German edition, S. 267-268). See also Aloysius Spindeler, *Cur Verbum caro factum? Das Motiv der Menschwerdung und das Verhältnis der Erlösung zur Menschwerdung Gottes in den christologischen Glaubenskämpfen des vierten und fünften christlichen Jahrhunderts* (Forschungen zur Christlichen Literatur- und Dogmengeschichte, herausgegeben von Erhard und Kirsch, XVIII. 2), 1938.

[4]On the notion of the circular motion in Aristotle see O. Hamelin, *Le Système d'Aristote* (2 ed., Paris 1831), p. 336ss.; J. Chevalier, *La Notion du Necessaire chez Aristote et chez ses prédecesseurs, particulièrement chez Platon* (Paris 1915), p. 160ss., 180ss.; R. Mugnier, *La Théorie du Premier Moteur et l'Évolution de la Pensée Aristotelienne* (Paris 1930). p. 24ss.

[5]See Pierre Duhem, *Le Système du Monde, Histoire des Doctrines Cosmologiques de Platon à Copernic* (t. I, Paris 1914), pp. 65ss., 275-296, and especially t. II, Paris 1914, p. 447ss.,—*Les Pères de l'Église et la Grande Année.* Cf. Hans Meyer, *Zur Lehre von der ewigen Wiederkunft aller Dinge,* in Festgabe A. Ehrhard (Bonn 1922), p. 359ff.

[6]See Oepke, s. v. ἀποκατάστασις, in Kittel, I, S. 389: "Vor allem wird

ἀποκατάστασις terminus technicus für die Wiederherstellung des kosmischen Zyklus."

[7]A. Lossev, *Essays in Ancient Symbolism and Mythology* (t. I, Moscow 1930 [in Russian]), p. 643. This book is one of the most valuable contributions to the modern discussion of Platonism, including Christian Platonism. It is utterly rare. The book, and other valuable writings of Lossev in the same field, is obtainable in Fritz Lieb's Library, at the University of Basel.

[8]Cf. my article, "The Idea of Creation in Christian Philosophy," in the *Eastern Churches Quarterly* (Vol. VIII, 1949), 3 Supplementary issue, "Nature and Grace."

[9]See Büchsel, s. v. ἀπολύτρωσις, in Kittel, IV, 355.

[10]Cf. the most interesting remarks of E. Gilson in his Gifford lectures: *L'Esprit de la Philosophie Médiévale* (2nd edition, Paris, 1944), the whole of chapter IX, "L'anthropologie chrétienne," p. 175 ss. Gilson seems to have underestimated the Aristotelian elements in Early Patristics, but he gives an excellent *mis au point* of the whole problem.

[11]R. D. Hicks, in the Introduction to his edition of *De anima*, Cambridge, at the University Press, 1934, p. LVI. Cf. Anton C. Pegis, *Saint Thomas and the Greeks*, The Aquinas Lecture, 1939, 3rd printing (Marquette University Press, Milwaukee, 1951), p. 171. Already E. Rohde, *Psyche, Seelencult und Unsterblichkeitsglaube der Griechen* (3. Aufl. 1903, Bd. II), p. 305, suggested that the whole doctrine of *Nous* was simply a survival of Aristotle's early Platonism. This idea was recently upheld by Werner Jäger, *Aristotle, Fundamentals of the History of his Development*, translation, by Richard Robinson, 2nd edition (Oxford, at the Clarendon Press, 1948), p. 332f.

[12]Hegel, *Vorlesungen über die Asthetik, Sämtliche Werke*, Bd. X. 2, p. 377; cf. the whole section on Sculpture, which was for Hegel a peculiarly "classical art," p. 353f.

[13]Lossev, *Essays in Ancient Symbolism and Mythology*, I, p. 670, 632, 633,—in Russian.

[14]On the Aristotelian background of Athenagoras' conception see Max Pohlenz, in *Zeitschrift für die wissenschaftliche Theologie*, Bd. 47, p. 241ff.; cf. E. Schwarz, *index graecus* to his edition of Athenagoras, in *Texte und Untersuchungen*, IV. 2, 1891, s. v. εἶδος, S. 105. Cf. E. Gilson, *L'Esprit de la Philosophie Médiévale*, p .197. "Lorsqu'on pèse les expressions d'Athénagoras, la profondeur de l'influence exercée par la Bonne Nouvelle sur la pensée philosophique apparait à plein. Crée par Dieu comme une individualité distincte, conservé par un acte de création continuée dans l'être qu'il a reçu de lui, l'homme est desormais le personnage d'un drame qui est celui de sa propre destinée. Comme il ne dependait pas de nous d'exister, il ne depend pas de nous de ne pas exister. Le décret divin nous a condamné à l'être; faits par la création, refraits par la redemption, et à quel prix. Nous n'avons le choix qu'entre une misère ou une béatitude également éternelles. Rien de plus resistant qu'une individualité de ce genre, prévue, voulue, élue par

Dieu, indestructible comme le decret divin lui-même qui l'a fait naître; mais rien aussi qui soit plus étranger à la philosophie de Platon comme à celle d'Aristote. Là encore, à partir du moment où elle visait une pleine justification rationelle de son espérance, la pensée chrétienne se trouvait contrainte à l'originalité."

THE ANTHROPOMORPHITES
IN THE EGYPTIAN DESERT

[1]O. Chadwick, *John Cassian. A Study in Primitive Monasticism* (Cambridge, 1950), p. 16, n. 3; cf. p. 34-35.

[2]A. Lieske, "Die Theologie der Logosmystik bei Origenes," *Münsterische Beiträge zur Theologie* (Heft 22, 1938), p. 45 ff., 133 ff. *"Bei aller Liebe zum gekreuzigten Christus und zum Gottmenschen ... tritt auf dieser höheren Stufe der Glaubenserkenntnis doch das Interesse und die Hochschätzung für das Gottmenschentum Jesu Christi zurück"* (p. 47).

[3]W. Voelker, *Das Vollkommenheitsideal des Origenes* (Tübingen 1931), pp. 109-110. The opposite view is strongly presented by H. De Lubac, *Histoire et Esprit. L'intelligence de l'Écriture d'après Origène* (Paris 1950), and also by F. Bertrand, *Mystique de Jesus chez Origène* (Paris 1951).

[4]Chadwick, p. 149.

[5]See J. Lebreton, *Le désaccord de la foi populaire et de la théologie savante dans l'Église chrétienne du III siècle, Rev. Hist. Eccl.* 19 (1923) and 20 (1924); cf. also his earlier article, "Les Degrés de la connaissance d'après Origène," *Recherches de Science Religieuse* 13 (1922).

[6]A. Struker, *Die Gottebenbildlichkeit des Menschen in der christlichen Literatur der ersten zwei Jahrhunderte* (Münster i. W. 1913), pp. 39-42.

[7]Cf. H. Crouzel, *Théologie de l'Image de Dieu chez Origène* (Paris 1956), p. 153-179, 257ss.

[8]D. Cairns, *The Image of God in Man* (New York 1953), p. 77.

[9]Cf. Struker, s. 76-128; also E. Klebba, *Die Anthropologie des hl. Irenaeus* (Münster i. W. 1894 [= Kirchengeschichtliche Studien, II. 3]), p. 22 ff.; J. Lawson, *The Biblical Theology of Saint Irenaeus* (London 1948), p. 198 ff.; G. Wingren, *Maenniskan och Inkarnationen enligt Irenaeus* (Lund 1947), p. 37-49; Engl. transl.: *Man and the Incarnation. A study in the Biblical Theology of Irenaeus* (Edinburgh-London 1959), pp. 14-26.

THEOPHILUS OF ALEXANDRIA
AND APA APHOU OF PEMDJE

[1]E. Revillout, "La Vie du bienheureux Aphou, Evêque de Pemdje (Oxyrinque)," in *Revue Egyptologique*, III, 1, 27-33.

[2]Francesco Rossi, "Trascrizione di tre manoscritti Copti del Museo Egizio di Torino, con traduzione italiana," in *Memorie della Reale Accademia delle Scienze di Torino*, Serie II, XXXVII, 67-84 (text) and 145-150 (translation). Rossi published in the same *Memorie* several other documents from the Turin collection. There is a separate edition: *I papiri copti del Museo egizio di Torino, trascritti e tradotti*, 2 vols. (Torino, 1887, 1892). Cf. Robert Atkinson, "On Professor Rossi's Publication of South Coptic texts," in the *Proceedings of the Royal Irish Academy*, III (Dublin, 1895-1898), 25-99.—A minor, but rather important, emendation of Rossi's text was suggested by Oscar von Lemm, "Koptische Miscellen," XLVI, in *Bulletin de l'Académie Impériale des Sciences de St. Petersbourg*, VI série, II, 7, 15 Avril 1908, 596-598.

[3]V. Bolotov, "Iz tserkovnoj istorii Egipta: II. Zhitie blazhennago Afu, episkopa Pemdzhskago," in *Khristianskoe Chtenie* (1886, 3/4), 334-377.

[4]E. Drioton, "La.discussion d'un moine anthropomorphite audien avec le Patriarche Théophile d'Alexandrie en l'année 399," in *Revue de l'Orient Chrétien*, Deuxième série, X [XX], (1915-1917), 92-100 and 113-128.

[5]"Manoscritti copti esistenti nel Museo Egizio nella Biblioteca Nazionale di Torino, raccolti da Bernardino Drovetti e indicati dal Prof. Francesco Rossi," in *Rivista delle Biblioteche e degli Archivi*, X, 9, Settembre 1899, 114.

[6]*Catalogus Codicum Copticorum manu scriptorum qui in Museo Borgiano Veletris adservantur, auctore Georgio Zoega Dano* (Romae, MDCCCX), p. 169.

[7]See Francesco Rossi, "Trascrizione di un Codice Copto del Museo Egizio di Torino," in *Memorie*, Ser. II, XXXV (1884), 165-167, and also: "Trascrizione di alcuni testi copti tirati dai papiri del Museo Egizio di Torino," in *Memorie*, Ser. II, XXXVI (1885), 89-91.

[8]Amedeo Peyron, "Saggio di studi sopra papiri codici cotti ed un stella trilingue del Reale Museo Egiziano," in *Memorie*, XXIX (1825), 78, and also: *Lexicon Linguae Copticae, studio Amedei Peyron* (Taurini, 1835), pp. XXV-XXVI.

[9]Rossi, in *Memorie*, Serie II, XXXV (1884), 166.

[10]E. Revillout, "Le Concile de Nicée, d'après les textes coptes," in *Journal Asiatique*, VII série, I (1873), 2, 217-222: Revillout gives here a transcription of the dedicatory note; at that time he thought that the whole collection was completed already in the *early years* of St. Cyril. Later on he became more

cautious and spoke of *the end* of St. Cyril's pontificate: *Le Concile de Nicée d'après les textes coptes et les divers collections canoniques* (Paris, 1881), p. 112, note I. In the preface to his publication of the "Life" of Aphou he says simply: *before the schism,—Revue Egyptologique*, III, I, p. 28.

[11]Cf. V. Bolotov, "Iz tserkovnoj istorii Egipta: I. 'Razskasy Dioskora o Khalkidonskom Sobore,'" in *Kristianskoe Chtenie* 1/2 (1885), 89-92.

[12]See Th. Lefort, "'Ισον = *Exemplum, Exemplar*," in *Le Muséon*, XLVII, 1/2, 58: "vraisemblablement aux environs du VIIe siècle." It is just a casual remark: Lefort gives no reasons for his dating.

[13]Zoëga, *Catalogus*, p. 4.

[14]Bolotov assumed that the Arabic *Synaxarion* of Michael, Bishop of Atrib and Malig (XIII century), was based on the Macarian version. See now Georg Graf, *Geschichte der Christlichen Arabischen Literatur*, II (Città del Vaticano, 1947), 416 ff. The history of the Arabic *Synaxaria*, however, cannot be traced in full.

[15]Bolotov, *Zhitie*, pp. 340-343.

[16]Bolotov, *ibid.*, pp. 343-346.

[17]Drioton, pp. 93-94. Marcel Richard thinks that Drioton had exaggerated a bit the historical value of the "Life": "Les Écrits de Théophile d'Alexandrie," in *Le Muséon*, LII, 1/2 (1937), 36, note 16.

[18]Zoëga, *Catalogus*, pp. 363-370 (Codex. Sahid. CLXXII); E. Amélineau, "Monuments pour servir à l'Histoire de l'Egypte Chrétienne," in *Mémoires publiés par les membres de la Mission Archéologique Française au Caire*, IV, 2 (Paris, 1895), 515-516 (Introduction) and 759-769 (text and translation).

[19]See De Lacy O'Leary, *The Saints of Egypt* (London, 1937), pp. 223-224 and 106-107; Hugh G. Evelyn White, *The Monasteries of the Wadi 'n Natrun*, Part II: The History of the Monasteries of Nitria and Scete (New York, 1932), pp. 158 ff; also in the Arabic *Synaxarium Alexandrinum*, under the 7 Paopi,—*Corpus Scriptorum Christianorum Orientalium, Scriptores Arabici*, Ser. III, t. 18 (Roma, 1922), Latin translation by J. Forget, pp. 58-59.

[20]Amélineau, *Monuments*, p. 516.

[21]The English translation quoted in the text was kindly made for me by Professor Thomas O. Lambdin, of Harvard University, to whom I want to extend my warmest thanks.

[22]See, for instance, the chapter "On Holy Anchorites." The Greek text was published by F. Nau: "Le chapitre περὶ ἀναχωρητῶν ἀγίων et les sources de la Vie de Saint Paul de Thèbes," in *Revue de l'Orient Chrétien*, X (1905), 387-417. Nau contended that it was one of the earliest ascetical writings in Egypt, and was used by St. Jerome: "un des premiers écrits ascétiques de l'Egypte" (387). A certain Anchorite is relating his experiences in the desert: ὁρῶ βουβάλους ἐρχομένους καὶ τὸν δοῦλον τοῦ Θεοῦ γυμνὸν (410); ἦν τις ἀναχωρητὴς βοσκόμενος μετὰ τῶν βουβάλων

(414, note 22). An ancient Latin version of this chapter, by subdeacon John, was published already by Rosweyde, *De vitis Patrum,* liber VI, libellus 3,—reprinted in *ML* LXXIII, 1004-1014: *"vidi bubalos venientes, et illum servum De: venientem cum eis nudum"* (1009); *"vidit... hominem pascentem tanquam bestiam"* (1008). Some fragments of a Coptic translation were published already by Mingarelli, *Aegyptiorum Codicum Reliquiae Venetis in Bibliotheca Naniana asservatae* (Bononiae, 1785), pp. CCCXXXVII-CCCXLIII. A Syriac version is in Anon Isho's *Paradisus Patrum:* published by Bedjan, *Acta Martyrum et Sanctorum,* VII (Paris, 1897), 252-260, and, together with an English translation, by E. W. Budge, *The Book of Paradise* etc., (London, 1904), I, 358-362 (translation). There are several stories told by different people; one of them is attributed to Apa Macarius of Egypt. The same material is used in the "Life and Conversation" of Apa Onouphrius (or Benofer). The Coptic text was published twice: by E. Amélineau, "Voyage d'un moine égyptien dans le désert," in *Recueil de Travaux relatifs à la Philologie et à l'Archéologie Egyptiennes et Assyriennes* V (Paris, 1884), 166-194, and then by E. W. Budge, *Coptic Martyrdoms, etc., in the dialect of Upper Egypt* (London, 1914), pp. 455-473. In fact, it is a description of a journey in the desert by Apa Paphnutius. An ancient Latin translation was also published by Rosweyde,—reprinted in *ML* LXXIII, 211-222.—An interesting pericope on wandering hermits is found among the new *Apophthegmata* in the Greek manuscript in the archives of the Library Company in Philadelphia (Greek Commentary 1141),—see Edwin C. Tappert, "A Greek Hagiological Manuscript in Philadelphia," in *Transactions of the American Philological Association* LXVIII (1937), 264-276. A selection of passages from this manuscript is given in English translation by E. Tappert, "Desert Wisdom: The Sayings of the Anchorites," in *The Lutheran Quarterly* IX (1957), 157-172. "Now men set snares there and caught antelopes, and the monk, too, was caught. And his reasoning said to him, 'Put forth thy hand and release thyself.' But he said to his reasoning, 'If thou art a man, release thyself and go to men. But if thou art an antelope, thou hast no hands.' And he stayed in the snare until morning. When the men came to catch the antelopes and saw the monk ensnared, they were struck with fear. He himself said nothing, and they released him and let him go. And he went off, running behind the antelopes into the wilderness." (p. 168).

[23]W. Bousset, "Das Mönchtum der sketischen Wüste," in *Zeitschrift für Kirchengeschichte* XLII (1923), 31 ff.; cf. Hans Frhr. von Campenhausen, *Die asketische Heimatslösigkeit im altkirchlichen und frühmittelalterlichen Mönchtum* (1930), now reprinted in *Tradition und Leben, Kräfte der Kirchengeschichte, Aufsätze und Vorträge* (Tübingen, 1960), pp. 293-294.

[24]See Arthur Vööbus, *History of Asceticism in the Syrian Orient,* I (Louvain, 1958—*C.S.C.O.,* Subsidia 14), 138 ff., and II (Louvain, 1960—*C.S.C.O.,* Subsidia 17), 19 ff. Professor Vööbus discusses at length the wild and exotic character of the early Syrian anchoritism: "The same wildness also becomes manifest in the way in which these texts draw a comparison between the life in monasticism and the life of animals. A frequently occurring feature in these sources is this, that the monks have become the companions of wild animals. Ephrem invites his readers to make the tour with him to see these monks and adds: 'Behold, they mingle with stags and are leaping with fawns.' Moreover it is stated that a life close to animals and nature

is the prerequisite to that sole sphere in which repentance can be obtained"
(II, p. 27).

[25]See B. Steidle, *O.S.B.*, "Homo Dei Antonius," in *Antonius Magnus Eremita* (356-1956); *Studia Anselmiana*, 38 (Roma, 1956), 148-200.

[26]The word μοναστήριον appears for the first time in Philo, *De Vita Contemplativa*, M. 475.13: οἴκημα ἱερόν, ὃ καλεῖται σεμνεῖον καὶ μοναστήριον. It denoted here a private chamber, or a closet, reserved for solitary meditation and worship (cf. ταμεῖον in Mt. 6:6, 24:26, Lk. 12:3). This passage of Philo was quoted by Eusebius, *HE*, II, 17, 9. The word does not occur in any other Greek text till the end of the third century, and at that time it acquires the meaning of an accommodation for a single monk or hermit. In this sense the word was used by St. Athanasius, and also in the *Historia Lausiaca*. See the note of Fred. C. Conybeare, in his edition, *Philo About the Contemplative Life* (Oxford, 1895), p. 211. Cf. also *Vita Epiphanii*, cap. 27: *Epiphanius* visited Hierakas ἐν τῷ μοναστηρίῳ αὐτοῦ. But by the end of the fourth century the word μοναστήριον came to mean "monastery."

[27]Cf. Georg Pfeilschifter, "Oxyrhynchos, Seine Kirchen und Klöster, Auf Grund der Papyrfunde," in *Festgabe Alois Knöpfler* (Freiburg i/Br., 1917), pp. 248-264.

[28]Cf. *Hist. monach.*, V: *ipsi quoque magistratus et principales civitatis et reliqui cives studiose per singulas portas statuunt qui observent ut sicubi apparuit peregrinus aut pauper, certatim ad eum qui praeoccupaverit adductus quae sunt necessaria consequatur.*—This description of Oxyrhynchus refers to the last decades of the fourth century.

[29]The Greek spelling of the name is ᾽Απφύ.

[30]*Mystic Treatises by Isaac of Nineveh*, translated from Bedjan's Syriac text, with an Introduction and Registers, by A.J. Wensinck (Amsterdam, 1923) (=*Verhandelingen der K. Akademie van Wetenschappen*, Afdeeling Letterkunde, N.R. Deel XXIII), pp. 166-167; cf. the Greek version, ed. Nicephorus Theotoki (Leipzig, 1770), pp. 500-501.

[31]Drioton, pp. 116-118.—The best up-to-date summary of information on the Audians is by H.-Ch. Puech, in the *Reallexikon für Antike und Christentum, sub voce*, I (1950), coll. 910-915. Puech warns against the indiscriminate identification of Audians with the Egyptian Anthropomorphites, but admits, referring to Drioton's article, a possibility of some Audian influence in Egypt. The Audian movement, which only gradually developed into a "sect," originated in Mesopotamia, and then expanded to Syria and later to Scythia, where Audius was banished.—H. G. Opitz, in his article on Theophilus, in Pauly-Wissowa-Kroll *Realenzyclopädie*, II R., Hb. 10 (1934), sp. 2154, reserves his opinion on this point: "es ist nicht leicht zu entscheiden, ob Aphou wirklich Audianer war"; Agostino Favale, *Teofilo d'Alessandria* (345-412), *Scritti, Vita e Dottrina* (Torino, 1958), quotes Drioton, but is not certain about the Audian character of the Anthropomorphite monks (pp. 93-95). Giuseppe Lazzati, *Teofilo d'Alessandria* (Milano, 1935), does not mention Aphou at all and only briefly mentions the Anthropomorphite conflict (pp. 31-33).

[32]Cf. Karl Holl, *Enthusiasmus und Bussgewalt beim Griechischen Mönchtum* (Leipzig, 1898), pp. 141 ff., 183 ff.

[33]R. Reitzenstein, "Des Athanasius Werk über das Leben des Antonius," in *Sitzungsberichte der Heidelberger Akademie der Wissenschaften*, Phil.-Hist. Klasse (1914), No. 8, pp. 54 ff.

[34]R. Reitzenstein, *Historia Monachorum und Historia Lausiaca* (Göttingen, 1916), p. 89; cf. the whole chapter 4, "Der Mönch als Apostel."

[35]Cf. *Les Pères du Désert*. Textes choisis et présentés par René Draguet (Paris 1942), p. XXXV: "Dans les documents pachomiens, le cenobitisme strict est communément appelé 'la voie apostolique, la voie supérieure des apôtres.'" See also Louis Bouyer, *La Spiritualité du Nouveau Testament et des Pères* (Paris, 1960), p. 369, and Dom Germain Morin, *L'idéal monastique e. la vie Chrétienne des premiers jours*, Troisième édition (Paris, 1921), pp. 66 ff. In this sense the word "apostolic life" was used still by Rupert of Deutz in his treatise *De vita vere apostolica* (*ML* CLXX, 611-664).

[36]The "Life of Blessed Aphou" was never translated into English. Père Pierre de Bourguet, S.J., of the Musée du Louvre, was kind enough to provide me with a French translation from the original. I wish to express my warmest gratitude for his gracious assistance. The English version given in the text was established on the basis of Père de Bourguet's translation, collated with the earlier translations: Russian by Bolotov and Italian by Rossi. Professor Thomas O. Lambdin checked the translation against the Coptic original, for which I am deeply thankful. My best and cordial thanks to my friend and colleague, Ralph Lazzaro, of Harvard Divinity School, for his generous and devoted help in translation. I have to thank also Père Jean Daniélou, S.J., for introducing me and my query to Père de Bourguet.

[37]This passage was misunderstood by all previous translators: Bolotov, Rossi, and Drioton. They missed the point: τὸ ἴσον is a legal term and denotes the original of a document, which is supposed to be deposited in the archives, as an *exemplum*, as *scriptum authenticum*, as a standard. Aphou wanted to check whether that to which he so firmly objected was *in the original* (ἴσον) or whether it was only in that *particular copy* which was sent to Oxyrhynchus, having crept in there by a *lapsus calami* of the scribe, συγγραφεύς. He wanted to know the *official text*. In fact, the "preaching" to which he objected was not a sermon, but rather the formal Paschal Epistle of the Archbishop, that is, an official document which had to be deposited in the archieves of the Archdiocese. See Bernhard Kübler, ""Ισον und ᾿Απογραφή" in *Zeitschrift der Savigny-Stiftung für Rechtsgeschichte*, Roman. Abt., LIII (1933), 64-98, and Th. Lefort, ""Ισον = Exemplum, Exemplar," in *Le Muséon*, XLVII, 1/2, 57-60.

[38]Drioton also puts the conversation *before* the intervention of monks, p 121. On the contrary, Felix Haase suggested that it took place shortly *after—kurz nachher*, which is hardly probable: *Altchristliche Kirchengeschichte nach Orientalischen Quellen* (Leipzig, 1925), p. 201.

[39]Cf. Berthold Altaner, *Patrologie*, 5th edition (München, 1958), p. 282, and Johannes Quasten, *Patrology*, III (1960), pp. 386-388.

[40]Cf. Henri Crouzel, *Théologie de Dieu chez Origène* (Paris, 1956), especially pp. 206-211; a brief summary of the book is given in the article of Crouzel "L'image de Dieu dans la théologie d'Origène," in *Studia Patristica*, II (Berlin, 1957), 194-201. See also Th. Camelot, "La Théologie de l'Image de Dieu," in *Revue des Sciences Philosophiques et Théologiques*, XL (1956), 443-471.

[41]Cf. my essay, "The Concept of Creation in St. Athanasius," in *Studia Patristica*, VI (1962), 36-57. Also in this volume.

[42]Cf. Régis Bernard, *L'image de Dieu d'après St. Athanase* (Paris, 1952), pp. 48-54, 62-79, 131 ff. See also the article of Père Camelot, quoted above, and Julius Gross, *Entstehungsgeschichte des Erbsündendogmas*, I (München-Basel, 1960), pp. 125-132.

[43]Cf. Walter J. Burghardt, S.J., *The Image of God in Man according to Cyril of Alexandria* (Washington, 1957), pp. 141-159.—It should be mentioned here that Saint Cyril continued the struggle against the Anthropomorphites in the monastic circles of Egypt. His treatise *Adversus Anthropomorphitas* is actually a later compilation in which his two epistles addressed to a certain Deacon Tiberius and his associates were fused together; see the critical edition by Philip E. Pusey, *Cyrilli Archiepiscopi Alexandrini in D. Ioannis Evangelium*, III (Oxonii, 1872).

[44]W. Bousset, *Apophthegmata, Studien zur Geschichte des ältesten Mönchtums* (Tübingen, 1923), p. 83.

[45]See my essay, "The Anthropomorphites in the Egyptian Desert," in the *Akten des XI Internationalen Byzantinisten-Kongresses*, 1958 (München, 1960), pp. 154-159. Also in this volume.

[46]Tillemont, *Mémoires pour servir à l'Histoire Ecclésiastique des six premiers siècles*, XI (Paris, 1706), 463.

[47]We find a similar phrase in the Coptic record of conversations of Cyril and Theophilus with the monks, published and translated in German by W. E. Crum: Theophilus says to Apa Horsiesius; "So wie der Herr der Sonne, Christus, als er zu dem Himmel auffuhr, ebenso bist du vor mir heute"—*Der Papyruscodex saec. VI-VII der Phillippsbibliothek in Cheltenham*, herausgegeben und übersetzt von W. E. Crum (Strassburg, 1915) (= Schriften der Wissenschaftlichen Gesellschaft in Strassburg, Heft 15), p. 67; also quoted in Haase, *op. cit.*, p. 201.

[48]They are for the years 401 (= Hieron. ep. 96) and 404 (= ep. 100). See Marcel Richard, the article quoted above, and also R. Delobel & Marcel Richard, under the name of Theophilus, in the *Dictionnaire de Théologie Catholique*, XV, I (1946).

[49]Draguet, *Les Pères du Désert*, p. XV: "Écrivant vingt ou trente ans après son voyage, le pieux journaliste a mis du sien dans son reportage: le mythe de la parfaite objectivité ne pourrait d'ailleurs tromper que les pauvres psychologues que nous sommes. Cassien ne cache pas que c'est à travers sa propre expérience qu'il se remémore celle de ses maîtres égyptiens; ce qu'il savait moins, peut-être, et qui ne l'aurait troublé d'aucune sorte, c'est que,

dans les Conférences, il peignait le rustique asceticisme de Scète avec la palette brillante des Alexandrins plus savants."

[50]D. Salvatore Marsili, O.S.B., *Giovanni Cassiano ed Evagrio Pontico, Dottrina sulla carità e contemplazione* (Romae, 1936) (= Studia Anselmiana, V), p. 161; cf. also Owen Chadwick, *John Cassian, A Study in Primitive Monasticism* (Cambridge, 1950).

[51]See especially R. Draguet, "L'Histoire Lausiaque, une oeuvre écrite dans l'esprit d'Evagre," in *Revue d'Histoire Ecclésiastique* (Louvain, 1946), 321-364, and (1947), 5-49.

WESTERN INFLUENCES IN RUSSIAN THEOLOGY

[1]*Otzyvy eparkhial'nykh arkhiereev po voprosu o cherkovnoi reformy,* II (Petersburg, 1906), pp. 142-143. See the brochure by Tarasii (Kurganskii): *"Perelom v drevnerusskom bogoslovii,"* in the edition containing a "Foreword" by Metropolitan Anthony (Warsaw, 1927).

[2]For the early period see B. Leib, *Rome Kiev et Byzance à la fin du 11 siècle* (Petersburg, 1924). This work contains a good bibliography.

[3]See A. A. Pokrovskii, *Drevnee Pskovsko-Novgorodskoe pis'mennoe nasledie, obozrenie pergamentnykh rukopisei Tipografskoi i Patriashei biblioteki. Trudy 15-go arkheologicheskogo s'ezda v Novgorode* (Moscow, 1916), II; I. P. Popov, *O vozniknovenii Moskovskoi Sinodal'noi (Patriarshei) Biblioteki. Sbornik statei* [in honor of A. S. Orlov] (Leningrad, 1934), pp. 29-38.

[4]See especially the works by I. E. Evseev, *Rukopisnoe predanie Slavianskoi biblioteki, Khristianskoe chtenie* (1911); *Ocherki po istorii Slavianskogo perevoda biblioteki, Khristianskoe chtenie* (1912 and 1913); *Genadievskaia Bibliia 1499 goda. Trudy 15-go arkheologicheskogo s'ezda v Novgorode,* II, 1 (1914); see also I. A. Chistovich, *Ispravlenie teksta Slavianskoi biblii pered izdaniem 1751. goda,* Pravoslavnoe obozrenie, 1860, April and May.

[5]B. N. Beneshevich, *K istorii perevodnoi literatury v Novgorode v 15. stoletii, Sbornik statei v chest' A. I. Sobolevskogo* (1928); Slovo-Kratko" published by A. D. Grigoriev, *Chteniia v Moskovskom Obschestve Istorii i Drevnostei* (1902); see V. Valdenberg, *Drevne-russkoe uchenie o predelakh tserkovnoi vlasti* (M. 1916); A. D. Sedelenikov, "K izuchen'iu 'Slovo-Kratko' i deiatel'nosti dominikantsa Veniamina," *Izvestiia Otdeleniia Russkogo Iazyka i Slovesnosti Rossiiskoi Akademii Nauk,* XXX (1925); *Ocherki katolicheskogo vliianiia v Novgorode v 15-16 vekakh.* Doklady R. Akademii Nauk, 1929.

[6]N. Andreev, O dele d'iaka Viskovatogo, *Seminarium Kondakovianum,* V (1932); "Rozysk" po delu Viskovatogo iz *Chteniia Moskovskogo Obschestva Istorii i Drevnostii* (1847;—and better, 1858); Buslaev, *Istoricheskie ocherki,* II, and in *Istoriia russkogo iskustva* by I. Grabar', Vol. VI.

[7]P. Pierling, La Russie et le Saint-Siège, I (1896).

[8]See his letter in the Appendix to *Tvoreniia Sv. Ottsov,* XVII, 2, p. 190.

[9]The "Apokrisis" was translated into modern Russian and newly published in 1869. See N. Skaballanovich, *Ob Apokrisise Khristofora Filaleta* (Petersburg, 1873); concerning the compiler see J. Tretjak, *Piotr Skarga w dziejach i literaturze unii Brzeskiej* (Krakow, 1913); see also M. Hrusevskii, *Istoriia Ukrainy-Rusi,* VI (1907). On Prince Ostrozhskii see K. V. Lewicki, *Ks. Konstanty Ostrogski a Unia Brzeska 1596* (Lemberg, 1933).

[10]Hyp. Pociei, *Kazania i Homilie,* p. 539—quoted from Josef Tretjak, *Piotr Skarga* (Krakow, 1913), p. 222.

[11]On Peter Mogila see the basic but unfinished work: S. T. Golubev, *Petr Mogila i ego spodvizhniki,* 2 vols. (Kiev, 1833 and 1897); quite important is the book by E. F. Shmurlo, *Rimskaia kuriia na russkom pravoslavnom vostoke v 1609-1654 godakh* (Prague, 1928); "Pravoslavnoe ispovedanie" (Greek) in the collections of E. Kimmel, *Monumenta fidei Ecclesiae Orientalis* (1850), or J. Michalcescu, Θησαυρὸς τῆς 'Ορθοδοξίας (1904), or recently in J. Karmiris, Τὰ δογματικὰ καὶ Συμβολικὰ Μνημεῖα τῆς 'Ορθόδοξου Καθολικῆς 'Εκκλησίας, 1. II, Athens 1952. See also the edition of the Latin text with notes and a foreword by A. Malvy, S.J. and M. Viller, S.J. in *Orientalia Christiana,* X, 39 (1927); on Peter Mogila's *Euchologion* see E. M. Kryzhanovskii, *Povrezhdenie tserkovnoi obriadnosti i religioznykh obychaev v iuzhno-russkoi mitropolii, Rukovodstvo dlia sel'skikh pastyrei* (1860) and *Sobranie Sochinenii,* I (1890). See my *Puti russkogo bogosloviia* [*Ways of Russian Theology*] for the literature on the Kievan Academy.

[12]See, for a precise analysis of *"Kamen' very,"* I. Morevi, *Kamen' very mitr. Stefana Iavorskogo* (Petersburg, 1904); see also the well-known book by Iurii Samarin, *Stefan Iavorskii i Theofan Prokopovich, Sobranie Sochinenii,* V (1880); S. I. Maslov, *Biblioteka Stefana Iavorskogo, Chtenie v obshchestve Nestora Letopissa,* 24, 2 (1914); Hans Koch, *Die russische Orthodoxie im Petrinischen Zeitalter* (Breslau, 1929).

[13]The basic work is: P. V. Znamenskii, *Dukhovnye shkoly v Rossi do reformy 1808 goda* (Kazan', 1881); S. T. Golubev, *Kievskaia akademiia v pervoi polovine 18-go stoletiia* (Kiev, 1903); N. I. Petrov, *Kievskaia akademiia v kontse 17-go i nachale 18-go stoletiia* (Kiev, 1901); D. Vishnevskii, *Znachenie Kievskoi akademii v razvitii dukhovnoi shkoly v Rossii s ucherezheleniia St. Sinoda,* Trudy Kievskoi dukhovnoi Akademii (1904, 4 and 5); *Kievskaia akademiia v getmanstvo K. G. Razumovskogo,* Trudy (1905), 5; *Kievskaia Dukh. Akademiia v tsarstvovanie Imp. Ekateriny* II, Trudy (1906), 7, 8-9, 11; V. Serebrennikov, *Kievskaia akademiia v polovine 18-go veka do preobrazovaniia v 1819 godu* (Kiev, 1897); S. K. Smirnov, *Istoriia Moskovskoi Slaviano-Greko-Latinskoi Akademii* (Moscow, 1855); *Istoriia Troitskoi Lavrskoi seminarii* (Moscow, 1867); see also the works of the history of specific seminaries: the Vladimir Seminary by K. F. Nadezhin (1875) and by N. V. Malitskii (1900); the Suzdal' Seminary by N. V. Malitskii (1900); the Tver' Seminary by V. Kolosov (1889); the Riazan' Seminary by Agntsev (1889).

[14]There is a rather comprehensive work on Theophan Prokopovich: Ia. Samarin, *Stefan Iavorskii i Feofan Prokopovich, Sobranie Sochinenii,* V (1880); I. V. Chistovich, *Feofan Prokopovich i ego vremiia* (Petersburg, 1866); on Theophan's "theological system" see the article by Pl. Cherviakovskii, *"Khrist. Chtenie,"* (1876-1878); F. A. Tikhomirov, *Traktaty Feofana Prokopovicha— o Boge edinom po sushchestvu i troichnom v litsakh* (Petersburg, 1884); A. I. Kartashev, *K voprosu pravoslaviia Feofana Prokopovicha, Sbornik statei v chest D. A. Kobeko* (1913); P. V. Verkhovskoi, *Ucherezhdenie Dukhovnoi kollegii i Dukhovnyi Reglament,* I and II (Rostov-on-Don,

1916); Hans Koch, *Die russische Orthodoxie* (Breslau, 1929); see also the interesting essays by R. Stupperich in *ZoG,* V and IX in *Zeitschrift für slavische Philologie,* XII, 332 ff., also in *Kyrios* (1936), 4; also R. Stupperich, *Staatsgedanke und Religionspolitik Peters des Grossen* (Königsberg, 1936); and also the article by V. Titlinov in the *Russkii Biograficheskii Slovar'.*

[15]See Filaret (Gumilevskii), *Obzor russkoi dukhovnoi literatury,* II, 3 (1884); on Metropolitan Platon see I. M. Snegirev, *Zhizn' mitr. Moskovskogo Platona,* 1-2 (Moscow, 1856); F. Nadezhdin, *M. Platon Levshin, kak propovednik* (Kazan', 1882); N. P. Rozanov, *M. M. Platon* (Moscow, 1913); V. P. Vinogradov, *Platon i Filaret, Mitropolity Moskovskie, Sravnitel'niia kharakteristika ikh nravstvennogo oblika* in *Bogoslovskii Vestnik,* 1913 1-2. See also "Iz vospominanii pokoinogo Filareta, mitrop. Moskov.," *Pravoslav. Obozreniia* (1868, August)—("iz zapisok A. V. Gorskogo").

[16]See the entirety of chapter V—"Bor'ba za Bogoslovie"—in my book *Puti Russkogo Bogosloviia* [*Ways of Russian Theology*], pp. 128-233.

[17]Aleksei I. Vvedenskii, "K voprosu o metodologicheskoi reforme pravoslavnoi dogmatiki," *Bogoslovskii Vestnik* (April, 1914); also published separately.

[18]N. Gilarov-Platonov, *Iz perezhitogo. Avtobiograficheskiia vospominaniia* (Moscow, 1886), pp. 279-280.